Cram101 Textbook Outlines to accompany:

Abnormal Psychology:The Problem Of Maladaptive Behavior

Sarason, Sarason, 11th Edition

An Academic Internet Publishers (AIPI) publication (c) 2007.

You have a discounted membership at www.Cram101.com with this book.

Get all of the practice tests for the chapters of this textbook, and access in-depth reference material for writing essays and papers. Here is an example from a Cram101 Biology text:

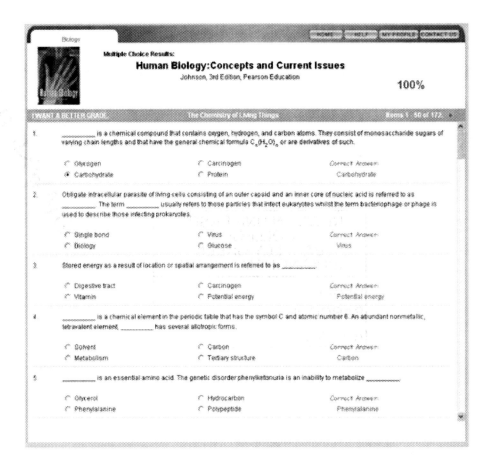

When you need problem solving help with math, stats, and other disciplines, www.Cram101.com will walk through the formulas and solutions step by step.

With Cram101.com online, you also have access to extensive reference material.

You will nail those essays and papers. Here is an example from a Cram101 Biology text:

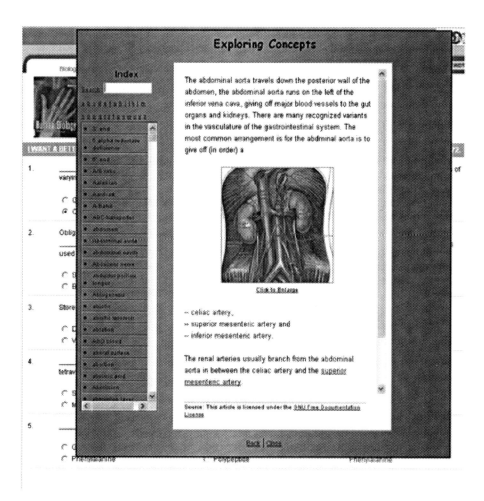

Learning System

Cram101 Textbook Outlines is a learning system. The notes in this book are the highlights of your textbook, you will never have to highlight a book again.

How to use this book. Take this book to class, it is your notebook for the lecture. The notes and highlights on the left hand side of the pages follow the outline and order of the textbook. All you have to do is follow along while your intructor presents the lecture. Circle the items emphasized in class and add other important information on the right side. With Cram101 Textbook Outlines you'll spend less time writing and more time listening. Learning becomes more efficient.

Cram101.com Online

Increase your studying efficiency by using Cram101.com's practice tests and online reference material. It is the perfect complement to Cram101 Textbook Outlines. Use self-teaching matching tests or simulate in-class testing with comprehensive multiple choice tests, or simply use Cram's true and false tests for quick review. Cram101.com even allows you to enter your in-class notes for an integrated studying format combining the textbook notes with your class notes.

Visit **www.Cram101.com**, click Sign Up at the top of the screen, and enter **DK73DW3343** in the promo code box on the registration screen. Access to www.Cram101.com is normally $9.95, but because you have purchased this book, your access fee is only $4.95. Sign up and stop highlighting textbooks forever.

Abnormal Psychology:The Problem Of Maladaptive Behavior
Sarason, Sarason, 11th

CONTENTS

1. Introduction 2
2. Theoretical Perspectives on Maladaptive Behavior 22
3. The Therapeutic Enterprise: Choices, Techniques, Evaluation 58
4. Classification and Assessment 80
5. Stress, Coping, and Maladaptive Behavior 98
6. Bodily Maladaptations: Eating, Sleeping, and Psychophysiological Disorders 110
7. Disorders of Bodily Preoccupation 132
8. Anxiety Disorders 144
9. Sexual Variants and Disorders 160
10. Personality Disorders 180
11. Mood Disorders and Suicide 194
12. Schizophrenia and Other Psychotic Disorders 216
13. Cognitive Impairment Disorders 238
14. Substance-Related Disorders 256
15. Disorders of Childhood and Adolescence 284
16. Pervasive Developmental Disorders and Mental Retardation 302
17. Society`s Response to Maladaptive Behavior 322

Depression	In everyday language depression refers to any downturn in mood, which may be relatively transitory and perhaps due to something trivial. This is differentiated from Clinical depression which is marked by symptoms that last two weeks or more and are so severe that they interfere with daily living.
Antidepressant	An antidepressant is a medication used primarily in the treatment of clinical depression. They are not thought to produce tolerance, although sudden withdrawal may produce adverse effects. They create little if any immediate change in mood and require between several days and several weeks to take effect.
Abnormal behavior	An action, thought, or feeling that is harmful to the person or to others is called abnormal behavior.
Perception	Perception is the process of acquiring, interpreting, selecting, and organizing sensory information.
Habit	A habit is a response that has become completely separated from its eliciting stimulus. Early learning theorists used the term to describe S-R associations, however not all S-R associations become a habit, rather many are extinguished after reinforcement is withdrawn.
Hallucination	A hallucination is a sensory perception experienced in the absence of an external stimulus, as distinct from an illusion, which is a misperception of an external stimulus. They may occur in any sensory modality - visual, auditory, olfactory, gustatory, tactile, or mixed.
Delusion	A false belief, not generally shared by others, and that cannot be changed despite strong evidence to the contrary is a delusion.
Maladjustment	Maladjustment is the condition of being unable to adapt properly to your environment with resulting emotional instability.
Mental disorder	Mental disorder refers to a disturbance in a person's emotions, drives, thought processes, or behavior that involves serious and relatively prolonged distress and/or impairment in ability to function, is not simply a normal response to some event or set of events in the person's environment.
Abnormal psychology	The scientific study whose objectives are to describe, explain, predict, and control behaviors that are considered strange or unusual is referred to as abnormal psychology.
Mental illness	Mental illness is the term formerly used to mean psychological disorder but less preferred because it implies that the causes of the disorder can be found in a medical disease process.
Maladaptive	In psychology, a behavior or trait is adaptive when it helps an individual adjust and function well within their social environment. A maladaptive behavior or trait is counterproductive to the individual.
Society	The social sciences use the term society to mean a group of people that form a semi-closed (or semi-open) social system, in which most interactions are with other individuals belonging to the group.
Stereotype	A stereotype is considered to be a group concept, held by one social group about another. They are often used in a negative or prejudicial sense and are frequently used to justify certain discriminatory behaviors. This allows powerful social groups to legitimize and protect their dominant position
Attitude	An enduring mental representation of a person, place, or thing that evokes an emotional response and related behavior is called attitude.
Prejudice	Prejudice in general, implies coming to a judgment on the subject before learning where the preponderance of the evidence actually lies, or formation of a judgement without direct experience.
Population	Population refers to all members of a well-defined group of organisms, events, or things.
Psychotherapy	Psychotherapy is a set of techniques based on psychological principles intended to improve mental health, emotional or behavioral issues.
Mood disorder	A mood disorder is a condition where the prevailing emotional mood is distorted or inappropriate to the circumstances.

Schizophrenia	Schizophrenia is characterized by persistent defects in the perception or expression of reality. A person suffering from untreated schizophrenia typically demonstrates grossly disorganized thinking, and may also experience delusions or auditory hallucinations
Alcoholism	A disorder that involves long-term, repeated, uncontrolled, compulsive, and excessive use of alcoholic beverages and that impairs the drinker's health and work and social relationships is called alcoholism.
Mania	Mania is a medical condition characterized by severely elevated mood. Mania is most usually associated with bipolar disorder, where episodes of mania may cyclically alternate with episodes of depression.
Clinician	A health professional authorized to provide services to people suffering from one or more pathologies is a clinician.
Discrimination	In Learning theory, discrimination refers the ability to distinguish between a conditioned stimulus and other stimuli. It can be brought about by extensive training or differential reinforcement. In social terms, it is the denial of privileges to a person or a group on the basis of prejudice.
Self-esteem	Self-esteem refers to a person's subjective appraisal of himself or herself as intrinsically positive or negative to some degree.
Socialization	Social rules and social relations are created, communicated, and changed in verbal and nonverbal ways creating social complexity useful in identifying outsiders and intelligent breeding partners. The process of learning these skills is called socialization.
Affect	A subjective feeling or emotional tone often accompanied by bodily expressions noticeable to others is called affect.
Suicide	Suicide behavior is rare in childhood but escalates in adolescence. The suicide rate increases in a linear fashion from adolescence through late adulthood.
Adaptation	Adaptation is a lowering of sensitivity to a stimulus following prolonged exposure to that stimulus. Behavioral adaptations are special ways a particular organism behaves to survive in its natural habitat.
Species	Species refers to a reproductively isolated breeding population.
Gene	A gene is an ultramicroscopic area of the chromosome. It is the smallest physical unit of the DNA molecule that carries a piece of hereditary information.
Adaptive behavior	An adaptive behavior increases the probability of the individual or organism to survive or exist within its environment.
Insight	Insight refers to a sudden awareness of the relationships among various elements that had previously appeared to be independent of one another.
Brain	The brain controls and coordinates most movement, behavior and homeostatic body functions such as heartbeat, blood pressure, fluid balance and body temperature. Functions of the brain are responsible for cognition, emotion, memory, motor learning and other sorts of learning. The brain is primarily made up of two types of cells: glia and neurons.
Chronic	Chronic refers to a relatively long duration, usually more than a few months.
Attention	Attention is the cognitive process of selectively concentrating on one thing while ignoring other things. Psychologists have labeled three types of attention: sustained attention, selective attention, and divided attention.
Theories	Theories are logically self-consistent models or frameworks describing the behavior of a certain natural or social phenomenon. They are broad explanations and predictions concerning phenomena of interest.
Trephination	Trephination a form of surgery in which a hole is drilled or scraped into the skull, leaving the membrane around the brain intact.

Trephining	Trephining is a form of surgery in which a hole is drilled or scraped into the skull, leaving the membrane around the brain intact. It addresses health problems that relate to abnormal intracranial pressure.
Motivation	In psychology, motivation is the driving force (desire) behind all actions of an organism.
Scientific method	Psychologists gather data in order to describe, understand, predict, and control behavior. Scientific method refers to an approach that can be used to discover accurate information. It includes these steps: understand the problem, collect data, draw conclusions, and revise research conclusions.
Psychotic behavior	A psychotic behavior is a severe psychological disorder characterized by hallucinations and loss of contact with reality.
Punishment	Punishment is the addtion of a stimulus that reduces the frequency of a response, or the removal of a stimulus that results in a reduction of the response.
Hippocrates	Hippocrates was an ancient Greek physician, commonly regarded as one of the most outstanding figures in medicine of all time; he has been called "the father of medicine."
Seizure	A seizure is a temporary alteration in brain function expressed as a changed mental state, tonic or clonic movements and various other symptoms. They are due to temporary abnormal electrical activity of a group of brain cells.
Aristotle	Aristotle can be credited with the development of the first theory of learning. He concluded that ideas were generated in consciousness based on four principlesof association: contiguity, similarity, contrast, and succession. In contrast to Plato, he believed that knowledge derived from sensory experience and was not inherited.
Reasoning	Reasoning is the act of using reason to derive a conclusion from certain premises. There are two main methods to reach a conclusion,deductive reasoning and inductive reasoning.
Plato	According to Plato, people must come equipped with most of their knowledge and need only hints and contemplation to complete it. Plato suggested that the brain is the mechanism of mental processes and that one gained knowledge by reflecting on the contents of one's mind.
Emotion	An emotion is a mental states that arise spontaneously, rather than through conscious effort. They are often accompanied by physiological changes.
Consciousness	The awareness of the sensations, thoughts, and feelings being experienced at a given moment is called consciousness.
Pupil	In the eye, the pupil is the opening in the middle of the iris. It appears black because most of the light entering it is absorbed by the tissues inside the eye. The size of the pupil is controlled by involuntary contraction and dilation of the iris, in order to regulate the intensity of light entering the eye. This is known as the pupillary reflex.
Temperament	Temperament refers to a basic, innate disposition to change behavior. The activity level is an important dimension of temperament.
Humors	The four humors were four fluids that were thought to permeate the body and influence its health. The concept was developed by ancient Greek thinkers around 400 BC and was directly linked with another popular theory of the four elements. Paired qualities were associated with each humour and its season.
Scheme	According to Piaget, a hypothetical mental structure that permits the classification and organization of new information is called a scheme.
Psychoanalytic	Freud's theory that unconscious forces act as determinants of personality is called psychoanalytic theory. The theory is a developmental theory characterized by critical stages of development.
Mental processes	The thoughts, feelings, and motives that each of us experiences privately but that cannot be observed directly are called mental processes.

Introspection	Introspection is the self report or consideration of one's own thoughts, perceptions and mental processes. Classic introspection was done through trained observers.
Motives	Needs or desires that energize and direct behavior toward a goal are motives.
Authoritarian	The term authoritarian is used to describe a style that enforces strong and sometimes oppressive measures against those in its sphere of influence, generally without attempts at gaining their consent.
Demonology	Demonology refers to the doctrine that a person's abnormal behavior is caused by an autonomous evil spirit.
Hysteria	Hysteria is a diagnostic label applied to a state of mind, one of unmanageable fear or emotional excesses. The fear is often centered on a body part, most often on an imagined problem with that body part.
Humanism	Humanism refers to the philosophy and school of psychology that asserts that people are conscious, self-aware, and capable of free choice, self-fulfillment, and ethical behavior.
Nightmare	Nightmare was the original term for the state later known as waking dream, and more currently as sleep paralysis, associated with rapid eye movement (REM) periods of sleep.
Psychosis	Psychosis is a generic term for mental states in which the components of rational thought and perception are severely impaired. Persons experiencing a psychosis may experience hallucinations, hold paranoid or delusional beliefs, demonstrate personality changes and exhibit disorganized thinking. This is usually accompanied by features such as a lack of insight into the unusual or bizarre nature of their behavior, difficulties with social interaction and impairments in carrying out the activities of daily living.
Paranoia	In popular culture, the term paranoia is usually used to describe excessive concern about one's own well-being, sometimes suggesting a person holds persecutory beliefs concerning a threat to themselves or their property and is often linked to a belief in conspiracy theories.
Epilepsy	Epilepsy is a chronic neurological condition characterized by recurrent unprovoked neural discharges. It is commonly controlled with medication, although surgical methods are used as well.
Subjective experience	Subjective experience refers to reality as it is perceived and interpreted, not as it exists objectively.
Direct observation	Direct observation refers to assessing behavior through direct surveillance.
Physiology	The study of the functions and activities of living cells, tissues, and organs and of the physical and chemical phenomena involved is referred to as physiology.
Spinoza	Spinoza was a determinist who held that absolutely everything that happens occurs through the operation of necessity. All behavior is fully determined, freedom being our capacity to know we are determined and to understand why we act as we do.
Psychoanalyst	A psychoanalyst is a specially trained therapist who attempts to treat the individual by uncovering and revealing to the individual otherwise subconscious factors that are contributing to some undesirable behavor.
Reflection	Reflection is the process of rephrasing or repeating thoughts and feelings expressed, making the person more aware of what they are saying or thinking.
Scientific observation	An empirical investigation that is structured to answer questions about the world is a scientific observation.
Physiognomy	Physiognomy is a pseudoscience, based upon the belief that the study and judgement of a person's outer appearance, primarily the face, reflects their character or personality.
Personality	Personality refers to the pattern of enduring characteristics that differentiates a person, the

patterns of behaviors that make each individual unique.

Gall	Gall most noted for introducing phrenology, was correct in assigning the brain the role of the seat of mental activities, and although he was wrong in detail due to a faulty methodology, the possibility of the localization of brain functions is widely accepted today.
Phrenology	Phrenology is a theory which claims to be able to determine character, personality traits, and criminality on the basis of the shape of the head (reading "bumps"). Developed by Gall around 1800, and very popular in the 19th century, it is now discredited as a pseudoscience.
Nervous system	The body's electrochemical communication circuitry, made up of billions of neurons is a nervous system.
Mesmer	Mesmer discovered what he called animal magnetism and others often called mesmerism. The evolution of Mesmer's ideas and practices led James Braid to develop hypnosis in 1842.
Testimonial	A testimonial or endorsement is a written or spoken statement, sometimes from a public figure, sometimes from a private citizen, extolling the virtue of some product, which is used in the promotion and advertising of that product.
Animal magnetism	Animal magnetism is both a synonym for Mesmerism as well as the 18th century term for the supposed ethereal medium postulated by Franz Mesmer as a therapeutic agent. Its existence was examined by a French royal commission in 1784, and the commission concluded there was no evidence of its existence.
Hypnosis	Hypnosis is a psychological state whose existence and effects are strongly debated. Some believe that it is a state under which the subject's mind becomes so suggestible that the hypnotist, the one who induces the state, can establish communication with the subconscious mind of the subject and command behavior that the subject would not choose to perform in a conscious state.
Pinel	Pinel is regarded as the father of modern psychiatry. He was a clinician believing that medical truth derived from clinical experience. While at Bicêtre, Pinel did away with bleeding, purging, and blistering in favor a therapy that involved close contact with and careful observation of patients.
Bedlam	Bedlam is the world's oldest psychiatric hospital. It became famous and afterwards infamous for the brutal ill-treatment meted out to the insane.
Asylums	Asylums are hospitals specializing in the treatment of persons with mental illness. Psychiatric wards differ only in that they are a unit of a larger hospital.
Benjamin Rush	Benjamin Rush was far ahead of his time in the treatment of mental illness. In fact, he is considered the Father of American Psychiatry, publishing the first textbook on the subject in the United States, Medical Inquiries and Observations upon the Diseases of the Mind (1812).
Senses	The senses are systems that consist of a sensory cell type that respond to a specific kind of physical energy, and that correspond to a defined region within the brain where the signals are received and interpreted.
Bipolar disorder	Bipolar Disorder is a mood disorder typically characterized by fluctuations between manic and depressive states; and, more generally, atypical mood regulation and mood instability.
Anchor	An anchor is a sample of work or performance used to set the specific performance standard for a rubric level .
Frontal lobe	The frontal lobe comprises four major folds of cortical tissue: the precentral gyrus, superior gyrus and the middle gyrus of the frontal gyri, the inferior frontal gyrus. It has been found to play a part in impulse control, judgement, language, memory, motor function, problem solving, sexual behavior, socialization and spontaneity.
Lobotomy	A lobotomy is the intentional severing of the prefrontal cortex from the thalamic region of the brain. The frontal lobe of the brain controls a number of advanced cognitive functions, as well as motor control. Today, lobotomy is very infrequently practised. It may be a treatment of last resort for obsessive-compulsive sufferers, and may also be used for people suffering chronic pain.

Thalamus	An area near the center of the brain involved in the relay of sensory information to the cortex and in the functions of sleep and attention is the thalamus.
Nerve	A nerve is an enclosed, cable-like bundle of nerve fibers or axons, which includes the glia that ensheath the axons in myelin. Neurons are sometimes called nerve cells, though this term is technically imprecise since many neurons do not form nerves.
Variable	A variable refers to a measurable factor, characteristic, or attribute of an individual or a system.
Biopsychosocial	The biopsychosocial model is a way of looking at the mind and body of a patient as two important systems that are interlinked. The biopsychosocial model draws a distinction between the actual pathological processes that cause disease, and the patient's perception of their health and the effects on it, called the illness.
Causation	Causation concerns the time order relationship between two or more objects such that if a specific antecendent condition occurs the same consequent must always follow.
Life span	Life span refers to the upper boundary of life, the maximum number of years an individual can live. The maximum life span of human beings is about 120 years of age. Females live an average of 6 years longer than males.
Stages	Stages represent relatively discrete periods of time in which functioning is qualitatively different from functioning at other periods.
Heredity	Heredity is the transfer of characteristics from parent to offspring through their genes.
Protective factors	Protective factors are influences that reduce the impact of early stress and tend to lead to positive outcomes.
Resilient children	Resilient children weather adverse circumstances, function well despite challenges or threats, or bounce back from traumatic events.
Autonomy	Autonomy is the condition of something that does not depend on anything else.
Sympathetic	The sympathetic nervous system activates what is often termed the "fight or flight response". It is an automatic regulation system, that is, one that operates without the intervention of conscious thought.
Epidemiology	Epidemiology is the study of the distribution and determinants of disease and disorders in human populations, and the use of its knowledge to control health problems.Epidemiology is considered the cornerstone methodology in all of public health research, and is highly regarded in evidence-based clinical medicine for identifying risk factors for disease and determining optimal treatment approaches to clinical practice.
Anxiety	Anxiety is a complex combination of the feeling of fear, apprehension and worry often accompanied by physical sensations such as palpitations, chest pain and/or shortness of breath.
Epidemiological research	The study of the rate and distribution of mental disorders in a population is referred to as epidemiological research.
Substance abuse	Substance abuse refers to the overindulgence in and dependence on a stimulant, depressant, or other chemical substance, leading to effects that are detrimental to the individual's physical or mental health, or the welfare of others.
Validity	The extent to which a test measures what it is intended to measure is called validity.
Paranoid schizophrenia	Paranoid schizophrenia is a type of schizophrenia characterized primarily by delusions-commonly of persecution-and by vivid hallucinations .
Psychiatrist	A psychiatrist is a physician who specializes in the diagnosis and treatment of psychological disorders.
Tact	The word tact, another of Skinner's intentionally "nonsense" words, comes from the notion of the

child's making "conTACT" with the nonverbal environment. The tact is verbal behavior that is under the control of the nonverbal environment and includes nouns, actions, adjectives, pronouns, relations, and others.

Deinstitutio-alization	The transfer of former mental patients from institutions into the community is referred to as deinstitutionalization.
Clinical psychologist	A psychologist, usually with a Ph.D, whose training is in the diagnosis, treatment, or research of psychological and behavioral disorders is a clinical psychologist.
Psychiatric social worker	A mental health professional trained to apply social science principles to help patients in clinics and hospitals is the psychiatric social worker.
American Psychological Association	The American Psychological Association is a professional organization representing psychology in the US. The mission statement is to "advance psychology as a science and profession and as a means of promoting health, education , and human welfare".
Survey	A method of scientific investigation in which a large sample of people answer questions about their attitudes or behavior is referred to as a survey.
Psychological test	Psychological test refers to a standardized measure of a sample of a person's behavior.
Ethnicity	Ethnicity refers to a characteristic based on cultural heritage, nationality characteristics, race, religion, and language.
Ethnic group	An ethnic group is a culture or subculture whose members are readily distinguishable by outsiders based on traits originating from a common racial, national, linguistic, or religious source. Members of an ethnic group are often presumed to be culturally or biologically similar, although this is not in fact necessarily the case.
Norms	In testing, standards of test performance that permit the comparison of one person's score on the test to the scores of others who have taken the same test are referred to as norms.
Reliability	Reliability means the extent to which a test produces a consistent , reproducible score .
Inference	Inference is the act or process of drawing a conclusion based solely on what one already knows.
Hypothesis	A specific statement about behavior or mental processes that is testable through research is a hypothesis.
Independent variable	A condition in a scientific study that is manipulated (assigned different values by a researcher) so that the effects of the manipulation may be observed is called an independent variable.
Dependent variable	A measure of an assumed effect of an independent variable is called the dependent variable.
Inferential statistics	Inferential statistics is the branch of statistics that is concerned with the degree of confidence that conclusions drawn about samples can be extended to the populations from which the samples were drawn .
Descriptive statistic	A simple numerical description of observations, such as the mean of a distribution of scores, used to summarize the observations is a descriptive statistic.
Statistics	Statistics is a type of data analysis which practice includes the planning, summarizing, and interpreting of observations of a system possibly followed by predicting or forecasting of future events based on a mathematical model of the system being observed.
Statistic	A statistic is an observable random variable of a sample.
Case study	A carefully drawn biography that may be obtained through interviews, questionnaires, and psychological tests is called a case study.
Correlation	A statistical technique for determining the degree of association between two or more variables is

referred to as correlation.

Experimental group	Experimental group refers to any group receiving a treatment effect in an experiment.
Child abuse	Child abuse is the physical or psychological maltreatment of a child.
Positive correlation	A relationship between two variables in which both vary in the same direction is called a positive correlation.
Guilt	Guilt describes many concepts related to a negative emotion or condition caused by actions which are believed to be, morally wrong. According to Freud, the avoidance of guilt is the basis for moral behavior.
Longitudinal study	Longitudinal study is a type of developmental study in which the same group of participants is followed and measured for an extended period of time, often years.
Control group	A group that does not receive the treatment effect in an experiment is referred to as the control group or sometimes as the comparison group.
Cross-sectional study	A type of developmental study in which researchers compare groups of participants of different ages on certain characteristics to determine age related differences is called a cross-sectional study.
Attachment	Attachment is the tendency to seek closeness to another person and feel secure when that person is present.
Social skills	Social skills are skills used to interact and communicate with others to assist status in the social structure and other motivations.
Generalizability	The ability to extend a set of findings observed in one piece of research to other situations and groups is called generalizability.
Research design	A research design tests a hypothesis. The basic typess are: descriptive, correlational, and experimental.
Representative sample	Representative sample refers to a sample of participants selected from the larger population in such a way that important subgroups within the population are included in the sample in the same proportions as they are found in the larger population.
Random assignment	Assignment of participants to experimental and control groups by chance is called random assignment. Random assigment reduces the likelihood that the results are due to preexisiting systematic differences between the groups.
Statistical significance	The condition that exists when the probability that the observed findings are due to chance is very low is called statistical significance.
Experimental manipulation	The change that an experimenter deliberately produces in a situation under study is called the experimental manipulation.
Amphetamine	Amphetamine is a synthetic stimulant used to suppress the appetite, control weight, and treat disorders including narcolepsy and ADHD. It is also used recreationally and for performance enhancement.
Stimulant	A stimulant is a drug which increases the activity of the sympathetic nervous system and produces a sense of euphoria or awakeness.
Antipsychotic	The term antipsychotic is applied to a group of drugs used to treat psychosis.
Insomnia	Insomnia is a sleep disorder characterized by an inability to sleep and/or to remain asleep for a reasonable period during the night.
Chronic insomnia	Insomnia that persists for more than 3 weeks is referred to as chronic insomnia.
Placebo	Placebo refers to a bogus treatment that has the appearance of being genuine.

Go to **Cram101.com** for the Practice Tests for this Chapter.

Double-blind	In a double-blind experiment, neither the individuals nor the researchers know who belongs to the control group. Only after all the data are recorded may researchers be permitted to learn which individuals are which. Performing an experiment in double-blind fashion is a way to lessen the influence of prejudices and unintentional physical cues on the results.
Scientific research	Research that is objective, systematic, and testable is called scientific research.
Confounding variable	A confounding variable is a variable which is the common cause of two things that may falsely appear to be in a causal relationship. It is the cause of a spurious relationship.
Internal validity	Internal validity is a term pertaining to scientific research that signifies the extent to which the conditions within a research design were conducive to drawing the conclusions the researcher was interested in drawing.
Central tendency	In statistics, central tendency is an average of a set of measurements, the word average being variously construed as mean, median, or other measure of location, depending on the context. Central tendency is a descriptive statistic analogous to center of mass in physical terms.
Variability	Statistically, variability refers to how much the scores in a distribution spread out, away from the mean.
Standard deviation	In probability and statistics, the standard deviation is the most commonly used measure of statistical dispersion. Simply put, it measures how spread out the values in a data set are.
Socioeconomic Status	A family's socioeconomic status is based on family income, parental education level, parental occupation, and social status in the community. Those with high status often have more success in preparing their children for school because they have access to a wide range of resources.
Statistical test	One may be faced with the problem of making a definite decision with respect to an uncertain hypothesis which is known only through its observable consequences. A statistical test is an algorithm to state the alternative (for or against the hypothesis) which minimizes certain risks.
Null hypothesis	Null hypothesis refers to hypothesis that the differences between two or more population parameters are zero. Used nontechnically to refer to the condition that no differences exist between groups in an experiment.
Correlation coefficient	Correlation coefficient refers to a number from +1.00 to -1.00 that expresses the direction and extent of the relationship between two variables. The closer to 1, the stronger the relationship. The sign, + or -, indicates the direction.
Psychoanalysis	Psychoanalysis refers to the school of psychology that emphasizes the importance of unconscious motives and conflicts as determinants of human behavior. It was Freud's method of exploring human personality.
Tranquilizer	A sedative, or tranquilizer, is a drug that depresses the central nervous system (CNS), which causes calmness, relaxation, reduction of anxiety, sleepiness, slowed breathing, slurred speech, staggering gait, poor judgment, and slow, uncertain reflexes.
Socioeconomic	Socioeconomic pertains to the study of the social and economic impacts of any product or service offering, market intervention or other activity on an economy as a whole and on the companies, organization and individuals who are its main economic actors.
Psychological view	The belief or theory that mental disorders are caused by psychological and emotional factors, rather than organic or biological factors is called the psychological view.
Psychodynamic	Most psychodynamic approaches are centered around the idea of a maladapted function developed early in life (usually childhood) which are at least in part unconscious. This maladapted function (a.k.a. defense mechanism) does not do well in place of a normal/healthy one.
Learning	Learning is a relatively permanent change in behavior that results from experience. Thus, to attribute a behavioral change to learning, the change must be relatively permanent and must result from

	experience.
Anatomy	Anatomy is the branch of biology that deals with the structure and organization of living things. It can be divided into animal anatomy (zootomy) and plant anatomy (phytonomy). Major branches of anatomy include comparative anatomy, histology, and human anatomy.
Sigmund Freud	Sigmund Freud was the founder of the psychoanalytic school, based on his theory that unconscious motives control much behavior, that particular kinds of unconscious thoughts and memories are the source of neurosis, and that neurosis could be treated through bringing these unconscious thoughts and memories to consciousness in psychoanalytic treatment.
Counseling psychologist	A doctoral level mental health professional whose training is similar to that of a clinical psychologist, though usually with less emphasis on research and serious psychopathology is referred to as a counseling psychologist.
Informed consent	The term used by psychologists to indicate that a person has agreed to participate in research after receiving information about the purposes of the study and the nature of the treatments is informed consent. Even with informed consent, subjects may withdraw from any experiment at any time.

Clinician	A health professional authorized to provide services to people suffering from one or more pathologies is a clinician.
Theories	Theories are logically self-consistent models or frameworks describing the behavior of a certain natural or social phenomenon. They are broad explanations and predictions concerning phenomena of interest.
Abnormal psychology	The scientific study whose objectives are to describe, explain, predict, and control behaviors that are considered strange or unusual is referred to as abnormal psychology.
Maladaptive	In psychology, a behavior or trait is adaptive when it helps an individual adjust and function well within their social environment. A maladaptive behavior or trait is counterproductive to the individual.
Perception	Perception is the process of acquiring, interpreting, selecting, and organizing sensory information.
Attention	Attention is the cognitive process of selectively concentrating on one thing while ignoring other things. Psychologists have labeled three types of attention: sustained attention, selective attention, and divided attention.
Clinical psychologist	A psychologist, usually with a Ph.D, whose training is in the diagnosis, treatment, or research of psychological and behavioral disorders is a clinical psychologist.
Psychiatrist	A psychiatrist is a physician who specializes in the diagnosis and treatment of psychological disorders.
Abnormal behavior	An action, thought, or feeling that is harmful to the person or to others is called abnormal behavior.
Validity	The extent to which a test measures what it is intended to measure is called validity.
Attitude	An enduring mental representation of a person, place, or thing that evokes an emotional response and related behavior is called attitude.
Psychological disorder	Mental processes and/or behavior patterns that cause emotional distress and/or substantial impairment in functioning is a psychological disorder.
Psychoanalysis	Psychoanalysis refers to the school of psychology that emphasizes the importance of unconscious motives and conflicts as determinants of human behavior. It was Freud's method of exploring human personality.
Variable	A variable refers to a measurable factor, characteristic, or attribute of an individual or a system.
Shaping	The concept of reinforcing successive, increasingly accurate approximations to a target behavior is called shaping. The target behavior is broken down into a hierarchy of elemental steps, each step more sophisticated then the last. By successively reinforcing each of the the elemental steps, a form of differential reinforcement, until that step is learned while extinguishing the step below, the target behavior is gradually achieved.
Physiology	The study of the functions and activities of living cells, tissues, and organs and of the physical and chemical phenomena involved is referred to as physiology.
Genetics	Genetics is the science of genes, heredity, and the variation of organisms.
Anatomy	Anatomy is the branch of biology that deals with the structure and organization of living things. It can be divided into animal anatomy (zootomy) and plant anatomy (phytonomy). Major branches of anatomy include comparative anatomy, histology, and human anatomy.
Mental retardation	Mental retardation refers to having significantly below-average intellectual functioning and limitations in at least two areas of adaptive functioning. Many categorize retardation as

mild, moderate, severe, or profound.

Metabolic disorder	A metabolic disorder is a medical disorder which affects the production of energy within individual human (or animal) cells. Most metabolic disorders are genetic, though a few are "acquired" as a result of diet, toxins, infections, etc.
Phenylketonuria	Phenylketonuria is a genetic disorder in which an individual cannot properly metabolize amino acids. The disorder is now easily detected but, if left untreated, results in mental retardation and hyperactivity.
Heredity	Heredity is the transfer of characteristics from parent to offspring through their genes.
Brain	The brain controls and coordinates most movement, behavior and homeostatic body functions such as heartbeat, blood pressure, fluid balance and body temperature. Functions of the brain are responsible for cognition, emotion, memory, motor learning and other sorts of learning. The brain is primarily made up of two types of cells: glia and neurons.
Endocrine gland	An endocrine gland is one of a set of internal organs involved in the secretion of hormones into the blood. The other major type of gland is the exocrine glands, which secrete substances—usually digestive juices—into the digestive tract or onto the skin.
Nervous system	The body's electrochemical communication circuitry, made up of billions of neurons is a nervous system.
Gene	A gene is an ultramicroscopic area of the chromosome. It is the smallest physical unit of the DNA molecule that carries a piece of hereditary information.
Nerve	A nerve is an enclosed, cable-like bundle of nerve fibers or axons, which includes the glia that ensheath the axons in myelin. Neurons are sometimes called nerve cells, though this term is technically imprecise since many neurons do not form nerves.
Schizophrenia	Schizophrenia is characterized by persistent defects in the perception or expression of reality. A person suffering from untreated schizophrenia typically demonstrates grossly disorganized thinking, and may also experience delusions or auditory hallucinations
Depression	In everyday language depression refers to any downturn in mood, which may be relatively transitory and perhaps due to something trivial. This is differentiated from Clinical depression which is marked by symptoms that last two weeks or more and are so severe that they interfere with daily living.
Biological Determinism	Biological Determinism refers to the type of determinism that stresses the biochemical , genetic , physiological , or anatomical causes of behavior
Chromosome	The DNA which carries genetic information in biological cells is normally packaged in the form of one or more large macromolecules called a chromosome. Humans normally have 46.
Human genome	The complete sequence or mapping of genes in the human body and their locations is the human genome. It is made up of 23 chromosome pairs with a total of about 3 billion DNA base pairs.
Karyotype	A karyotype is the complete set of all chromosomes of a cell of any living organism. The chromosomes are arranged and displayed in a standard format: in pairs, ordered by size. Karyotypes are examined in searches for chromosomal aberrations, and may be used to determine other macroscopically visible aspects of an individual's genotype.
Genetic testing	Genetic testing allows the genetic diagnosis of vulnerabilities to inherited diseases, and can also be used to determine a person's ancestry. Every person carries two copies of every gene, one inherited from their mother, one inherited from their father.
DNA sequence	A DNA sequence is a succession of letters representing the primary structure of a real or hypothetical DNA molecule or strand.

Deoxyribonuc-eic acid	Deoxyribonucleic acid contains the genetic instructions specifying the biological development of all cellular forms of life. It is often referred to as the molecule of heredity, as it is responsible for the genetic propagation of most inherited traits.
Double helix	The double helix is the structure of DNA. Each of the two strands forms a helix, and the two helices are held together through hydrogen bonds, ionic forces, hydrophobic interactions, and van der Waals forces forming a double helix.
Trait	An enduring personality characteristic that tends to lead to certain behaviors is called a trait. The term trait also means a genetically inherited feature of an organism.
Heritability	Heritability It is that proportion of the observed variation in a particular phenotype within a particular population, that can be attributed to the contribution of genotype. In other words: it measures the extent to which differences between individuals in a population are due their being different genetically.
Population	Population refers to all members of a well-defined group of organisms, events, or things.
Protein	A protein is a complex, high-molecular-weight organic compound that consists of amino acids joined by peptide bonds. It is essential to the structure and function of all living cells and viruses. Many are enzymes or subunits of enzymes.
Species	Species refers to a reproductively isolated breeding population.
Genotype	The genotype is the specific genetic makeup of an individual, usually in the form of DNA. It codes for the phenotype of that individual. Any given gene will usually cause an observable change in an organism, known as the phenotype.
Allele	An allele is any one of a number of alternative forms of the same gene (sometimes the term refers to a non-gene sequence) occupying a given locus (position) on a chromosome.
Monozygotic	Identical twins occur when a single egg is fertilized to form one zygote, calld monozygotic, but the zygote then divides into two separate embryos. The two embryos develop into foetuses sharing the same womb. Monozygotic twins are genetically identical unless there has been a mutation in development, and they are almost always the same gender.
Dizygotic	Fraternal twins (commonly known as "non-identical twins") usually occur when two fertilized eggs are implanted in the uterine wall at the same time. The two eggs form two zygotes, and these twins are therefore also known as dizygotic.
Identical twins	Identical twins occur when a single egg is fertilized to form one zygote (monozygotic) but the zygote then divides into two separate embryos. The two embryos develop into foetuses sharing the same womb. Monozygotic twins are genetically identical unless there has been a mutation in development, and they are almost always the same gender.
Concordance	Concordance as used in genetics means the presence of the same trait in both members of a pair of twins, or in sets of individuals. A twin study examines the concordance rates of twins having the same trait, especially a disease, which can help determine how much the disease is affected by genetics versus environment.
Chronic disorders	Chronic disorders are characterized by slow onset and long duration. They are rare in early adulthood, they increase during middle adulthood, and they become common in late adulthood.
Hallucination	A hallucination is a sensory perception experienced in the absence of an external stimulus, as distinct from an illusion, which is a misperception of an external stimulus. They may occur in any sensory modality - visual, auditory, olfactory, gustatory, tactile, or mixed.
Affective	Affective is the way people react emotionally, their ability to feel another living thing's pain or joy.
Autism	Autism is a neurodevelopmental disorder that manifests itself in markedly abnormal social

Chapter 2. Theoretical Perspectives on Maladaptive Behavior

Go to **Cram101.com** for the Practice Tests for this Chapter.

	interaction, communication ability, patterns of interests, and patterns of behavior.
Alcoholism	A disorder that involves long-term, repeated, uncontrolled, compulsive, and excessive use of alcoholic beverages and that impairs the drinker's health and work and social relationships is called alcoholism.
Affect	A subjective feeling or emotional tone often accompanied by bodily expressions noticeable to others is called affect.
Nurture	Nurture refers to the environmental influences on behavior due to nutrition, culture, socioeconomic status, and learning.
Nature versus nurture	Nature versus nurture is a shorthand expression for debates about the relative importance of an individual's innate makeup versus personal experiences in determining or causing physical and behavioral traits.
Critical period	A period of time when an innate response can be elicited by a particular stimulus is referred to as the critical period.
Innate	Innate behavior is not learned or influenced by the environment, rather, it is present or predisposed at birth.
Nonshared environment	A home environment that is unique to an individual, not shared by a sibling, for instance is a called a nonshared environment.
Personality	Personality refers to the pattern of enduring characteristics that differentiates a person, the patterns of behaviors that make each individual unique.
Neuron	The neuron is the primary cell of the nervous system. They are found in the brain, the spinal cord, in the nerves and ganglia of the peripheral nervous system. It is a specialized cell that conducts impulses through the nervous system and contains three major parts: cell body, dendrites, and an axon. It can have many dendrites but only one axon.
Peripheral nervous system	The peripheral nervous system consists of the nerves and neurons that serve the limbs and organs. It is not protected by bone or the blood-brain barrier, leaving it exposed to toxins and mechanical injuries. The peripheral nervous system is divided into the somatic nervous system and the autonomic nervous system.
Central nervous system	The vertebrate central nervous system consists of the brain and spinal cord.
Sensory receptor	A sensory receptor is a structure that recognizes a stimulus in the environment of an organism. In response to stimuli the sensory receptor initiates sensory transduction by creating graded potentials or action potentials in the same cell or in an adjacent one.
Spinal cord	The spinal cord is a part of the vertebrate nervous system that is enclosed in and protected by the vertebral column (it passes through the spinal canal). It consists of nerve cells. The spinal cord carries sensory signals and motor innervation to most of the skeletal muscles in the body.
Gland	A gland is an organ in an animal's body that synthesizes a substance for release such as hormones, often into the bloodstream or into cavities inside the body or its outer surface.
Brain stem	The brain stem is the stalk of the brain below the cerebral hemispheres. It is the major route for communication between the forebrain and the spinal cord and peripheral nerves. It also controls various functions including respiration, regulation of heart rhythms, and primary aspects of sound localization.
Dendrite	A dendrite is a slender, typically branched projection of a nerve cell, or "neuron," which conducts the electrical stimulation received from other cells to the body or soma of the cell from which it projects. This stimulation arrives through synapses, which typically are

	located near the tips of the dendrites and away from the soma.
Axon	An axon, or "nerve fiber," is a long slender projection of a nerve cell, or "neuron," which conducts electrical impulses away from the neuron's cell body or soma.
Receptor	A sensory receptor is a structure that recognizes a stimulus in the internal or external environment of an organism. In response to stimuli the sensory receptor initiates sensory transduction by creating graded potentials or action potentials in the same cell or in an adjacent one.
Synapse	A synapse is specialized junction through which cells of the nervous system signal to one another and to non-neuronal cells such as muscles or glands.
Neurotransmitter	A neurotransmitter is a chemical that is used to relay, amplify and modulate electrical signals between a neurons and another cell.
Receptor site	A location on the dendrite of a receiving neuron that is tailored to receive a specific neurotransmitter is a receptor site.
Enzyme	An enzyme is a protein that catalyzes, or speeds up, a chemical reaction. Enzymes are essential to sustain life because most chemical reactions in biological cells would occur too slowly, or would lead to different products, without enzymes.
Chlorpromazine	Chlorpromazine was the first antipsychotic drug, used during the 1950s and 1960s. Used as chlorpromazine hydrochloride and sold under the tradenames Largactil (the "liquid cosh") and Thorazine, it has sedative, hypotensive and antiemetic properties as well as anticholinergic and antidopaminergic effects. Today, Chlorpromazine is considered a typical antipsychotic.
Anxiety	Anxiety is a complex combination of the feeling of fear, apprehension and worry often accompanied by physical sensations such as palpitations, chest pain and/or shortness of breath.
Anxiety disorder	Anxiety disorder is a blanket term covering several different forms of abnormal anxiety, fear, phobia and nervous condition, that come on suddenly and prevent pursuing normal daily routines.
Norepinephrine	Norepinephrine is released from the adrenal glands as a hormone into the blood, but it is also a neurotransmitter in the nervous system. As a stress hormone, it affects parts of the human brain where attention and impulsivity are controlled. Along with epinephrine, this compound effects the fight-or-flight response, activating the sympathetic nervous system to directly increase heart rate, release energy from fat, and increase muscle readiness.
Serotonin	Serotonin, a neurotransmitter, is believed to play an important part of the biochemistry of depression, bipolar disorder and anxiety. It is also believed to be influential on sexuality and appetite.
Dopamine	Dopamine is critical to the way the brain controls our movements and is a crucial part of the basal ganglia motor loop. It is commonly associated with the 'pleasure system' of the brain, providing feelings of enjoyment and reinforcement to motivate us to do, or continue doing, certain activities.
Phineas Gage	As a result of an injury to his brain, Phineas Gage reportedly had significant changes in personality and temperament, which provided some of the first evidence that specific parts of the brain, particularly the frontal lobes, might be involved in specific psychological processes dealing with emotion, personality and problem solving.
Frontal lobe	The frontal lobe comprises four major folds of cortical tissue: the precentral gyrus, superior gyrus and the middle gyrus of the frontal gyri, the inferior frontal gyrus. It has been found to play a part in impulse control, judgement, language, memory, motor function, problem solving, sexual behavior, socialization and spontaneity.

Consciousness	The awareness of the sensations, thoughts, and feelings being experienced at a given moment is called consciousness.
Left hemisphere	The left hemisphere of the cortex controls the right side of the body, coordinates complex movements, and, in 95% of people, controls the production of speech and written language.
Parietal lobe	The parietal lobe is positioned above (superior to) the occipital lobe and behind (posterior to) the frontal lobe. It plays important roles in integrating sensory information from various senses, and in the manipulation of objects.
Brain trauma	Brain Trauma, also called acquired brain injury, intracranial injury, or simply head injury, occurs when a sudden trauma causes damage to the brain.
Insight	Insight refers to a sudden awareness of the relationships among various elements that had previously appeared to be independent of one another.
Cerebral hemisphere	Either of the two halves that make up the cerebrum is referred to as a cerebral hemisphere. The hemispheres operate together, linked by the corpus callosum, a very large bundle of nerve fibers, and also by other smaller commissures.
Cerebral cortex	The cerebral cortex is the outermost layer of the cerebrum and has a grey color. It is made up of four lobes and it is involved in many complex brain functions including memory, perceptual awareness, "thinking", language and consciousness. The cerebral cortex receives sensory information from many different sensory organs eg: eyes, ears, etc. and processes the information.
Gray matter	Gray matter is a category of nervous tissue with many nerve cell bodies and few myelinated axons. Generally, gray matter can be understood as the parts of the brain responsible for information processing; whereas, white matter is responsible for information transmission. In addition, gray matter does not have a myelin sheath and does not regenerate after injury unlike white matter.
Sensation	Sensation is the first stage in the chain of biochemical and neurologic events that begins with the impinging of a stimulus upon the receptor cells of a sensory organ, which then leads to perception, the mental state that is reflected in statements like "I see a uniformly blue wall."
Tumor	A tumor is an abnormal growth that when located in the brain can either be malignant and directly destroy brain tissue, or be benign and disrupt functioning by increasing intracranial pressure.
Electroencep-alogram	Electroencephalography is the neurophysiologic measurement of the electrical activity of the brain by recording from electrodes placed on the scalp, or in the special cases on the cortex. The resulting traces are known as an electroencephalogram and represent so-called brainwaves.
Epilepsy	Epilepsy is a chronic neurological condition characterized by recurrent unprovoked neural discharges. It is commonly controlled with medication, although surgical methods are used as well.
Alpha wave	The brain wave associated with deep relaxation is referred to as the alpha wave. Recorded by electroencephalography (EEG) , they are synchronous and coherent (regular like sawtooth) and in the frequency range of 8 - 12 Hz. It is also called Berger's wave in memory of the founder of EEG.
Deep sleep	Deep sleep refers to stage 4 sleep; the deepest form of normal sleep.
Electrode	Any device used to electrically stimulate nerve tissue or to record its activity is an electrode.

Limbic system	The limbic system is a group of brain structures that are involved in various emotions such as aggression, fear, pleasure and also in the formation of memory. The limbic system affects the endocrine system and the autonomic nervous system. It consists of several subcortical structures located around the thalamus.
Hypothalamus	The hypothalamus is a region of the brain located below the thalamus, forming the major portion of the ventral region of the diencephalon and functioning to regulate certain metabolic processes and other autonomic activities.
Reinforcer	In operant conditioning, a reinforcer is any stimulus that increases the probability that a preceding behavior will occur again. In Classical Conditioning, the unconditioned stimulus (US) is the reinforcer.
Addiction	Addiction is an uncontrollable compulsion to repeat a behavior regardless of its consequences. Many drugs or behaviors can precipitate a pattern of conditions recognized as addiction, which include a craving for more of the drug or behavior, increased physiological tolerance to exposure, and withdrawal symptoms in the absence of the stimulus.
Opium	Opium is a narcotic analgesic drug which is obtained from the unripe seed pods of the opium poppy. Regular use, even for a few days, invariably leads to physical tolerance and dependence. Various degrees of psychological addiction can occur, though this is relatively rare when opioids are properly used..
Opiates	A group of narcotics derived from the opium poppy that provide a euphoric rush and depress the nervous system are referred to as opiates.
Drug addiction	Drug addiction, or substance dependence is the compulsive use of drugs, to the point where the user has no effective choice but to continue use.
Endorphin	An endorphin is an endogenous opioid biochemical compound. They are peptides produced by the pituitary gland and the hypothalamus, and they resemble the opiates in their abilities to produce analgesia and a sense of well-being. In other words, they work as "natural pain killers."
Plasticity	The capacity for modification and change is referred to as plasticity.
Learning	Learning is a relatively permanent change in behavior that results from experience. Thus, to attribute a behavioral change to learning, the change must be relatively permanent and must result from experience.
Habit	A habit is a response that has become completely separated from its eliciting stimulus. Early learning theorists used the term to describe S-R associations, however not all S-R associations become a habit, rather many are extinguished after reinforcement is withdrawn.
Social development	The person's developing capacity for social relationships and the effects of those relationships on further development is referred to as social development.
Liver	The liver plays a major role in metabolism and has a number of functions in the body including detoxification, glycogen storage and plasma protein synthesis. It also produces bile, which is important for digestion. The liver converts most carbohydrates, proteing, and fats into glucose.
Lungs	The lungs are the essential organs of respiration. Its principal function is to transport oxygen from the atmosphere into the bloodstream, and excrete carbon dioxide from the bloodstream into the atmosphere.
Endocrine system	The endocrine system is a control system of ductless endocrine glands that secrete chemical messengers called hormones that circulate within the body via the bloodstream to affect distant organs. It does not include exocrine glands such as salivary glands, sweat glands and glands within the gastrointestinal tract.

Pancreas	The pancreas is a retroperitoneal organ that serves two functions: it produces juice containing digestive enzymes; and it produces several important hormones including insulin, glucagon, and several other hormones.
Thyroid	In anatomy, the thyroid is the largest endocrine gland in the body. The primary function of the thyroid is production of hormones.
Hormone	A hormone is a chemical messenger from one cell (or group of cells) to another. The best known are those produced by endocrine glands, but they are produced by nearly every organ system. The function of hormones is to serve as a signal to the target cells; the action of the hormone is determined by the pattern of secretion and the signal transduction of the receiving tissue.
Adaptation	Adaptation is a lowering of sensitivity to a stimulus following prolonged exposure to that stimulus. Behavioral adaptations are special ways a particular organism behaves to survive in its natural habitat.
Pituitary gland	The pituitary gland is an endocrine gland about the size of a pea that sits in the small, bony cavity at the base of the brain. The pituitary gland secretes hormones regulating a wide variety of bodily activities, including trophic hormones that stimulate other endocrine glands.
Adrenal cortex	Adrenal cortex refers to the outer layer of the adrenal glands, which produces hormones that affect salt intake, reactions to stress, and sexual development.
Steroid	A steroid is a lipid characterized by a carbon skeleton with four fused rings. Different steroids vary in the functional groups attached to these rings. Hundreds of distinct steroids have been identified in plants and animals. Their most important role in most living systems is as hormones.
Neuroscience	A field that combines the work of psychologists, biologists, biochemists, medical researchers, and others in the study of the structure and function of the nervous system is neuroscience.
Mental illness	Mental illness is the term formerly used to mean psychological disorder but less preferred because it implies that the causes of the disorder can be found in a medical disease process.
Substantia nigra	The substantia nigra is a portion of the midbrain thought to be involved in certain aspects of movement and attention. Degeneration of cells in this region is the principle pathology that underlies Parkinson's disease.
Cognition	The intellectual processes through which information is obtained, transformed, stored, retrieved, and otherwise used is cognition.
Brain imaging	Brain imaging is a fairly recent discipline within medicine and neuroscience. Brain imaging falls into two broad categories -- structural imaging and functional imaging.
Behavioral observation	A form of behavioral assessment that entails careful observation of a person's overt behavior in a particular situation is behavioral observation.
Lesion	A lesion is a non-specific term referring to abnormal tissue in the body. It can be caused by any disease process including trauma (physical, chemical, electrical), infection, neoplasm, metabolic and autoimmune.
Computerized axial tomography	Computerized axial tomography is a medical imaging method employing tomography where digital processing is used to generate a three-dimensional image of the internals of an object from a large series of two-dimensional X-ray images taken around a single axis of rotation.
Neuroimaging	Neuroimaging comprises all invasive, minimally invasive, and non-invasive methods for obtaining structural and functional images of the nervous system's major subsystems: the brain, the

Go to **Cram101.com** for the Practice Tests for this Chapter.

	peripheral nervous system, and the spinal cord.
Magnetic resonance imaging	Magnetic resonance imaging is a method of creating images of the inside of opaque organs in living organisms as well as detecting the amount of bound water in geological structures. It is primarily used to demonstrate pathological or other physiological alterations of living tissues and is a commonly used form of medical imaging.
Photon	A photon is a quantum of the electromagnetic field, for instance light. In some respects a photon acts as a particle, for instance when registered by the light sensitive device in a camera. It also acts like a wave, as when passing through the optics in a camera.
Positron emission tomography	Positron Emission Tomography measures emissions from radioactively labeled chemicals that have been injected into the bloodstream. The greatest benefit is that different compounds can show blood flow and oxygen and glucose metabolism in the tissues of the working brain.
Mental disorder	Mental disorder refers to a disturbance in a person's emotions, drives, thought processes, or behavior that involves serious and relatively prolonged distress and/or impairment in ability to function, is not simply a normal response to some event or set of events in the person's environment.
Metabolism	Metabolism is the biochemical modification of chemical compounds in living organisms and cells.
Emotion	An emotion is a mental states that arise spontaneously, rather than through conscious effort. They are often accompanied by physiological changes.
Antidepressant	An antidepressant is a medication used primarily in the treatment of clinical depression. They are not thought to produce tolerance, although sudden withdrawal may produce adverse effects. They create little if any immediate change in mood and require between several days and several weeks to take effect.
Agonist	Agonist refers to a drug that mimics or increases a neurotransmitter's effects.
Psychoneuroi-munology	Psychoneuroimmunology is a specialist field of research that studies the connection between the brain, or mental states, and the immunal and hormonal systems of the human body.
Immune system	The most important function of the human immune system occurs at the cellular level of the blood and tissues. The lymphatic and blood circulation systems are highways for specialized white blood cells. These cells include B cells, T cells, natural killer cells, and macrophages. All function with the primary objective of recognizing, attacking and destroying bacteria, viruses, cancer cells, and all substances seen as foreign.
Lymphocyte	A lymphocyte is a type of white blood cell involved in the human body's immune system. There are two broad categories, namely T cells and B cells. The lymphocyte play an important and integral part of the body's defenses.
Psychoactive drug	A psychoactive drug or psychotropic substance is a chemical that alters brain function, resulting in temporary changes in perception, mood, consciousness, or behavior. Such drugs are often used for recreational and spiritual purposes, as well as in medicine, especially for treating neurological and psychological illnesses.
Antipsychotic	The term antipsychotic is applied to a group of drugs used to treat psychosis.
Psychodynamic	Most psychodynamic approaches are centered around the idea of a maladapted function developed early in life (usually childhood) which are at least in part unconscious. This maladapted function (a.k.a. defense mechanism) does not do well in place of a normal/healthy one.
Dichotomy	A dichotomy is the division of a proposition into two parts which are both mutually exclusive – i.e. both cannot be simultaneously true – and jointly exhaustive – i.e. they cover the full range of possible outcomes. They are often contrasting and spoken of as "opposites".

Darwin	Darwin achieved lasting fame as originator of the theory of evolution through natural selection. His book Expression of Emotions in Man and Animals is generally considered the first text on comparative psychology.
Psychotherapy	Psychotherapy is a set of techniques based on psychological principles intended to improve mental health, emotional or behavioral issues.
Sigmund Freud	Sigmund Freud was the founder of the psychoanalytic school, based on his theory that unconscious motives control much behavior, that particular kinds of unconscious thoughts and memories are the source of neurosis, and that neurosis could be treated through bringing these unconscious thoughts and memories to consciousness in psychoanalytic treatment.
Neurologist	A physician who studies the nervous system, especially its structure, functions, and abnormalities is referred to as neurologist.
Hysteria	Hysteria is a diagnostic label applied to a state of mind, one of unmanageable fear or emotional excesses. The fear is often centered on a body part, most often on an imagined problem with that body part.
Hypnosis	Hypnosis is a psychological state whose existence and effects are strongly debated. Some believe that it is a state under which the subject's mind becomes so suggestible that the hypnotist, the one who induces the state, can establish communication with the subconscious mind of the subject and command behavior that the subject would not choose to perform in a conscious state.
Determinism	Determinism is the philosophical proposition that every event, including human cognition and action, is causally determined by an unbroken chain of prior occurrences.
Preconscious	In psychodynamic theory, material that is not in awareness but that can be brought into awareness by focusing one's attention is referred to as preconscious.
Intrapsychic conflict	In psychoanalysis, the struggles among the id, ego, and superego are an intrapsychic conflict.
Stanley Hall	His laboratory at Johns Hopkins is considered to be the first American laboratory of psychology. In 1887 Stanley Hall founded the American Journal of Psychology. His interests centered around child development and evolutionary theory
Jung	Jung was in some aspects a response to Sigmund Freud's psychoanalysis. He proposed and developed the concepts of the extroverted and introverted personality, archetypes, and the collective unconscious. His work has been influential in psychiatry and in the study of religion, literature, and related fields.
Ernest Jones	Ernest Jones was arguably the best-known follower of Freud. His writings on the subject of psychoanalysis prompted him to launch The International Journal of Psychoanalysis in 1920.
American Psychological Association	The American Psychological Association is a professional organization representing psychology in the US. The mission statement is to "advance psychology as a science and profession and as a means of promoting health, education , and human welfare".
Unconscious thought	Unconscious thought is Freud's concept of a reservoir of unacceptable wishes, feelings, and thoughts that are beyond conscious awareness.
Libido	Sigmund Freud suggested that libido is the instinctual energy or force that can come into conflict with the conventions of civilized behavior. Jung, condidered the libido as the free creative, or psychic, energy an individual has to put toward personal development, or individuation.
Psychoanalytic	Freud's theory that unconscious forces act as determinants of personality is called psychoanalytic theory. The theory is a developmental theory characterized by critical stages

Go to **Cram101.com** for the Practice Tests for this Chapter.

of development.

Psychosexual development	In psychodynamic theory, the process by which libidinal energy is expressed through different erogenous zones during different stages of development is called psychosexual development.
Stages	Stages represent relatively discrete periods of time in which functioning is qualitatively different from functioning at other periods.
Erogenous zone	An erogenous zone is an area of the human body that has heightened sensitivity and stimulation normally results in sexual response.
Psychosexual stages	In Freudian theory each child passes through five psychosexual stages. During each stage, the id focuses on a distinct erogenous zone on the body. Suffering from trauma during any of the first three stages may result in fixation in that stage. Freud related the resolutions of the stages with adult personalities and personality disorders.
Genitals	Genitals refers to the internal and external reproductive organs.
Adolescence	The period of life bounded by puberty and the assumption of adult responsibilities is adolescence.
Latency	In child development, latency refers to a phase of psychosexual development characterized by repression of sexual impulses. In learning theory, latency is the delay between stimulus (S) and response (R), which according to Hull depends on the strength of the association.
Genital stage	The genital stage in psychology is the term used by Sigmund Freud to describe the final stage of human psychosexual development. It is characterized by the expression of libido through intercourse with an adult of the other gender.
Fixation	Fixation in abnormal psychology is the state where an individual becomes obsessed with an attachment to another human, animal or inanimate object. Fixation in vision refers to maintaining the gaze in a constant direction. .
Superego	Frued's third psychic structure, which functions as a moral guardian and sets forth high standards for behavior is the superego.
Ego	In Freud's view the Ego serves to balance our primitive needs and our moral beliefs and taboos. Relying on experience, a healthy Ego provides the ability to adapt to reality and interact with the outside world.
Guilt	Guilt describes many concepts related to a negative emotion or condition caused by actions which are believed to be, morally wrong. According to Freud, the avoidance of guilt is the basis for moral behavior.
Infancy	The developmental period that extends from birth to 18 or 24 months is called infancy.
Pleasure principle	The pleasure principle is the tendency to seek pleasure and avoid pain. In Freud's theory, this principle rules the Id, but is at least partly repressed by the reality principle.
Primary process	The primary process in psychoanalytic theory, is one of the id's means of reducing tension by imagining what it desires.
Psychoanalyst	A psychoanalyst is a specially trained therapist who attempts to treat the individual by uncovering and revealing to the individual otherwise subconscious factors that are contributing to some undesirable behavor.
Defense mechanism	A Defense mechanism is a set of unconscious ways to protect one's personality from unpleasant thoughts and realities which may otherwise cause anxiety. The notion is an integral part of the psychoanalytic theory.
Adaptive behavior	An adaptive behavior increases the probability of the individual or organism to survive or exist within its environment.

Repression	A defense mechanism, repression involves moving thoughts unacceptable to the ego into the unconscious, where they cannot be easily accessed.
Motivated forgetting	Forgetting through suppression or repression in order to protect oneself from material that is too painful, anxiety- or guilt-producing, or otherwise unpleasant is called motivated forgetting.
Early childhood	Early childhood refers to the developmental period extending from the end of infancy to about 5 or 6 years of age; sometimes called the preschool years.
Free association	In psychoanalysis, the uncensored uttering of all thoughts that come to mind is called free association.
Anna Freud	Anna Freud was a pioneer of child psychoanalysis. She popularized the notion that adolescence is a period that includes rapid mood fluctuation with enormous uncertainty about self.
Displacement	An unconscious defense mechanism in which the individual directs aggressive or sexual feelings away from the primary object to someone or something safe is referred to as displacement. Displacement in linguistics is simply the ability to talk about things not present.
Reaction formation	In Freud's psychoanalytic theory, reaction formation is a defense mechanism in which anxiety-producing or unacceptable emotions are replaced by their direct opposites.
Denial	Denial is a psychological defense mechanism in which a person faced with a fact that is uncomfortable or painful to accept rejects it instead, insisting that it is not true despite what may be overwhelming evidence.
Projection	Attributing one's own undesirable thoughts, impulses, traits, or behaviors to others is referred to as projection.
Regression	Return to a form of behavior characteristic of an earlier stage of development is called regression.
Sublimation	Sublimation is a coping mechanism. It refers to rechanneling sexual or aggressive energy into pursuits that society considers acceptable or admirable.
Rationalization	Rationalization is the process of constructing a logical justification for a decision that was originally arrived at through a different mental process. It is one of Freud's defense mechanisms.
The Interpretation of Dreams	The Interpretation of Dreams is a book by Sigmund Freud. The book introduces the Id, the Ego, and the Superego, and describes Freud's theory of the unconscious with respect to Dream interpretation. Widely considered to be his most important contribution to Psychology.
Adler	Adler argued that human personality could be explained teleologically, separate strands dominated by the guiding purpose of the individual's unconscious self ideal to convert feelings of inferiority to superiority (or rather completeness). The desires of the self ideal were countered by social and ethical demands.
Human nature	Human nature is the fundamental nature and substance of humans, as well as the range of human behavior that is believed to be invariant over long periods of time and across very different cultural contexts.
Collective unconscious	Collective unconscious is a term of analytical psychology, originally coined by Carl Jung. It refers to that part of a person's unconscious which is common to all human beings. It contains archetypes, which are forms or symbols that are manifested by all people in all cultures.
Erik Erikson	Erik Erikson conceived eight stages of development, each confronting the individual with its own psychosocial demands, that continued into old age. Personality development, according to

Go to **Cram101.com** for the Practice Tests for this Chapter.

	Erikson, takes place through a series of crises that must be overcome and internalized by the individual in preparation for the next developmental stage. Such crisis are not catastrophes but vulnerabilities.
Acquisition	Acquisition is the process of adapting to the environment, learning or becoming conditioned. In classical conditoning terms, it is the initial learning of the stimulus response link, which involves a neutral stimulus being associated with a unconditioned stimulus and becoming a conditioned stimulus.
Self-concept	Self-concept refers to domain-specific evaluations of the self where a domain may be academics, athletics, etc.
Autonomy	Autonomy is the condition of something that does not depend on anything else.
Ego psychology	Ego psychology was derived from psychoanalysis. The theory emphasizes the role of the ego in development and attributes psychological disorders to failure of the ego to manage impulses and internal conflicts.
Object relation	Object relation theory is the idea that the ego-self exists only in relation to other objects, which may be external or internal.
Melanie Klein	Melanie Klein built on the work of Sigmund Freud and was one of the theoretical cofounders of object relations theory. Her insistence on regarding aggression as an important force in its own right when analyzing children brought her into conflict with Anna Freud.
Kohut	Kohut was a pioneer in the fields of psychology and psychiatry. He established the school of Self Psychology as a branch of psychoanalysis. Where Freud empahasized guilt in the etiology of emotional disorders, Kohut saw shame as more central.
Maturation	The orderly unfolding of traits, as regulated by the genetic code is called maturation.
Psychopathology	Psychopathology refers to the field concerned with the nature and development of mental disorders.
Motivation	In psychology, motivation is the driving force (desire) behind all actions of an organism.
Scientific method	Psychologists gather data in order to describe, understand, predict, and control behavior. Scientific method refers to an approach that can be used to discover accurate information. It includes these steps: understand the problem, collect data, draw conclusions, and revise research conclusions.
Behaviorism	The school of psychology that defines psychology as the study of observable behavior and studies relationships between stimuli and responses is called behaviorism. Behaviorism relied heavily on animal research and stated the same principles governed the behavior of both nonhumans and humans.
Overt behavior	An action or response that is directly observable and measurable is an overt behavior.
Conditioning	Conditioning describes the process by which behaviors can be learned or modified through interaction with the environment.
Reinforcement	In operant conditioning, reinforcement is any change in an environment that (a) occurs after the behavior, (b) seems to make that behavior re-occur more often in the future and (c) that reoccurence of behavior must be the result of the change.
Classical conditioning	Classical conditioning is a simple form of learning in which an organism comes to associate or anticipate events. A neutral stimulus comes to evoke the response usually evoked by a natural or unconditioned stimulus by being paired repeatedly with the unconditioned stimulus.
Stimulus	A change in an environmental condition that elicits a response is a stimulus.
Pavlov	Pavlov first described the phenomenon now known as classical conditioning in experiments with

	dogs.
Conditioned stimulus	A previously neutral stimulus that elicits the conditioned response because of being repeatedly paired with a stimulus that naturally elicited that response, is called a conditioned stimulus.
Unconditioned response	An Unconditioned Response is the response elicited to an unconditioned stimulus. It is a natural, automatic response.
Unconditioned stimulus	In classical conditioning, an unconditioned stimulus elicits a response from an organism prior to conditioning. It is a naturally occurring stimulus and a naturally occurring response..
Conditioned response	A conditioned response is the response to a stimulus that occurs when an animal has learned to associate the stimulus with a certain positive or negative effect.
Generalization	In conditioning, the tendency for a conditioned response to be evoked by stimuli that are similar to the stimulus to which the response was conditioned is a generalization. The greater the similarity among the stimuli, the greater the probability of generalization.
Instrumental conditioning	Operant conditioning, sometimes called instrumental conditioning, was first extensively studied by Thorndike. In instrumental conditioning, the organism must act in a certain way before it is reinforced; that is, reinforcement is contingent on the organism's behavior.
Operant Conditioning	A simple form of learning in which an organism learns to engage in behavior because it is reinforced is referred to as operant conditioning. The consequences of a behavior produce changes in the probability of the behavior's occurence.
Skinner	Skinner conducted research on shaping behavior through positive and negative reinforcement, and demonstrated operant conditioning, a technique which he developed in contrast with classical conditioning.
Skinner box	An operant conditioning chamber, or Skinner box, is an experimental apparatus used to study conditioning in animals. Chambers have at least one operandum that can automatically detect the occurrence of a behavioral response or action. The other minimal requirement of a conditioning chamber is that it have a means of delivering a primary reinforcer or unconditioned stimulus like food or water.
Punishment	Punishment is the addtion of a stimulus that reduces the frequency of a response, or the removal of a stimulus that results in a reduction of the response.
Extinction	In operant extinction, if no reinforcement is delivered after the response, gradually the behavior will no longer occur in the presence of the stimulus. The process is more rapid following continuous reinforcement rather than after partial reinforcement. In Classical Conditioning, repeated presentations of the CS without being followed by the US results in the extinction of the CS.
Negative reinforcer	Negative reinforcer is a reinforcer that when removed increases the frequency of an response.
Pupil	In the eye, the pupil is the opening in the middle of the iris. It appears black because most of the light entering it is absorbed by the tissues inside the eye. The size of the pupil is controlled by involuntary contraction and dilation of the iris, in order to regulate the intensity of light entering the eye. This is known as the pupillary reflex.
Aversive stimulus	A stimulus that elicits pain, fear, or avoidance is an aversive stimulus.
Schedule of reinforcement	A schedule of reinforcement is either continuous (the behavior is reinforced each time it occurs) or intermittent (the behavior is reinforced only on certain occasions).

Go to **Cram101.com** for the Practice Tests for this Chapter.

Intermittent reinforcement	In an intermittent reinforcement schedule, a designated response is reinforced only some of the time.
Fixed-ratio	In a fixed-ratio schedule, reinforcement is provided after a fixed number of correct responses.
Fixed-interval	A reinforcement schedule in which a fixed amount of time must elapse between the previous and subsequent times that reinforcement is available is the fixed-interval schedule.
Variable-ratio	In a variable-ratio schedule of reinforcement reinforcement is provided after a variable number of correct responses.
Variable-interval	A reinforcement schedule in which a variable amount of time must elapse between the previous and subsequent times that reinforcement is available is a variable-interval schedule.
Variable interval	In a variable interval schedule of reinforcement, reinforcement occurs after the passage of a varying length of time around an average, provided that at least one response occurred in that period.
Negative Reinforcement	During negative reinforcement, a stimulus is removed and the frequency of the behavior or response increases.
Deprivation	Deprivation, is the loss or withholding of normal stimulation, nutrition, comfort, love, and so forth; a condition of lacking. The level of stimulation is less than what is required.
Social-cognitive theory	Social-cognitive theory, a school of psychology in the behaviorist tradition, includes cognitive factors in the explanation and prediction of behavior. It is a cognitively oriented learning theory in with observational learning and person variables such as values and expectances.
Observational learning	The acquisition of knowledge and skills through the observation of others rather than by means of direct experience is observational learning. Four major processes are thought to influence the observational learning: attentional, retentional, behavioral production, and motivational.
Bandura	Bandura is best known for his work on social learning theory or Social Cognitivism. His famous Bobo doll experiment illustrated that people learn from observing others.
Self-esteem	Self-esteem refers to a person's subjective appraisal of himself or herself as intrinsically positive or negative to some degree.
Phobia	A persistent, irrational fear of an object, situation, or activity that the person feels compelled to avoid is referred to as a phobia.
Social norm	A social norm, is a rule that is socially enforced. In social situations, such as meetings, they are unwritten and often unstated rules that govern individuals' behavior. A social norm is most evident when not followed or broken.
Cognitive psychology	Cognitive psychology is the psychological science which studies the mental processes that are hypothesised to underlie behavior. This covers a broad range of research domains, examining questions about the workings of memory, attention, perception, knowledge representation, reasoning, creativity and problem solving.
Mental processes	The thoughts, feelings, and motives that each of us experiences privately but that cannot be observed directly are called mental processes.
Schemata	Cognitive categories or frames of reference are called schemata.
Schema	Schema refers to a way of mentally representing the world, such as a belief or an expectation, that can influence perception of persons, objects, and situations.
Cognitive	According to Piaget, the number of schemata available to an organism at any given time

structure	constitutes that organism's cognitive structure. How the organism interacts with its environment depends on the current cognitive structure available. As the cognitive structure develops, new assimilations can occur.
Personality disorder	A mental disorder characterized by a set of inflexible, maladaptive personality traits that keep a person from functioning properly in society is referred to as a personality disorder.
Cognitive therapy	Cognitive therapy is a kind of psychotherapy used to treat depression, anxiety disorders, phobias, and other forms of mental disorder. It involves recognizing distorted thinking and learning how to replace it with more realistic thoughts and actions.
Aaron Beck	Aaron Beck was initially trained as a psychoanalyst and conducted research on the psychoanalytic treatment of depression. With out the strong ability to collect data to this end, he began exploring cognitive approaches to treatment and originated cognitive behavior therapy.
Cognitive approach	A cognitive approach focuses on the mental processes involved in knowing: how we direct our attention, perceive, remember, think, and solve problems.
Social influence	Social influence is when the actions or thoughts of individual(s) are changed by other individual(s). Peer pressure is an example of social influence.
All-or-none	All-or-none indicates a situation in which there are two possibilities (a binary choice set), one of which is 100% and one of which is 0%. It is a phrase commonly used to describe action potentials of neurons, which, if they fire at all, propagate from the beginning to the end of the axonal process.
Overgenerali- ation	Overgeneralization is concluding that all instances of some kind of event will turn out a certain way because one or more in the past did. For instance, a class goes badly one day and I conclude, "I'll never be a good teacher."
Humanistic	Humanistic refers to any system of thought focused on subjective experience and human problems and potentials.
Self- actualization	Self-actualization (a term originated by Kurt Goldstein) is the instinctual need of a human to make the most of their unique abilities. Maslow described it as follows: Self Actualization is the intrinsic growth of what is already in the organism, or more accurately, of what the organism is.
Pathology	Pathology is the study of the processes underlying disease and other forms of illness, harmful abnormality, or dysfunction.
Humanistic psychology	Humanistic psychology refers to the school of psychology that focuses on the uniqueness of human beings and their capacity for choice, growth, and psychological health.
Self- understanding	Self-understanding is a child's cognitive representation of the self, the substance and content of the child's self-conceptions.
Carl Rogers	Carl Rogers was instrumental in the development of non-directive psychotherapy, also known as "client-centered" psychotherapy. Rogers' basic tenets were unconditional positive regard, genuineness, and empathic understanding, with each demonstrated by the counselor.
Self-image	A person's self-image is the mental picture, generally of a kind that is quite resistant to change, that depicts not only details that are potentially available to objective investigation by others, but also items that have been learned by that person about himself or herself.
Humanistic theories	Humanistic theories focus attention on the whole, unique person, especially on the person's conscious understanding of his or her self and the world.
Existentialism	The view that people are completely free and responsible for their own behavior is

existentialism.

Logotherapy	Developed by Viktor Frankl, Logotherapy is considered the "third Viennese school of psychotherapy" after Freud's psychoanalysis and Adler's individual psychology. It is a type of Existential Analysis that focuses on a "will to meaning" as opposed to Adler's Nietzschian doctrine of "will to power" or Freud's of "will to pleasure".
Community psychology	Community psychology is the study of how to use the principles of psychology to create communities of all sizes that promote mental health of their members.
Causation	Causation concerns the time order relationship between two or more objects such that if a specific antecendent condition occurs the same consequent must always follow.
Prejudice	Prejudice in general, implies coming to a judgment on the subject before learning where the preponderance of the evidence actually lies, or formation of a judgement without direct experience.
Socioeconomic	Socioeconomic pertains to the study of the social and economic impacts of any product or service offering, market intervention or other activity on an economy as a whole and on the companies, organization and individuals who are its main economic actors.
Social role	Social role refers to expected behavior patterns associated with particular social positions.
Script	A schema, or behavioral sequence, for an event is called a script. It is a form of schematic organization, with real-world events organized in terms of temporal and causal relations between component acts.
Role-playing	Role-playing refers to a technique that teaches people to behave in a certain way by encouraging them to pretend that they are in a particular situation; it helps people acquire complex behaviors in an efficient way.
Discrimination	In Learning theory, discrimination refers the ability to distinguish between a conditioned stimulus and other stimuli. It can be brought about by extensive training or differential reinforcement. In social terms, it is the denial of privileges to a person or a group on the basis of prejudice.
Social policy	Social policy is the study of the welfare state, and the range of responses to social need.
Child development	Scientific study of the processes of change from conception through adolescence is called child development.
Social skills	Social skills are skills used to interact and communicate with others to assist status in the social structure and other motivations.
Control group	A group that does not receive the treatment effect in an experiment is referred to as the control group or sometimes as the comparison group.
Experimental group	Experimental group refers to any group receiving a treatment effect in an experiment.
Community intervention	An approach to treating and preventing disorders by directing action at the organizational, agency, and community levels rather than at individuals is called a community intervention.
Temperament	Temperament refers to a basic, innate disposition to change behavior. The activity level is an important dimension of temperament.
Mind-body relationship	Mind-body relationship is the philosophical issue regarding whether the mind and body operate indistinguishably as a single system or whether they act as two separate systems.
Longitudinal study	Longitudinal study is a type of developmental study in which the same group of participants is followed and measured for an extended period of time, often years.

Go to **Cram101.com** for the Practice Tests for this Chapter.

Psychosocial stages	Erikson's eight developmental stages through the life span, each defined by a conflict that must be resolved satisfactorily in order for healthy personality development to occur are called psychosocial stages.
Object relations theory	Object relations theory holds that the ego-self exists only in relation to other objects, which may be external or internal. The internal objects are internalized versions of external objects, primarily formed from early interactions with the parents.
Social learning	Social learning is learning that occurs as a function of observing, retaining and replicating behavior observed in others. Although social learning can occur at any stage in life, it is thought to be particularly important during childhood, particularly as authority becomes important.
Problem solving	An attempt to find an appropriate way of attaining a goal when the goal is not readily available is called problem solving.
Maladjustment	Maladjustment is the condition of being unable to adapt properly to your environment with resulting emotional instability.
Humanistic perspective	The approach that suggests that all individuals naturally strive to grow, develop, and be in control of their lives and behavior is called the humanistic perspective.
Social support	Social Support is the physical and emotional comfort given by family, friends, co-workers and others. Research has identified three main types of social support: emotional, practical, sharing points of view.

Go to **Cram101.com** for the Practice Tests for this Chapter.

Psychotherapy	Psychotherapy is a set of techniques based on psychological principles intended to improve mental health, emotional or behavioral issues.
Group therapy	Group therapy is a form of psychotherapy during which one or several therapists treat a small group of clients together as a group. This may be more cost effective than individual therapy, and possibly even more effective.
Clinical psychologist	A psychologist, usually with a Ph.D, whose training is in the diagnosis, treatment, or research of psychological and behavioral disorders is a clinical psychologist.
Attention	Attention is the cognitive process of selectively concentrating on one thing while ignoring other things. Psychologists have labeled three types of attention: sustained attention, selective attention, and divided attention.
Depression	In everyday language depression refers to any downturn in mood, which may be relatively transitory and perhaps due to something trivial. This is differentiated from Clinical depression which is marked by symptoms that last two weeks or more and are so severe that they interfere with daily living.
Anxiety	Anxiety is a complex combination of the feeling of fear, apprehension and worry often accompanied by physical sensations such as palpitations, chest pain and/or shortness of breath.
Nightmare	Nightmare was the original term for the state later known as waking dream, and more currently as sleep paralysis, associated with rapid eye movement (REM) periods of sleep.
Maladaptive	In psychology, a behavior or trait is adaptive when it helps an individual adjust and function well within their social environment. A maladaptive behavior or trait is counterproductive to the individual.
Schema	Schema refers to a way of mentally representing the world, such as a belief or an expectation, that can influence perception of persons, objects, and situations.
Guilt	Guilt describes many concepts related to a negative emotion or condition caused by actions which are believed to be, morally wrong. According to Freud, the avoidance of guilt is the basis for moral behavior.
Emotion	An emotion is a mental states that arise spontaneously, rather than through conscious effort. They are often accompanied by physiological changes.
Fixation	Fixation in abnormal psychology is the state where an individual becomes obsessed with an attachment to another human, animal or inanimate object. Fixation in vision refers to maintaining the gaze in a constant direction. .
Negative schema	Negative schema are automatic, enduring, and stable negative cognitive biases.
Validity	The extent to which a test measures what it is intended to measure is called validity.
Empathy	Empathy is the recognition and understanding of the states of mind, including beliefs, desires and particularly emotions of others without injecting your own.
Motives	Needs or desires that energize and direct behavior toward a goal are motives.
Self-esteem	Self-esteem refers to a person's subjective appraisal of himself or herself as intrinsically positive or negative to some degree.
Clinician	A health professional authorized to provide services to people suffering from one or more pathologies is a clinician.
Variable	A variable refers to a measurable factor, characteristic, or attribute of an individual or a system.

Theories	Theories are logically self-consistent models or frameworks describing the behavior of a certain natural or social phenomenon. They are broad explanations and predictions concerning phenomena of interest.
Control group	A group that does not receive the treatment effect in an experiment is referred to as the control group or sometimes as the comparison group.
Placebo	Placebo refers to a bogus treatment that has the appearance of being genuine.
Double-blind	In a double-blind experiment, neither the individuals nor the researchers know who belongs to the control group. Only after all the data are recorded may researchers be permitted to learn which individuals are which. Performing an experiment in double-blind fashion is a way to lessen the influence of prejudices and unintentional physical cues on the results.
Spontaneous remission	Spontaneous remission is a catch-all expression by the medical faculty for any healing with no obvious conventional explanation.
Schizophrenia	Schizophrenia is characterized by persistent defects in the perception or expression of reality. A person suffering from untreated schizophrenia typically demonstrates grossly disorganized thinking, and may also experience delusions or auditory hallucinations
Population	Population refers to all members of a well-defined group of organisms, events, or things.
Antidepressant	An antidepressant is a medication used primarily in the treatment of clinical depression. They are not thought to produce tolerance, although sudden withdrawal may produce adverse effects. They create little if any immediate change in mood and require between several days and several weeks to take effect.
Mood disorder	A mood disorder is a condition where the prevailing emotional mood is distorted or inappropriate to the circumstances.
Self-concept	Self-concept refers to domain-specific evaluations of the self where a domain may be academics, athletics, etc.
Psychodynamic therapy	Psychodynamic therapy uses a range of different techniques, applied to the client considering his or her needs. Most approaches are centered around the idea of a maladapted function developed early in life which are at least in part unconscious.
Psychoanalysis	Psychoanalysis refers to the school of psychology that emphasizes the importance of unconscious motives and conflicts as determinants of human behavior. It was Freud's method of exploring human personality.
Sigmund Freud	Sigmund Freud was the founder of the psychoanalytic school, based on his theory that unconscious motives control much behavior, that particular kinds of unconscious thoughts and memories are the source of neurosis, and that neurosis could be treated through bringing these unconscious thoughts and memories to consciousness in psychoanalytic treatment.
Free association	In psychoanalysis, the uncensored uttering of all thoughts that come to mind is called free association.
Psychodynamic	Most psychodynamic approaches are centered around the idea of a maladapted function developed early in life (usually childhood) which are at least in part unconscious. This maladapted function (a.k.a. defense mechanism) does not do well in place of a normal/healthy one.
Psychodynamic psychotherapy	The "goal" of psychodynamic therapy is the experience of "truth." This "truth" must be encountered through the breakdown of psychological defenses. Psychodynamic psychotherapy involves a great idea of introspection and reflection from the client.
Displacement	An unconscious defense mechanism in which the individual directs aggressive or sexual feelings away from the primary object to someone or something safe is referred to as displacement. Displacement in linguistics is simply the ability to talk about things not

present.

Transference	Transference is a phenomenon in psychology characterized by unconscious redirection of feelings from one person to another.
Affect	A subjective feeling or emotional tone often accompanied by bodily expressions noticeable to others is called affect.
Countertrans-erence	Feelings that the psychoanalyst unconsciously directs to the analysis, stemming from his or her own emotional vulnerabilities and unresolved conflicts are countertransference effects.
Psychoanalyst	A psychoanalyst is a specially trained therapist who attempts to treat the individual by uncovering and revealing to the individual otherwise subconscious factors that are contributing to some undesirable behavor.
Motivation	In psychology, motivation is the driving force (desire) behind all actions of an organism.
Insight	Insight refers to a sudden awareness of the relationships among various elements that had previously appeared to be independent of one another.
Attitude	An enduring mental representation of a person, place, or thing that evokes an emotional response and related behavior is called attitude.
Acquisition	Acquisition is the process of adapting to the environment, learning or becoming conditioned. In classical conditoning terms, it is the initial learning of the stimulus response link, which involves a neutral stimulus being associated with a unconditioned stimulus and becoming a conditioned stimulus.
Early childhood	Early childhood refers to the developmental period extending from the end of infancy to about 5 or 6 years of age; sometimes called the preschool years.
Repression	A defense mechanism, repression involves moving thoughts unacceptable to the ego into the unconscious, where they cannot be easily accessed.
Sexual abuse	Sexual abuse is a term used to describe non- consentual sexual relations between two or more parties which are considered criminally and/or morally offensive.
Hypnosis	Hypnosis is a psychological state whose existence and effects are strongly debated. Some believe that it is a state under which the subject's mind becomes so suggestible that the hypnotist, the one who induces the state, can establish communication with the subconscious mind of the subject and command behavior that the subject would not choose to perform in a conscious state.
Altered state of consciousness	Altered state of consciousness refers to a mental state other than ordinary waking consciousness, such as sleep, meditation, hypnosis, or a drug-induced state.
Infancy	The developmental period that extends from birth to 18 or 24 months is called infancy.
Reasoning	Reasoning is the act of using reason to derive a conclusion from certain premises. There are two main methods to reach a conclusion,deductive reasoning and inductive reasoning.
Amnesia	Amnesia is a condition in which memory is disturbed. The causes of amnesia are organic or functional. Organic causes include damage to the brain, through trauma or disease, or use of certain (generally sedative) drugs.
Role-playing	Role-playing refers to a technique that teaches people to behave in a certain way by encouraging them to pretend that they are in a particular situation; it helps people acquire complex behaviors in an efficient way.
Dissociation	Dissociation is a psychological state or condition in which certain thoughts, emotions, sensations, or memories are separated from the rest.

Humanistic and existential therapies	A generic term for insight psychotherapies that emphasize the individual's subjective experiences, free will, and ever-present ability to decide on a new life course are humanistic and existential therapies.
Humanistic	Humanistic refers to any system of thought focused on subjective experience and human problems and potentials.
Client-Centered Therapy	Client-Centered Therapy was developed by Carl Rogers. It is based on the principal of talking therapy and is a non-directive approach. The therapist encourages the patient to express their feelings and does not suggest how the person might wish to change, but by listening and then mirroring back what the patient reveals to them, helps them to explore and understand their feelings for themselves.
Humanistic therapy	The aim of much humanistic therapy is to give a holistic description of the person. By using phenomenological, intersubjective and first-person categories, the humanistic psychologist hopes to get a glimpse of the whole person and not just the fragmented parts of the personality.
Unconditional positive regard	Unqualified caring and nonjudgmental acceptance of another is called unconditional positive regard.
Gestalt therapy	Gestalt therapy is a form of psychotherapy, based on the experiential ideal of "here and now," and relationships with others and the world. By focusing the individual on their self-awareness as part of present reality, new insights can be made into their behavior, and they can engage in self-healing.
Perception	Perception is the process of acquiring, interpreting, selecting, and organizing sensory information.
Self-worth	In psychology, self-esteem or self-worth refers to a person's subjective appraisal of himself or herself as intrinsically positive or negative to some degree.
Aaron Beck	Aaron Beck was initially trained as a psychoanalyst and conducted research on the psychoanalytic treatment of depression. With out the strong ability to collect data to this end, he began exploring cognitive approaches to treatment and originated cognitive behavior therapy.
Suicide	Suicide behavior is rare in childhood but escalates in adolescence. The suicide rate increases in a linear fashion from adolescence through late adulthood.
Cognition	The intellectual processes through which information is obtained, transformed, stored, retrieved, and otherwise used is cognition.
Schemata	Cognitive categories or frames of reference are called schemata.
Interpersonal therapy	A brief psychotherapy designed to help depressed people better understand and cope with problems relating to their interpersonal relationships is referred to as interpersonal therapy.
Brief therapy	A primary approach of brief therapy is to open up the present to admit a wider context and more appropriate understandings (not necessarily at a conscious level), rather than formal analysis of historical causes.
Questionnaire	A self-report method of data collection or clinical assessment method in which the individual being studied checks off items on a printed list, answers multiple-choice questions, or writes out answers to essay questions aimed at producing a selfdescription is called questionnaire.
Psychiatrist	A psychiatrist is a physician who specializes in the diagnosis and treatment of psychological disorders.

Research design	A research design tests a hypothesis. The basic typess are: descriptive, correlational, and experimental.
Dependent variable	A measure of an assumed effect of an independent variable is called the dependent variable.
Meta-analysis	In statistics, a meta-analysis combines the results of several studies that address a set of related research hypotheses.
Standard deviation	In probability and statistics, the standard deviation is the most commonly used measure of statistical dispersion. Simply put, it measures how spread out the values in a data set are.
Effect size	An effect size is the strength or magnitude of the difference between two sets of data or, in outcome studies, between two time points for the same population. (The degree to which the null hypothesis is false).
Frequency distribution	In statistics, a frequency distribution is a list of the values that a variable takes in a sample. It is usually a list, ordered by quantity, showing the number of times each value appears.
Percentile rank	The percentile rank of a score is the percentage of scores in its frequency distribution which are lower.
Ethnicity	Ethnicity refers to a characteristic based on cultural heritage, nationality characteristics, race, religion, and language.
Syndrome	The term syndrome is the association of several clinically recognizable features, signs, symptoms, phenomena or characteristics which often occur together, so that the presence of one feature indicates the presence of the others.
Process research	Research on the mechanisms by which a therapy may bring improvement is called process research.
Behavior modification	Behavior Modification is a technique of altering an individual's reactions to stimuli through positive reinforcement and the extinction of maladaptive behavior.
Obedience	Obedience is the willingness to follow the will of others. Humans have been shown to be surprisingly obedient in the presence of perceived legitimate authority figures, as demonstrated by the Milgram experiment in the 1960s.
Direct observation	Direct observation refers to assessing behavior through direct surveillance.
Behavior therapy	Behavior therapy refers to the systematic application of the principles of learning to direct modification of a client's problem behaviors.
Classical conditioning	Classical conditioning is a simple form of learning in which an organism comes to associate or anticipate events. A neutral stimulus comes to evoke the response usually evoked by a natural or unconditioned stimulus by being paired repeatedly with the unconditioned stimulus.
Desensitization	Desensitization refers to the type of sensory or behavioral adaptation in which we become less sensitive to constant stimuli.
Operant learning	A simple form of learning in which an organism learns to engage in behavior because it is reinforced is referred to as operant learning. The consequences of a behavior produce changes in the probability of the behavior's occurence.
Operant Conditioning	A simple form of learning in which an organism learns to engage in behavior because it is reinforced is referred to as operant conditioning. The consequences of a behavior produce changes in the probability of the behavior's occurence.
Cognitive	A cognitive approach focuses on the mental processes involved in knowing: how we direct our

approach	attention, perceive, remember, think, and solve problems.
Schedules of Reinforcement	Different combinations of frequency and timing of reinforcement following a behavior are referred to as schedules of reinforcement. They are either continuous (the behavior is reinforced each time it occurs) or intermittent (the behavior is reinforced only on certain occasions).
Shaping	The concept of reinforcing successive, increasingly accurate approximations to a target behavior is called shaping. The target behavior is broken down into a hierarchy of elemental steps, each step more sophisticated then the last. By successively reinforcing each of the the elemental steps, a form of differential reinforcement, until that step is learned while extinguishing the step below, the target behavior is gradually achieved.
Abnormal behavior	An action, thought, or feeling that is harmful to the person or to others is called abnormal behavior.
Social learning	Social learning is learning that occurs as a function of observing, retaining and replicating behavior observed in others. Although social learning can occur at any stage in life, it is thought to be particularly important during childhood, particularly as authority becomes important.
Generalization	In conditioning, the tendency for a conditioned response to be evoked by stimuli that are similar to the stimulus to which the response was conditioned is a generalization. The greater the similarity among the stimuli, the greater the probability of generalization.
Reinforcer	In operant conditioning, a reinforcer is any stimulus that increases the probability that a preceding behavior will occur again. In Classical Conditioning, the unconditioned stimulus (US) is the reinforcer.
Token economy	An environmental setting that fosters desired behavior by reinforcing it with tokens that can be exchanged for other reinforcers is called a token economy.
Punishment	Punishment is the addtion of a stimulus that reduces the frequency of a response, or the removal of a stimulus that results in a reduction of the response.
Extinction	In operant extinction, if no reinforcement is delivered after the response, gradually the behavior will no longer occur in the presence of the stimulus. The process is more rapid following continuous reinforcement rather than after partial reinforcement. In Classical Conditioning, repeated presentations of the CS without being followed by the US results in the extinction of the CS.
Biofeedback	Biofeedback is the process of measuring and quantifying an aspect of a subject's physiology, analyzing the data, and then feeding back the information to the subject in a form that allows the subject to enact physiological change.
Cognitive-behavioral therapy	Cognitive-behavioral therapy refers to group of treatment procedures aimed at identifying and modifying faulty thought processes, attitudes and attributions, and problem behaviors.
Behavioral therapy	The treatment of a mental disorder through the application of basic principles of conditioning and learning is called behavioral therapy.
Relaxation training	Relaxation training is an intervention technique used for tics. The person is taught to relax the muscles involved in the tics.
Learning	Learning is a relatively permanent change in behavior that results from experience. Thus, to attribute a behavioral change to learning, the change must be relatively permanent and must result from experience.
Meditation	Meditation usually refers to a state in which the body is consciously relaxed and the mind is

allowed to become calm and focused.

Psychophysio-ogical disorder	Any physical disorder that has a strong psychological basis or component is called a psychophysiological disorder.
Migraine	Migraine is a form of headache, usually very intense and disabling. It is a neurologic disease.
Panic attack	An attack of overwhelming anxiety, fear, or terror is called panic attack.
Natural childbirth	The natural childbirth technique attempts to minimize medical intervention, particularly anaesthetics, during childbirth.
Sensation	Sensation is the first stage in the chain of biochemical and neurologic events that begins with the impinging of a stimulus upon the receptor cells of a sensory organ, which then leads to perception, the mental state that is reflected in statements like "I see a uniformly blue wall."
Exposure therapy	An exposure therapy is any method of treating fears, including flooding and systematic desensitization, that involves exposing the client to the feared object or situation so that the process of extinction or habituation of the fear response can occur.
In vivo	In vivo is used to indicate the presence of a whole/living organism, in distinction to a partial or dead organism, or a computer model. In vivo research is more suited to observe an overall effect than in vitro research, which is better suited to deduce mechanisms of action.
Exposure treatment	An exposure treatment is any method of treating fears, including flooding and systematic desensitization, that involves exposing the client to the feared object or situation so that the process of extinction or habituation of the fear response can occur.
Flooding	Flooding is a behavioral fear-reduction technique based on principles of classical conditioning. Fear-evoking stimuli are presented continuously in the absence of harm so that fear responses are extinguished. However, subjects tend to avoid the stimulus, making extinction difficult.
Systematic desensitization	Systematic desensitization refers to Wolpe's behavioral fear-reduction technique in which a hierarchy of fear-evoking stimuli are presented while the person remains relaxed. The fear-evoking stimuli thereby become associated with muscle relaxation.
Phobia	A persistent, irrational fear of an object, situation, or activity that the person feels compelled to avoid is referred to as a phobia.
Stimulus	A change in an environmental condition that elicits a response is a stimulus.
Habit	A habit is a response that has become completely separated from its eliciting stimulus. Early learning theorists used the term to describe S-R associations, however not all S-R associations become a habit, rather many are extinguished after reinforcement is withdrawn.
Social skills	Social skills are skills used to interact and communicate with others to assist status in the social structure and other motivations.
Positive reinforcement	In positive reinforcement, a stimulus is added and the rate of responding increases.
Adaptive behavior	An adaptive behavior increases the probability of the individual or organism to survive or exist within its environment.
Participant modeling	A behavior therapy in which an appropriate response is modeled in graduated steps and the client attempts each step, encouraged and supported by the therapist is participant modeling.
Behavioral rehearsal	Behavior therapy technique in which the client practices coping with troublesome or anxiety arousing situations in a safe and supervised situation is a behavioral rehearsal.

Assertiveness training	In behavior therapy, a direct method of training people to express their own desires and feelings and to maintain their own rights in interactions with others, while at the same time respecting the others' rights is called assertiveness training.
Positive feedback	When a change in a variable occurs in a system, the system responds. In the case of positive feedback the response of the system is to cause that variable to increase in the same direction.
Assertiveness	Assertiveness basically means the ability to express your thoughts and feelings in a way that clearly states your needs and keeps the lines of communication open with the other.
Case study	A carefully drawn biography that may be obtained through interviews, questionnaires, and psychological tests is called a case study.
Self-efficacy	Self-efficacy is the belief that one has the capabilities to execute the courses of actions required to manage prospective situations.
Cognitive therapy	Cognitive therapy is a kind of psychotherapy used to treat depression, anxiety disorders, phobias, and other forms of mental disorder. It involves recognizing distorted thinking and learning how to replace it with more realistic thoughts and actions.
Stress disorder	A significant emotional disturbance caused by stresses outside the range of normal human experience is referred to as stress disorder.
Reinforcement	In operant conditioning, reinforcement is any change in an environment that (a) occurs after the behavior, (b) seems to make that behavior re-occur more often in the future and (c) that reoccurence of behavior must be the result of the change.
Multimodal therapy	Multimodal Therapy is an approach to psychotherapy founded by Arnold Lazarus. It is based on the idea that humans are biological beings that think, feel, act, sense, imagine, and interact; and that each of these "modalities" should be addressed in psychological treatment.
Vicarious learning	Vicarious learning is learning without specific reinforcement for one's behavior. It is learning by observing others.
Self-understanding	Self-understanding is a child's cognitive representation of the self, the substance and content of the child's self-conceptions.
Feedback	Feedback refers to information returned to a person about the effects a response has had.
Self-disclosure	The process of revealing private thoughts, feelings, and one's personal history to others is referred to as self-disclosure.
Role-play	A training technique that involves having the trainee pretend to perform a task is called role-play.
Social reinforcement	Praise, attention, approval, and/or affection from others is referred to as social reinforcement.
Behavior rehearsal	A behavior therapy technique in which a client practices new behavior in the consulting room, often aided by demonstrations and role-play by the therapist is referred to as behavior rehearsal.
Family therapy	Family therapy is a branch of psychotherapy that treats family problems. Family therapists consider the family as a system of interacting members; as such, the problems in the family are seen to arise as an emergent property of the interactions in the system, rather than ascribed exclusively to the "faults" or psychological problems of individual members.
Individuality	According to Cooper, individuality consists of two dimensions: self-assertion and separateness.
Substance abuse	Substance abuse refers to the overindulgence in and dependence on a stimulant, depressant, or

	other chemical substance, leading to effects that are detrimental to the individual's physical or mental health, or the welfare of others.
Society	The social sciences use the term society to mean a group of people that form a semi-closed (or semi-open) social system, in which most interactions are with other individuals belonging to the group.
Homeostasis	Homeostasis is the property of an open system, especially living organisms, to regulate its internal environment so as to maintain a stable condition, by means of multiple dynamic equilibrium adjustments controlled by interrelated regulation mechanisms.
Acculturation	Acculturation is the obtainment of culture by an individual or a group of people.
Personal identity	The portion of the self-concept that pertains to the self as a distinct, separate individual is called personal identity.
Ethnic group	An ethnic group is a culture or subculture whose members are readily distinguishable by outsiders based on traits originating from a common racial, national, linguistic, or religious source. Members of an ethnic group are often presumed to be culturally or biologically similar, although this is not in fact necessarily the case.
Gender role	A cluster of behaviors that characterizes traditional female or male behaviors within a cultural setting is a gender role.
Couples therapy	Therapy with married or unmarried couples whose major problem is within their relationship is referred to as couples therapy.
Psychodrama	A therapy in which clients act out personal conflicts and feelings in the presence of others who play supporting roles is referred to as psychodrama.
Independent variable	A condition in a scientific study that is manipulated (assigned different values by a researcher) so that the effects of the manipulation may be observed is called an independent variable.
Inference	Inference is the act or process of drawing a conclusion based solely on what one already knows.
Homogeneous	In biology homogeneous has a meaning similar to its meaning in mathematics. Generally it means "the same" or "of the same quality or general property".
Overt behavior	An action or response that is directly observable and measurable is an overt behavior.
Social isolation	Social isolation refers to a type of loneliness that occurs when a person lacks a sense of integrated involvement. Being deprived of participation in a group or community involving companionship, shared interests, organized activities, and meaningful roles causes a person to feel alone.
Socioeconomic	Socioeconomic pertains to the study of the social and economic impacts of any product or service offering, market intervention or other activity on an economy as a whole and on the companies, organization and individuals who are its main economic actors.
Biological therapies	Treatments to reduce or eliminate the symptoms of psychological disorders by altering the way an individual's body functions are called biological therapies.
Electrode	Any device used to electrically stimulate nerve tissue or to record its activity is an electrode.
Brain	The brain controls and coordinates most movement, behavior and homeostatic body functions such as heartbeat, blood pressure, fluid balance and body temperature. Functions of the brain are responsible for cognition, emotion, memory, motor learning and other sorts of learning. The brain is primarily made up of two types of cells: glia and neurons.

Antianxiety drugs	Drugs that can reduce a person's level of excitability while increasing feelings of well-being are called antianxiety drugs.
Antipsychotic	The term antipsychotic is applied to a group of drugs used to treat psychosis.
Antidepressants	Antidepressants are medications used primarily in the treatment of clinical depression. Antidepressants create little if any immediate change in mood and require between several days and several weeks to take effect.
Drug dependence	Drug dependence refers to the condition, which may or may not stem from physiological withdrawal symptoms, in which a person feels compelled to take a particular drug on a regular basis.
Metabolism	Metabolism is the biochemical modification of chemical compounds in living organisms and cells.
Psychoactive drug	A psychoactive drug or psychotropic substance is a chemical that alters brain function, resulting in temporary changes in perception, mood, consciousness, or behavior. Such drugs are often used for recreational and spiritual purposes, as well as in medicine, especially for treating neurological and psychological illnesses.
Insomnia	Insomnia is a sleep disorder characterized by an inability to sleep and/or to remain asleep for a reasonable period during the night.
Tricyclic antidepressant	A tricyclic antidepressant is of a class of antidepressant drugs first used in the 1950s. They are named after the drugs' molecular structure, which contains three rings of atoms.
Panic disorder	A panic attack is a period of intense fear or discomfort, typically with an abrupt onset and usually lasting no more than thirty minutes. The disorder is strikingly different from other types of anxiety, in that panic attacks are very sudden, appear to be unprovoked, and are often disabling. People who have repeated attacks, or feel severe anxiety about having another attack are said to have panic disorder.
Tranquilizer	A sedative, or tranquilizer, is a drug that depresses the central nervous system (CNS), which causes calmness, relaxation, reduction of anxiety, sleepiness, slowed breathing, slurred speech, staggering gait, poor judgment, and slow, uncertain reflexes.
Trauma	Trauma refers to a severe physical injury or wound to the body caused by an external force, or a psychological shock having a lasting effect on mental life.
Bipolar disorder	Bipolar Disorder is a mood disorder typically characterized by fluctuations between manic and depressive states; and, more generally, atypical mood regulation and mood instability.
Lithium	Lithium salts are used as mood stabilizing drugs primarily in the treatment of bipolar disorder, depression, and mania; but also in treating schizophrenia. Lithium is widely distributed in the central nervous system and interacts with a number of neurotransmitters and receptors, decreasing noradrenaline release and increasing serotonin synthesis.
Tardive dyskinesia	Tardive dyskinesia is a serious neurological disorder caused by the long-term use of traditional antipsychotic drugs.
Psychopathology	Psychopathology refers to the field concerned with the nature and development of mental disorders.
Alcoholism	A disorder that involves long-term, repeated, uncontrolled, compulsive, and excessive use of alcoholic beverages and that impairs the drinker's health and work and social relationships is called alcoholism.
Affective	Affective is the way people react emotionally, their ability to feel another living thing's pain or joy.

Distinctive features	The characteristics of an object that differentiate it from other objects are distinctive features.
Acute	Acute means sudden, sharp, and abrupt. Usually short in duration.
Imipramine	Imipramine is the first antidepressant to be developed in the late 1950s. The drug became a prototypical drug for the development of the later released tricyclics. It is not as commonly used today but sometimes used to treat major depression as a second-line treatment.
Partial hospitalization	Partial hospitalization is a type of program used to treat mental illness and substance abuse. In partial hospitalization, the patient continues to reside at home, but commutes to a treatment center up to seven days a week. Since partial hospitalization focuses on the overall treatment of the individual, rather than purely on his or her safety, the program is not used for people who are acutely suicidal.
Chronic	Chronic refers to a relatively long duration, usually more than a few months.
Pinel	Pinel is regarded as the father of modern psychiatry. He was a clinician believing that medical truth derived from clinical experience. While at Bicêtre, Pinel did away with bleeding, purging, and blistering in favor a therapy that involved close contact with and careful observation of patients.
Adaptation	Adaptation is a lowering of sensitivity to a stimulus following prolonged exposure to that stimulus. Behavioral adaptations are special ways a particular organism behaves to survive in its natural habitat.
Clinical method	Studying psychological problems and therapies in clinical settings is referred to as the clinical method. It usually involves case histories, pathology, or non-experimentally controlled environments.
Social support	Social Support is the physical and emotional comfort given by family, friends, co-workers and others. Research has identified three main types of social support: emotional, practical, sharing points of view.
Personality	Personality refers to the pattern of enduring characteristics that differentiates a person, the patterns of behaviors that make each individual unique.
Cognitive restructuring	Cognitive restructuring refers to any behavior therapy procedure that attempts to alter the manner in which a client thinks about life so that he or she changes overt behavior and emotions.
Normative	The term normative is used to describe the effects of those structures of culture which regulate the function of social activity.
Deinstitutio-alization	The transfer of former mental patients from institutions into the community is referred to as deinstitutionalization.
Jung	Jung was in some aspects a response to Sigmund Freud's psychoanalysis. He proposed and developed the concepts of the extroverted and introverted personality, archetypes, and the collective unconscious. His work has been influential in psychiatry and in the study of religion, literature, and related fields.

Schizophrenia	Schizophrenia is characterized by persistent defects in the perception or expression of reality. A person suffering from untreated schizophrenia typically demonstrates grossly disorganized thinking, and may also experience delusions or auditory hallucinations
Medical model	The medical model views abnormal behavior as a disease.
Affective	Affective is the way people react emotionally, their ability to feel another living thing's pain or joy.
Clinician	A health professional authorized to provide services to people suffering from one or more pathologies is a clinician.
Anxiety	Anxiety is a complex combination of the feeling of fear, apprehension and worry often accompanied by physical sensations such as palpitations, chest pain and/or shortness of breath.
Depression	In everyday language depression refers to any downturn in mood, which may be relatively transitory and perhaps due to something trivial. This is differentiated from Clinical depression which is marked by symptoms that last two weeks or more and are so severe that they interfere with daily living.
Mental disorder	Mental disorder refers to a disturbance in a person's emotions, drives, thought processes, or behavior that involves serious and relatively prolonged distress and/or impairment in ability to function, is not simply a normal response to some event or set of events in the person's environment.
Maladaptive	In psychology, a behavior or trait is adaptive when it helps an individual adjust and function well within their social environment. A maladaptive behavior or trait is counterproductive to the individual.
Hippocrates	Hippocrates was an ancient Greek physician, commonly regarded as one of the most outstanding figures in medicine of all time; he has been called "the father of medicine."
Delusions of grandeur	Delusions of grandeur are a false belief that one is a famous person or a person who has some great knowledge, ability, or authority.
Abnormal psychology	The scientific study whose objectives are to describe, explain, predict, and control behaviors that are considered strange or unusual is referred to as abnormal psychology.
Scheme	According to Piaget, a hypothetical mental structure that permits the classification and organization of new information is called a scheme.
Mental illness	Mental illness is the term formerly used to mean psychological disorder but less preferred because it implies that the causes of the disorder can be found in a medical disease process.
Kraepelin	Kraepelin postulated that there is a specific brain or other biological pathology underlying each of the major psychiatric disorders. Just as his laboratory discovered the pathologic basis of what is now known as Alzheimers disease, Kraepelin was confident that it would someday be possible to identify the pathologic basis of each of the major psychiatric disorders.
Pathology	Pathology is the study of the processes underlying disease and other forms of illness, harmful abnormality, or dysfunction.
Brain	The brain controls and coordinates most movement, behavior and homeostatic body functions such as heartbeat, blood pressure, fluid balance and body temperature. Functions of the brain are responsible for cognition, emotion, memory, motor learning and other sorts of learning. The brain is primarily made up of two types of cells: glia and neurons.
Abnormal behavior	An action, thought, or feeling that is harmful to the person or to others is called abnormal behavior.

Go to **Cram101.com** for the Practice Tests for this Chapter.

DSM-IV TR	The current Diagnostic and Statistical Manual of Mental Disorders of the American Psychiatric Association is called DSM-IV TR.
Personality disorder	A mental disorder characterized by a set of inflexible, maladaptive personality traits that keep a person from functioning properly in society is referred to as a personality disorder.
Mental retardation	Mental retardation refers to having significantly below-average intellectual functioning and limitations in at least two areas of adaptive functioning. Many categorize retardation as mild, moderate, severe, or profound.
Adolescence	The period of life bounded by puberty and the assumption of adult responsibilities is adolescence.
Defense mechanism	A Defense mechanism is a set of unconscious ways to protect one's personality from unpleasant thoughts and realities which may otherwise cause anxiety. The notion is an integral part of the psychoanalytic theory.
Personality	Personality refers to the pattern of enduring characteristics that differentiates a person, the patterns of behaviors that make each individual unique.
Global Assessment of Functioning	Global Assessment of Functioning is a numeric scale (0 through 100) used by mental health clinicians and doctors to rate the social, occupational and psychological functioning of adults.
Paranoid	The term paranoid is typically used in a general sense to signify any self-referential delusion, or more specifically, to signify a delusion involving the fear of persecution.
Acute	Acute means sudden, sharp, and abrupt. Usually short in duration.
Psychiatrist	A psychiatrist is a physician who specializes in the diagnosis and treatment of psychological disorders.
Attention	Attention is the cognitive process of selectively concentrating on one thing while ignoring other things. Psychologists have labeled three types of attention: sustained attention, selective attention, and divided attention.
Trait	An enduring personality characteristic that tends to lead to certain behaviors is called a trait. The term trait also means a genetically inherited feature of an organism.
Infancy	The developmental period that extends from birth to 18 or 24 months is called infancy.
Autistic disorder	An autistic disorder is a neurodevelopmental disorder that manifests itself in markedly abnormal social interaction, communication ability, patterns of interests, and patterns of behavior.
Learning disorder	A disorder characterized by a discrepancy between one's academic achievement and one's intellectual ability is referred to as a learning disorder.
Delirium	Delirium is a medical term used to describe an acute decline in attention and cognition. Delirium is probably the single most common acute disorder affecting adults in general hospitals. It affects 10-20% of all adults in hospital, and 30-40% of older patients.
Dementia	Dementia is progressive decline in cognitive function due to damage or disease in the brain beyond what might be expected from normal aging.
Cognition	The intellectual processes through which information is obtained, transformed, stored, retrieved, and otherwise used is cognition.
Amphetamine	Amphetamine is a synthetic stimulant used to suppress the appetite, control weight, and treat disorders including narcolepsy and ADHD. It is also used recreationally and for performance enhancement.

Cocaine	Cocaine is a crystalline tropane alkaloid that is obtained from the leaves of the coca plant. It is a stimulant of the central nervous system and an appetite suppressant, creating what has been described as a euphoric sense of happiness and increased energy.
Social isolation	Social isolation refers to a type of loneliness that occurs when a person lacks a sense of integrated involvement. Being deprived of participation in a group or community involving companionship, shared interests, organized activities, and meaningful roles causes a person to feel alone.
Hallucination	A hallucination is a sensory perception experienced in the absence of an external stimulus, as distinct from an illusion, which is a misperception of an external stimulus. They may occur in any sensory modality - visual, auditory, olfactory, gustatory, tactile, or mixed.
Mood disorder	A mood disorder is a condition where the prevailing emotional mood is distorted or inappropriate to the circumstances.
Motivation	In psychology, motivation is the driving force (desire) behind all actions of an organism.
Perception	Perception is the process of acquiring, interpreting, selecting, and organizing sensory information.
Delusion	A false belief, not generally shared by others, and that cannot be changed despite strong evidence to the contrary is a delusion.
Affect	A subjective feeling or emotional tone often accompanied by bodily expressions noticeable to others is called affect.
Mania	Mania is a medical condition characterized by severely elevated mood. Mania is most usually associated with bipolar disorder, where episodes of mania may cyclically alternate with episodes of depression.
Gender identity disorder	Gender identity disorder is a condition where a person who has been assigned one gender but identifies as belonging to another gender, or does not conform with the gender role their respective society prescribes to them.
Consciousness	The awareness of the sensations, thoughts, and feelings being experienced at a given moment is called consciousness.
Eating disorders	Psychological disorders characterized by distortion of the body image and gross disturbances in eating patterns are called eating disorders.
Gender identity	Gender identity describes the gender with which a person identifies, but can also be used to refer to the gender that other people attribute to the individual on the basis of what they know from gender role indications.
Anorexia	Anorexia nervosa is an eating disorder characterized by voluntary starvation and exercise stress.
Binge	Binge refers to relatively brief episode of uncontrolled, excessive consumption.
Threshold	In general, a threshold is a fixed location or value where an abrupt change is observed. In the sensory modalities, it is the minimum amount of stimulus energy necessary to elicit a sensory response.
Early adulthood	The developmental period beginning in the late teens or early twenties and lasting into the thirties is called early adulthood; characterized by an increasing self-awareness.
Psychoanalytic	Freud's theory that unconscious forces act as determinants of personality is called psychoanalytic theory. The theory is a developmental theory characterized by critical stages of development.
Juvenile	Juvenile delinquency refers to a broad range of child and adolescent behaviors, including

delinquency	socially unacceptable behavior, status offenses, and criminal acts.
Etiology	Etiology is the study of causation. The term is used in philosophy, physics and biology in reference to the causes of various phenomena. It is generally the study of why things occur, or even the reasons behind the way that things act.
Theories	Theories are logically self-consistent models or frameworks describing the behavior of a certain natural or social phenomenon. They are broad explanations and predictions concerning phenomena of interest.
Attitude	An enduring mental representation of a person, place, or thing that evokes an emotional response and related behavior is called attitude.
Early childhood	Early childhood refers to the developmental period extending from the end of infancy to about 5 or 6 years of age; sometimes called the preschool years.
Reliability	Reliability means the extent to which a test produces a consistent , reproducible score .
Statistic	A statistic is an observable random variable of a sample.
Validity	The extent to which a test measures what it is intended to measure is called validity.
Causation	Causation concerns the time order relationship between two or more objects such that if a specific antecedent condition occurs the same consequent must always follow.
Population	Population refers to all members of a well-defined group of organisms, events, or things.
Major depression	Major depression is characterized by a severely depressed mood that persists for at least two weeks. Episodes of depression may start suddenly or slowly and can occur several times through a person's life. The disorder may be categorized as "single episode" or "recurrent" depending on whether previous episodes have been experienced before.
Society	The social sciences use the term society to mean a group of people that form a semi-closed (or semi-open) social system, in which most interactions are with other individuals belonging to the group.
Norms	In testing, standards of test performance that permit the comparison of one person's score on the test to the scores of others who have taken the same test are referred to as norms.
Sexual orientation	Sexual orientation refers to the sex or gender of people who are the focus of a person's amorous or erotic desires, fantasies, and spontaneous feelings, the gender(s) toward which one is primarily "oriented".
Social class	Social class describes the relationships between people in hierarchical societies or cultures. Those with more power usually subordinate those with less power.
Ethnic identity	An enduring, basic aspect of the self that includes a sense of membership in an ethnic group and the attitudes and feelings related to that membership is called an ethnic identity.
Self-concept	Self-concept refers to domain-specific evaluations of the self where a domain may be academics, athletics, etc.
Ethnic group	An ethnic group is a culture or subculture whose members are readily distinguishable by outsiders based on traits originating from a common racial, national, linguistic, or religious source. Members of an ethnic group are often presumed to be culturally or biologically similar, although this is not in fact necessarily the case.
Play therapy	Play therapy is often used to help the diagnostician to try to determine the cause of disturbed behavior in a child. Treatment therapists then used a type of systematic desensitization or relearning therapy to change the disturbing behavior, either systematically or in less formal social settings.

Psychological testing	Psychological testing is a field characterized by the use of small samples of behavior in order to infer larger generalizations about a given individual. The technical term for psychological testing is psychometrics.
Cultural values	The importance and desirability of various objects and activities as defined by people in a given culture are referred to as cultural values.
Reflection	Reflection is the process of rephrasing or repeating thoughts and feelings expressed, making the person more aware of what they are saying or thinking.
Emotion	An emotion is a mental states that arise spontaneously, rather than through conscious effort. They are often accompanied by physiological changes.
Guilt	Guilt describes many concepts related to a negative emotion or condition caused by actions which are believed to be, morally wrong. According to Freud, the avoidance of guilt is the basis for moral behavior.
Neuropsychol- gical test	A neuropsychological test use specifically designed tasks used to measure a psychological function known to be linked to a particular brain structure or pathway. They usually involve the systematic administration of clearly defined procedures in a formal environment.
Behavioral assessment	Direct measures of an individual's behavior used to describe characteristics indicative of personality are called behavioral assessment.
Intelligence test	An intelligence test is a standardized means of assessing a person's current mental ability, for example, the Stanford-Binet test and the Wechsler Adult Intelligence Scale.
Social development	The person's developing capacity for social relationships and the effects of those relationships on further development is referred to as social development.
Sleep patterns	The order and timing of daily sleep and waking periods are called sleep patterns.
Construct	A generalized concept, such as anxiety or gravity, is a construct.
Clinical psychologist	A psychologist, usually with a Ph.D, whose training is in the diagnosis, treatment, or research of psychological and behavioral disorders is a clinical psychologist.
Psychotherapy	Psychotherapy is a set of techniques based on psychological principles intended to improve mental health, emotional or behavioral issues.
Manic episode	A manic episode is a period of unusually high energy, sometimes including uncontrollable excitement. Such episodes most commonly occur as part of bipolar disorder. In extreme cases, the person may need to be hospitalized.
Insight	Insight refers to a sudden awareness of the relationships among various elements that had previously appeared to be independent of one another.
Structured interview	Structured interview refers to an interview in which the questions are set out in a prescribed fashion for the interviewer. It assists professionals in making diagnostic decisions based upon standardized criteria.
Psychological test	Psychological test refers to a standardized measure of a sample of a person's behavior.
Quantitative	A quantitative property is one that exists in a range of magnitudes, and can therefore be measured. Measurements of any particular quantitative property are expressed as as a specific quantity, referred to as a unit, multiplied by a number.
Individual differences	Individual differences psychology studies the ways in which individual people differ in their behavior. This is distinguished from other aspects of psychology in that although psychology is ostensibly a study of individuals, modern psychologists invariably study groups.

Personality inventory	A self-report questionnaire by which an examinee indicates whether statements assessing habitual tendencies apply to him or her is referred to as a personality inventory.
Alfred Binet	Alfred Binet published the first modern intelligence test, the Binet-Simon intelligence scale, in 1905. Binet stressed that the core of intelligence consists of complex cognitive processes, such as memory, imagery, comprehension, and judgment; and, that these developed over time in the individual.
Rorschach	The Rorschach inkblot test is a method of psychological evaluation. It is a projective test associated with the Freudian school of thought. Psychologists use this test to try to probe the unconscious minds of their patients.
Reasoning	Reasoning is the act of using reason to derive a conclusion from certain premises. There are two main methods to reach a conclusion, deductive reasoning and inductive reasoning.
Intelligence quotient	An intelligence quotient is a score derived from a set of standardized tests that were developed with the purpose of measuring a person's cognitive abilities ("intelligence") in relation to their age group.
Chronological age	Chronological age refers to the number of years that have elapsed since a person's birth.
Mental age	The mental age refers to the accumulated months of credit that a person earns on the Stanford-Binet Intelligence Scale.
Stanford-Binet	Terman released the "Stanford Revision of the Binet-Simon Scale" or the Stanford-Binet for short. Using validation experiments, he removed several of the Binet-Simon test items and added new ones. In 1985 it was revised to analyze an individual's responses in four content areas: verbal reasoning, quantitative reasoning, abstract reasoning, and short-term memory.
David Wechsler	David Wechsler developed two well-known intelligence scales, namely the Wechsler Adult Intelligence Scale and the Wechsler Intelligence Scale for Children. He held the view that human intelligence is not a single thing, but a mixture of many distinct -- and separately measurable -- human capabilities.
Wechsler Adult Intelligence Scale	Wechsler adult intelligence scale is an individual intelligence test for adults that yields separate verbal and performance IQ scores as well as an overall IQ score.
Life expectancy	The number of years that will probably be lived by the average person born in a particular year is called life expectancy.
Working Memory	Working memory is the collection of structures and processes in the brain used for temporarily storing and manipulating information. Working memory consists of both memory for items that are currently being processed, and components governing attention and directing the processing itself.
Coding	In senation, coding is the process by which information about the quality and quantity of a stimulus is preserved in the pattern of action potentials sent through sensory neurons to the central nervous system.
Cognitive development	The process by which a child's understanding of the world changes as a function of age and experience is called cognitive development.
Sensorimotor	The first of Piaget's stages is the Sensorimotor stage. This stage typically ranges from birth to 2 years. In this stage, children experience the world through their senses. During this stage, object permanence and stranger anxiety develop.
Tumor	A tumor is an abnormal growth that when located in the brain can either be malignant and directly destroy brain tissue, or be benign and disrupt functioning by increasing

intracranial pressure.

Bender Visual-Motor	The Bender Visual-Motor Gestalt test is a psychological assessment used to evaluate visual-motor functioning, visual-perceptual skills, neurological impairment, and emotional disturbances in children and adults ages three and older.
Reversibility	Reversibility according to Piaget, is recognition that processes can be undone, that things can be made as they were.
Behavioral observation	A form of behavioral assessment that entails careful observation of a person's overt behavior in a particular situation is behavioral observation.
Personality test	A personality test aims to describe aspects of a person's character that remain stable across situations.
Psychometric	Psychometric study is concerned with the theory and technique of psychological measurement, which includes the measurement of knowledge, abilities, attitudes, and personality traits. The field is primarily concerned with the study of differences between individuals
Questionnaire	A self-report method of data collection or clinical assessment method in which the individual being studied checks off items on a printed list, answers multiple-choice questions, or writes out answers to essay questions aimed at producing a selfdescription is called questionnaire.
Hypochondriasis	The persistent beliefs that one has a medical disorder despite lack of medical findings are called hypochondriasis.
Introversion	A personality trait characterized by intense imagination and a tendency to inhibit impulses is called introversion.
Hypomania	Hypomania is a state involving combinations of: elevated mood, irritability, racing thoughts, people-seeking, hypersexuality, grandiose thinking, religiosity, and pressured speech.
Paranoia	In popular culture, the term paranoia is usually used to describe excessive concern about one's own well-being, sometimes suggesting a person holds persecutory beliefs concerning a threat to themselves or their property and is often linked to a belief in conspiracy theories.
Hysteria	Hysteria is a diagnostic label applied to a state of mind, one of unmanageable fear or emotional excesses. The fear is often centered on a body part, most often on an imagined problem with that body part.
Psychopathology	Psychopathology refers to the field concerned with the nature and development of mental disorders.
Millon Clinical Multiaxial Inventory	The Millon Clinical Multiaxial Inventory is a self-report assessment of personality disorders and clinical syndromes. This is sometimes used as an adjunct instrument in comprehensive neuropsychological assessment.
Five-factor model	The five-factor model of personality proposes that there are five universal dimensions of personality: Neuroticism, Extraversion, Openness, Conscientiousness, and Agreeableness.
Openness to Experience	Openness to Experience, one of the big-five traits, describes a dimension of cognitive style that distinguishes imaginative, creative people from down-to-earth, conventional people.
Conscientiou-ness	Conscientiousness is one of the dimensions of the five-factor model of personality and individual differences involving being organized, thorough, and reliable as opposed to careless, negligent, and unreliable.
Agreeableness	Agreeableness, one of the big-five personality traits, reflects individual differences in concern with cooperation and social harmony. It is the degree individuals value getting along

with others.

Extroversion	Extroversion refers to the tendency to be outgoing, adaptable, and sociable.
Nicotine	Nicotine is an organic compound, an alkaloid found naturally throughout the tobacco plant, with a high concentration in the leaves. It is a potent nerve poison and is included in many insecticides. In lower concentrations, the substance is a stimulant and is one of the main factors leading to the pleasure and habit-forming qualities of tobacco smoking.
Halo effect	The halo effect occurs when a person's positive or negative traits seem to "spill over" from one area of their personality to another in others' perceptions of them.
Ambiguous stimuli	Patterns that allow more than one perceptual organization are called ambiguous stimuli.
Apperception	A newly experienced sensation is related to past experiences to form an understood situation. For Wundt, consciousness is composed of two "stages:" There is a large capacity working memory called the Blickfeld and the narrower consciousness called Apperception, or selective attention.
Paranoid schizophrenia	Paranoid schizophrenia is a type of schizophrenia characterized primarily by delusions-commonly of persecution-and by vivid hallucinations .
Motives	Needs or desires that energize and direct behavior toward a goal are motives.
Reinforcement	In operant conditioning, reinforcement is any change in an environment that (a) occurs after the behavior, (b) seems to make that behavior re-occur more often in the future and (c) that reoccurence of behavior must be the result of the change.
Subjective experience	Subjective experience refers to reality as it is perceived and interpreted, not as it exists objectively.
Inference	Inference is the act or process of drawing a conclusion based solely on what one already knows.
Baseline	Measure of a particular behavior or process taken before the introduction of the independent variable or treatment is called the baseline.
Behavior modification	Behavior Modification is a technique of altering an individual's reactions to stimuli through positive reinforcement and the extinction of maladaptive behavior.
Brain imaging	Brain imaging is a fairly recent discipline within medicine and neuroscience. Brain imaging falls into two broad categories -- structural imaging and functional imaging.
Physiological changes	Alterations in heart rate, blood pressure, perspiration, and other involuntary responses are physiological changes.
Pupil	In the eye, the pupil is the opening in the middle of the iris. It appears black because most of the light entering it is absorbed by the tissues inside the eye. The size of the pupil is controlled by involuntary contraction and dilation of the iris, in order to regulate the intensity of light entering the eye. This is known as the pupillary reflex.
Galvanic skin response	Galvanic skin response is a method of measuring the electrical resistance of the skin and interpreting it as an image of activity in certain parts of the body.
Polygraph	A polygraph is a device which measures and records several physiological variables such as blood pressure, heart rate, respiration and skin conductivity while a series of questions is being asked, in an attempt to detect lies.
Diastolic blood pressure	Blood pressure level when the heart is at rest or between heartbeats is called diastolic blood pressure.

Stimulus	A change in an environmental condition that elicits a response is a stimulus.
Suicide	Suicide behavior is rare in childhood but escalates in adolescence. The suicide rate increases in a linear fashion from adolescence through late adulthood.
Biofeedback	Biofeedback is the process of measuring and quantifying an aspect of a subject's physiology, analyzing the data, and then feeding back the information to the subject in a form that allows the subject to enact physiological change.
Diagnostic and Statistical Manual of Mental Disorders	The Diagnostic and Statistical Manual of Mental Disorders, published by the American Psychiatric Association, is the handbook used most often in diagnosing mental disorders in the United States and internationally.
Substance-related disorders	Substance-related disorders involve drugs such as alcohol and cocaine that are abused to such an extent that behavior becomes maladaptive. Social and occupational functioning are impaired, and control or abstinence becomes impossible.
Dissociative disorder	Psychological dysfunctions characterized by the separation of critical personality facets that are normally integrated, allowing stress avoidance by escape is a dissociative disorder.
Adjustment disorder	An emotional disturbance caused by ongoing stressors within the range of common experience is called an adjustment disorder.
Factitious disorder	A factitious disorder is an illness whose symptoms are either self-induced or falsified by the patient.
Somatoform disorder	Psychological difficulty that take on a physical form, but for which there is no medical cause is referred to as a somatoform disorder.
Anxiety disorder	Anxiety disorder is a blanket term covering several different forms of abnormal anxiety, fear, phobia and nervous condition, that come on suddenly and prevent pursuing normal daily routines.
Representative sample	Representative sample refers to a sample of participants selected from the larger population in such a way that important subgroups within the population are included in the sample in the same proportions as they are found in the larger population.
Sensation	Sensation is the first stage in the chain of biochemical and neurologic events that begins with the impinging of a stimulus upon the receptor cells of a sensory organ, which then leads to perception, the mental state that is reflected in statements like "I see a uniformly blue wall."

Attention	Attention is the cognitive process of selectively concentrating on one thing while ignoring other things. Psychologists have labeled three types of attention: sustained attention, selective attention, and divided attention.
Acute	Acute means sudden, sharp, and abrupt. Usually short in duration.
Attitude	An enduring mental representation of a person, place, or thing that evokes an emotional response and related behavior is called attitude.
Clinician	A health professional authorized to provide services to people suffering from one or more pathologies is a clinician.
Physiological changes	Alterations in heart rate, blood pressure, perspiration, and other involuntary responses are physiological changes.
Chronic	Chronic refers to a relatively long duration, usually more than a few months.
Social support	Social Support is the physical and emotional comfort given by family, friends, co-workers and others. Research has identified three main types of social support: emotional, practical, sharing points of view.
Temperament	Temperament refers to a basic, innate disposition to change behavior. The activity level is an important dimension of temperament.
Maladaptive	In psychology, a behavior or trait is adaptive when it helps an individual adjust and function well within their social environment. A maladaptive behavior or trait is counterproductive to the individual.
Insomnia	Insomnia is a sleep disorder characterized by an inability to sleep and/or to remain asleep for a reasonable period during the night.
Abnormal psychology	The scientific study whose objectives are to describe, explain, predict, and control behaviors that are considered strange or unusual is referred to as abnormal psychology.
Questionnaire	A self-report method of data collection or clinical assessment method in which the individual being studied checks off items on a printed list, answers multiple-choice questions, or writes out answers to essay questions aimed at producing a selfdescription is called questionnaire.
Perception	Perception is the process of acquiring, interpreting, selecting, and organizing sensory information.
Schizophrenia	Schizophrenia is characterized by persistent defects in the perception or expression of reality. A person suffering from untreated schizophrenia typically demonstrates grossly disorganized thinking, and may also experience delusions or auditory hallucinations
Denial	Denial is a psychological defense mechanism in which a person faced with a fact that is uncomfortable or painful to accept rejects it instead, insisting that it is not true despite what may be overwhelming evidence.
Emotion	An emotion is a mental states that arise spontaneously, rather than through conscious effort. They are often accompanied by physiological changes.
Psychiatrist	A psychiatrist is a physician who specializes in the diagnosis and treatment of psychological disorders.
Learning	Learning is a relatively permanent change in behavior that results from experience. Thus, to attribute a behavioral change to learning, the change must be relatively permanent and must result from experience.
Problem solving	An attempt to find an appropriate way of attaining a goal when the goal is not readily available is called problem solving.

Arousal response	A pattern of measurable physiological changes that helps prepare the body for the possible expenditure of a large amount of energy is referred to as the arousal response.
Personality	Personality refers to the pattern of enduring characteristics that differentiates a person, the patterns of behaviors that make each individual unique.
Social skills	Social skills are skills used to interact and communicate with others to assist status in the social structure and other motivations.
Social isolation	Social isolation refers to a type of loneliness that occurs when a person lacks a sense of integrated involvement. Being deprived of participation in a group or community involving companionship, shared interests, organized activities, and meaningful roles causes a person to feel alone.
Hormone	A hormone is a chemical messenger from one cell (or group of cells) to another. The best known are those produced by endocrine glands, but they are produced by nearly every organ system. The function of hormones is to serve as a signal to the target cells; the action of the hormone is determined by the pattern of secretion and the signal transduction of the receiving tissue.
Brain	The brain controls and coordinates most movement, behavior and homeostatic body functions such as heartbeat, blood pressure, fluid balance and body temperature. Functions of the brain are responsible for cognition, emotion, memory, motor learning and other sorts of learning. The brain is primarily made up of two types of cells: glia and neurons.
Stuttering	The term stuttering is most commonly associated with involuntary sound repetition, but it also encompasses the abnormal hesitation or pausing before speech.
Correlation	A statistical technique for determining the degree of association between two or more variables is referred to as correlation.
Anxiety	Anxiety is a complex combination of the feeling of fear, apprehension and worry often accompanied by physical sensations such as palpitations, chest pain and/or shortness of breath.
Depression	In everyday language depression refers to any downturn in mood, which may be relatively transitory and perhaps due to something trivial. This is differentiated from Clinical depression which is marked by symptoms that last two weeks or more and are so severe that they interfere with daily living.
Random sample	A sample drawn so that each member of a population has an equal chance of being selected to participate is referred to as a random sample.
Trauma	Trauma refers to a severe physical injury or wound to the body caused by an external force, or a psychological shock having a lasting effect on mental life.
Projection	Attributing one's own undesirable thoughts, impulses, traits, or behaviors to others is referred to as projection.
Date rape	Date rape refers to non-consensual sexual activity between people who are already acquainted, or who know each other socially where it is alleged that consent for sexual activity was not given, or was given under duress.
Rape	Rape is a crime where the victim is forced into sexual activity, in particular sexual penetration, against his or her will.
Classical conditioning	Classical conditioning is a simple form of learning in which an organism comes to associate or anticipate events. A neutral stimulus comes to evoke the response usually evoked by a natural or unconditioned stimulus by being paired repeatedly with the unconditioned stimulus.
Fear response	In the Mowrer-Miller theory, a response to a threatening or noxious situation that is covert

	but that is assumed to function as a stimulus to produce measurable physiological changes in the body and observable overt behavior is referred to as the fear response.
Stimulus	A change in an environmental condition that elicits a response is a stimulus.
Behavior therapy	Behavior therapy refers to the systematic application of the principles of learning to direct modification of a client's problem behaviors.
Sexual dysfunction	Sexual dysfunction or sexual malfunction is difficulty during any stage of the sexual act (which includes desire, arousal, orgasm, and resolution) that prevents the individual or couple from enjoying sexual activity.
Adjustment disorder	An emotional disturbance caused by ongoing stressors within the range of common experience is called an adjustment disorder.
Affective	Affective is the way people react emotionally, their ability to feel another living thing's pain or joy.
Pathology	Pathology is the study of the processes underlying disease and other forms of illness, harmful abnormality, or dysfunction.
Hallucination	A hallucination is a sensory perception experienced in the absence of an external stimulus, as distinct from an illusion, which is a misperception of an external stimulus. They may occur in any sensory modality - visual, auditory, olfactory, gustatory, tactile, or mixed.
Motives	Needs or desires that energize and direct behavior toward a goal are motives.
Psychotherapy	Psychotherapy is a set of techniques based on psychological principles intended to improve mental health, emotional or behavioral issues.
Ambivalence	The simultaneous holding of strong positive and negative emotional attitudes toward the same situation or person is called ambivalence.
Suicide	Suicide behavior is rare in childhood but escalates in adolescence. The suicide rate increases in a linear fashion from adolescence through late adulthood.
Self-concept	Self-concept refers to domain-specific evaluations of the self where a domain may be academics, athletics, etc.
Body image	A person's body image is their perception of their physical appearance. It is more than what a person thinks they will see in a mirror, it is inextricably tied to their self-esteem and acceptance by peers.
Early-maturing	Early-maturing girls tend to be more likely than their peers to engage in a number of deviant behaviors, such as being truant from school, getting drunk, and stealing.
Adolescence	The period of life bounded by puberty and the assumption of adult responsibilities is adolescence.
Individual differences	Individual differences psychology studies the ways in which individual people differ in their behavior. This is distinguished from other aspects of psychology in that although psychology is ostensibly a study of individuals, modern psychologists invariably study groups.
DSM-IV TR	The current Diagnostic and Statistical Manual of Mental Disorders of the American Psychiatric Association is called DSM-IV TR.
Acute stress disorder	Acute stress disorder is a psychological condition arising in response to a terrifying event.
Dissociative disorder	Psychological dysfunctions characterized by the separation of critical personality facets that are normally integrated, allowing stress avoidance by escape is a dissociative disorder.
Abnormal	An action, thought, or feeling that is harmful to the person or to others is called abnormal

behavior	behavior.
Menopause	Menopause is a stage of the human female reproductive cycle that occurs as the ovaries stop producing estrogen, causing the reproductive system to gradually shut down.
Norms	In testing, standards of test performance that permit the comparison of one person's score on the test to the scores of others who have taken the same test are referred to as norms.
Dissociation	Dissociation is a psychological state or condition in which certain thoughts, emotions, sensations, or memories are separated from the rest.
Mental processes	The thoughts, feelings, and motives that each of us experiences privately but that cannot be observed directly are called mental processes.
Personality trait	According to the Diagnostic and Statistical Manual of the American Psychiatric Association, a personality trait is a "prominent aspect of personality that is exhibited in a wide range of important social and personal contexts. ...".
Trait	An enduring personality characteristic that tends to lead to certain behaviors is called a trait. The term trait also means a genetically inherited feature of an organism.
Depersonaliz-tion	Depersonalization is the experience of feelings of loss of a sense of reality. A sufferer feels that they have changed and the world has become less real — it is vague, dreamlike, or lacking in significance.
Self-identity	The self-identity is the mental and conceptual awareness and persistent regard that sentient beings hold with regard to their own being.
Social role	Social role refers to expected behavior patterns associated with particular social positions.
Early childhood	Early childhood refers to the developmental period extending from the end of infancy to about 5 or 6 years of age; sometimes called the preschool years.
Affect	A subjective feeling or emotional tone often accompanied by bodily expressions noticeable to others is called affect.
Consciousness	The awareness of the sensations, thoughts, and feelings being experienced at a given moment is called consciousness.
Amnesia	Amnesia is a condition in which memory is disturbed. The causes of amnesia are organic or functional. Organic causes include damage to the brain, through trauma or disease, or use of certain (generally sedative) drugs.
Statistics	Statistics is a type of data analysis which practice includes the planning, summarizing, and interpreting of observations of a system possibly followed by predicting or forecasting of future events based on a mathematical model of the system being observed.
Statistic	A statistic is an observable random variable of a sample.
Dissociative amnesia	Dissociative amnesia is marked by loss of memory or self-identity, thought to stem from psychological conflict or trauma; skills and general knowledge are usually retained. Previously termed psychogenic amnesia.
Localized amnesia	Localized amnesia is most often an outcome of a particular event. The disease renders the afflicted unable to recall the details of an usually traumatic event, such as a violent incestual rape. This is undoubtably the most common type of amnesia.
Generalized amnesia	Condition in which one loses memory of all personal information, including one's own identity is generalized amnesia.
Continuous amnesia	Continuous amnesia is an inability to recall any events that have occurred between a specific time in the past and the present time. It is the least common form of psychogenic amnesia.

Dissociative fugue	Dissociative fugue is a state of mind where a person experiences a dissociative break in identity and attempts to run away from some perceived threat, usually something abstract such as the person's identity. People who enter into a fugue state may disappear, running away to a completely different geographical region, in unplanned travel, and assuming another identity.
Fugue state	A fugue state is a state of mind where a person experiences a dissociative break in identity and attempts to run away from some perceived threat, usually something abstract such as the person's identity.
Psychopathology	Psychopathology refers to the field concerned with the nature and development of mental disorders.
Dissociative identity disorder	Dissociative identity disorder refers to a disorder in which a person appears to have two or more distinct identities or personalities that may alternately emerge. Previously termed multiple personality.
Sexual orientation	Sexual orientation refers to the sex or gender of people who are the focus of a person's amorous or erotic desires, fantasies, and spontaneous feelings, the gender(s) toward which one is primarily "oriented".
Alcoholic	An alcoholic is dependent on alcohol as characterized by craving, loss of control, physical dependence and withdrawal symptoms, and tolerance.
Internalization	The developmental change from behavior that is externally controlled to behavior that is controlled by internal standards and principles is referred to as internalization.
Adaptation	Adaptation is a lowering of sensitivity to a stimulus following prolonged exposure to that stimulus. Behavioral adaptations are special ways a particular organism behaves to survive in its natural habitat.
Sexual abuse	Sexual abuse is a term used to describe non- consentual sexual relations between two or more parties which are considered criminally and/or morally offensive.
Validity	The extent to which a test measures what it is intended to measure is called validity.
Psychoanalysis	Psychoanalysis refers to the school of psychology that emphasizes the importance of unconscious motives and conflicts as determinants of human behavior. It was Freud's method of exploring human personality.
Sedative	A sedative is a drug that depresses the central nervous system (CNS), which causes calmness, relaxation, reduction of anxiety, sleepiness, slowed breathing, slurred speech, staggering gait, poor judgment, and slow, uncertain reflexes.
Hypnosis	Hypnosis is a psychological state whose existence and effects are strongly debated. Some believe that it is a state under which the subject's mind becomes so suggestible that the hypnotist, the one who induces the state, can establish communication with the subconscious mind of the subject and command behavior that the subject would not choose to perform in a conscious state.
Ego	In Freud's view the Ego serves to balance our primitive needs and our moral beliefs and taboos. Relying on experience, a healthy Ego provides the ability to adapt to reality and interact with the outside world.
Antidepressant	An antidepressant is a medication used primarily in the treatment of clinical depression. They are not thought to produce tolerance, although sudden withdrawal may produce adverse effects. They create little if any immediate change in mood and require between several days and several weeks to take effect.
Tranquilizer	A sedative, or tranquilizer, is a drug that depresses the central nervous system (CNS), which

	causes calmness, relaxation, reduction of anxiety, sleepiness, slowed breathing, slurred speech, staggering gait, poor judgment, and slow, uncertain reflexes.
Relaxation training	Relaxation training is an intervention technique used for tics. The person is taught to relax the muscles involved in the tics.
Autonomic nervous system	A division of the peripheral nervous system, the autonomic nervous system, regulates glands and activities such as heartbeat, respiration, digestion, and dilation of the pupils. It is responsible for homeostasis, maintaining a relatively constant internal environment .
Stages	Stages represent relatively discrete periods of time in which functioning is qualitatively different from functioning at other periods.
Empirical	Empirical means the use of working hypotheses which are capable of being disproved using observation or experiment.
Acquisition	Acquisition is the process of adapting to the environment, learning or becoming conditioned. In classical conditoning terms, it is the initial learning of the stimulus response link, which involves a neutral stimulus being associated with a unconditioned stimulus and becoming a conditioned stimulus.
Stress disorder	A significant emotional disturbance caused by stresses outside the range of normal human experience is referred to as stress disorder.
Nervous system	The body's electrochemical communication circuitry, made up of billions of neurons is a nervous system.
Systematic desensitization	Systematic desensitization refers to Wolpe's behavioral fear-reduction technique in which a hierarchy of fear-evoking stimuli are presented while the person remains relaxed. The fear-evoking stimuli thereby become associated with muscle relaxation.
Desensitization	Desensitization refers to the type of sensory or behavioral adaptation in which we become less sensitive to constant stimuli.

Chronic	Chronic refers to a relatively long duration, usually more than a few months.
Asthma	Asthma is a complex disease characterized by bronchial hyperresponsiveness (BHR), inflammation, mucus production and intermittent airway obstruction.
Anxiety	Anxiety is a complex combination of the feeling of fear, apprehension and worry often accompanied by physical sensations such as palpitations, chest pain and/or shortness of breath.
Psychiatrist	A psychiatrist is a physician who specializes in the diagnosis and treatment of psychological disorders.
Insight	Insight refers to a sudden awareness of the relationships among various elements that had previously appeared to be independent of one another.
Depression	In everyday language depression refers to any downturn in mood, which may be relatively transitory and perhaps due to something trivial. This is differentiated from Clinical depression which is marked by symptoms that last two weeks or more and are so severe that they interfere with daily living.
Emotion	An emotion is a mental states that arise spontaneously, rather than through conscious effort. They are often accompanied by physiological changes.
Learning	Learning is a relatively permanent change in behavior that results from experience. Thus, to attribute a behavioral change to learning, the change must be relatively permanent and must result from experience.
Affect	A subjective feeling or emotional tone often accompanied by bodily expressions noticeable to others is called affect.
Acute	Acute means sudden, sharp, and abrupt. Usually short in duration.
Social support	Social Support is the physical and emotional comfort given by family, friends, co-workers and others. Research has identified three main types of social support: emotional, practical, sharing points of view.
Attitude	An enduring mental representation of a person, place, or thing that evokes an emotional response and related behavior is called attitude.
Variable	A variable refers to a measurable factor, characteristic, or attribute of an individual or a system.
Mesmer	Mesmer discovered what he called animal magnetism and others often called mesmerism. The evolution of Mesmer's ideas and practices led James Braid to develop hypnosis in 1842.
Psychoanalytic	Freud's theory that unconscious forces act as determinants of personality is called psychoanalytic theory. The theory is a developmental theory characterized by critical stages of development.
Sigmund Freud	Sigmund Freud was the founder of the psychoanalytic school, based on his theory that unconscious motives control much behavior, that particular kinds of unconscious thoughts and memories are the source of neurosis, and that neurosis could be treated through bringing these unconscious thoughts and memories to consciousness in psychoanalytic treatment.
Hypnosis	Hypnosis is a psychological state whose existence and effects are strongly debated. Some believe that it is a state under which the subject's mind becomes so suggestible that the hypnotist, the one who induces the state, can establish communication with the subconscious mind of the subject and command behavior that the subject would not choose to perform in a conscious state.
Charcot	Charcot took an interest in the malady then called hysteria. It seemed to be a mental

disorder with physical manifestations, of immediate interest to a neurologist. He believed that hysteria was the result of a weak neurological system which was hereditary.

Intrapsychic conflict	In psychoanalysis, the struggles among the id, ego, and superego are an intrapsychic conflict.
Clinician	A health professional authorized to provide services to people suffering from one or more pathologies is a clinician.
Psychosomatic	A psychosomatic illness is one with physical manifestations and perhaps a supposed psychological cause. It is often diagnosed when any known or identifiable physical cause was excluded by medical examination.
Hypothesis	A specific statement about behavior or mental processes that is testable through research is a hypothesis.
Blocking	If the one of the two members of a compound stimulus fails to produce the CR due to an earlier conditioning of the other member of the compound stimulus, blocking has occurred.
Adrenal medulla	Composed mainly of hormone-producing chromaffin cells, the adrenal medulla is the principal site of the conversion of the amino acid tyrosine into the catecholamines epinephrine and norepinephrine (also called adrenaline and noradrenaline, respectively).
Endocrine gland	An endocrine gland is one of a set of internal organs involved in the secretion of hormones into the blood. The other major type of gland is the exocrine glands, which secrete substances—usually digestive juices—into the digestive tract or onto the skin.
Hormone	A hormone is a chemical messenger from one cell (or group of cells) to another. The best known are those produced by endocrine glands, but they are produced by nearly every organ system. The function of hormones is to serve as a signal to the target cells; the action of the hormone is determined by the pattern of secretion and the signal transduction of the receiving tissue.
Habit	A habit is a response that has become completely separated from its eliciting stimulus. Early learning theorists used the term to describe S-R associations, however not all S-R associations become a habit, rather many are extinguished after reinforcement is withdrawn.
Biopsychosocial	The biopsychosocial model is a way of looking at the mind and body of a patient as two important systems that are interlinked. The biopsychosocial model draws a distinction between the actual pathological processes that cause disease, and the patient's perception of their health and the effects on it, called the illness.
Brain	The brain controls and coordinates most movement, behavior and homeostatic body functions such as heartbeat, blood pressure, fluid balance and body temperature. Functions of the brain are responsible for cognition, emotion, memory, motor learning and other sorts of learning. The brain is primarily made up of two types of cells: glia and neurons.
Information processing	Information processing is an approach to the goal of understanding human thinking. The essence of the approach is to see cognition as being essentially computational in nature, with mind being the software and the brain being the hardware.
Homeostasis	Homeostasis is the property of an open system, especially living organisms, to regulate its internal environment so as to maintain a stable condition, by means of multiple dynamic equilibrium adjustments controlled by interrelated regulation mechanisms.
Individual differences	Individual differences psychology studies the ways in which individual people differ in their behavior. This is distinguished from other aspects of psychology in that although psychology is ostensibly a study of individuals, modern psychologists invariably study groups.
Personality	Personality refers to the pattern of enduring characteristics that differentiates a person,

the patterns of behaviors that make each individual unique.

Human immunodeficiency virus	The human immunodeficiency virus is a retrovirus that primarily infects vital components of the human immune system. It is transmitted through penetrative and oral sex; blood transfusion; the sharing of contaminated needles in health care settings and through drug injection; and, between mother and infant, during pregnancy, childbirth and breastfeeding.
Immune system	The most important function of the human immune system occurs at the cellular level of the blood and tissues. The lymphatic and blood circulation systems are highways for specialized white blood cells. These cells include B cells, T cells, natural killer cells, and macrophages. All function with the primary objective of recognizing, attacking and destroying bacteria, viruses, cancer cells, and all substances seen as foreign.
Acquired immune deficiency syndrome	Acquired Immune Deficiency Syndrome is defined as a collection of symptoms and infections resulting from the depletion of the immune system caused by infection with the human immunodeficiency virus, commonly called HIV.
Behavioral medicine	Behavioral medicine refers to an interdisciplinary field that focuses on developing and integrating behavioral and biomedical knowledge to promote health and reduce illness.
Health psychology	The field of psychology that studies the relationships between psychological factors and the prevention and treatment of physical illness is called health psychology.
Acquisition	Acquisition is the process of adapting to the environment, learning or becoming conditioned. In classical conditoning terms, it is the initial learning of the stimulus response link, which involves a neutral stimulus being associated with a unconditioned stimulus and becoming a conditioned stimulus.
Gender difference	A gender difference is a disparity between genders involving quality or quantity. Though some gender differences are controversial, they are not to be confused with sexist stereotypes.
Menopause	Menopause is a stage of the human female reproductive cycle that occurs as the ovaries stop producing estrogen, causing the reproductive system to gradually shut down.
Stress management	Stress management encompasses techniques intended to equip a person with effective coping mechanisms for dealing with psychological stress.
Ethnic group	An ethnic group is a culture or subculture whose members are readily distinguishable by outsiders based on traits originating from a common racial, national, linguistic, or religious source. Members of an ethnic group are often presumed to be culturally or biologically similar, although this is not in fact necessarily the case.
Population	Population refers to all members of a well-defined group of organisms, events, or things.
Life expectancy	The number of years that will probably be lived by the average person born in a particular year is called life expectancy.
Hypertension	Hypertension is a medical condition where the blood pressure in the arteries is chronically elevated. Persistent hypertension is one of the risk factors for strokes, heart attacks, heart failure and arterial aneurysm, and is a leading cause of chronic renal failure.
Discrimination	In Learning theory, discrimination refers the ability to distinguish between a conditioned stimulus and other stimuli. It can be brought about by extensive training or differential reinforcement. In social terms, it is the denial of privileges to a person or a group on the basis of prejudice.
Obesity	The state of being more than 20 percent above the average weight for a person of one's height is called obesity.
Diabetes	Diabetes is a medical disorder characterized by varying or persistent elevated blood sugar levels, especially after eating. All types of diabetes share similar symptoms and

	complications at advanced stages: dehydration and ketoacidosis, cardiovascular disease, chronic renal failure, retinal damage which can lead to blindness, nerve damage which can lead to erectile dysfunction, gangrene with risk of amputation of toes, feet, and even legs.
Liver	The liver plays a major role in metabolism and has a number of functions in the body including detoxification, glycogen storage and plasma protein synthesis. It also produces bile, which is important for digestion. The liver converts most carbohydrates, proteing, and fats into glucose.
Perception	Perception is the process of acquiring, interpreting, selecting, and organizing sensory information.
Nervous system	The body's electrochemical communication circuitry, made up of billions of neurons is a nervous system.
Lungs	The lungs are the essential organs of respiration. Its principal function is to transport oxygen from the atmosphere into the bloodstream, and excrete carbon dioxide from the bloodstream into the atmosphere.
Adrenal glands	The adrenal glands sit atop the kidneys. They are chiefly responsible for regulating the stress response through the synthesis of corticosteroids and catecholamines, including cortisol and adrenalin.
Stimulus	A change in an environmental condition that elicits a response is a stimulus.
Questionnaire	A self-report method of data collection or clinical assessment method in which the individual being studied checks off items on a printed list, answers multiple-choice questions, or writes out answers to essay questions aimed at producing a selfdescription is called questionnaire.
Eating disorders	Psychological disorders characterized by distortion of the body image and gross disturbances in eating patterns are called eating disorders.
Social skills	Social skills are skills used to interact and communicate with others to assist status in the social structure and other motivations.
Adolescence	The period of life bounded by puberty and the assumption of adult responsibilities is adolescence.
Self-esteem	Self-esteem refers to a person's subjective appraisal of himself or herself as intrinsically positive or negative to some degree.
Body image	A person's body image is their perception of their physical appearance. It is more than what a person thinks they will see in a mirror, it is inextricably tied to their self-esteem and acceptance by peers.
Anorexia	Anorexia nervosa is an eating disorder characterized by voluntary starvation and exercise stress.
Bulimia	Bulimia refers to a disorder in which a person binges on incredibly large quantities of food, then purges by vomiting or by using laxatives. Bulimia is often less about food, and more to do with deep psychological issues and profound feelings of lack of control.
Binge	Binge refers to relatively brief episode of uncontrolled, excessive consumption.
Society	The social sciences use the term society to mean a group of people that form a semi-closed (or semi-open) social system, in which most interactions are with other individuals belonging to the group.
Metabolism	Metabolism is the biochemical modification of chemical compounds in living organisms and cells.

Arrhythmia	Cardiac arrhythmia is a group of conditions in which muscle contraction of the heart is irregular for any reason.
Attention	Attention is the cognitive process of selectively concentrating on one thing while ignoring other things. Psychologists have labeled three types of attention: sustained attention, selective attention, and divided attention.
Epidemiology	Epidemiology is the study of the distribution and determinants of disease and disorders in human populations, and the use of its knowledge to control health problems.Epidemiology is considered the cornerstone methodology in all of public health research, and is highly regarded in evidence-based clinical medicine for identifying risk factors for disease and determining optimal treatment approaches to clinical practice.
Obsessive-compulsive disorder	Obsessive-compulsive disorder is an anxiety disorder manifested in a variety of forms, but is most commonly characterized by a subject's obsessive drive to perform a particular task or set of tasks, compulsions commonly termed rituals.
Control group	A group that does not receive the treatment effect in an experiment is referred to as the control group or sometimes as the comparison group.
Behavior modification	Behavior Modification is a technique of altering an individual's reactions to stimuli through positive reinforcement and the extinction of maladaptive behavior.
Psychotherapy	Psychotherapy is a set of techniques based on psychological principles intended to improve mental health, emotional or behavioral issues.
Contingency management	Providing a supply of reinforcers to promote and maintain desired behaviors, and the prompt removal of reinforcers that maintain undesired behaviors is called contingency management.
Behavior therapy	Behavior therapy refers to the systematic application of the principles of learning to direct modification of a client's problem behaviors.
Family therapy	Family therapy is a branch of psychotherapy that treats family problems. Family therapists consider the family as a system of interacting members; as such, the problems in the family are seen to arise as an emergent property of the interactions in the system, rather than ascribed exclusively to the "faults" or psychological problems of individual members.
Malnutrition	Malnutrition is a general term for the medical condition in a person or animal caused by an unbalanced diet—either too little or too much food, or a diet missing one or more important nutrients.
Satiety	Satiety refers to the state of being satisfied; fullness.
Suicide	Suicide behavior is rare in childhood but escalates in adolescence. The suicide rate increases in a linear fashion from adolescence through late adulthood.
Group therapy	Group therapy is a form of psychotherapy during which one or several therapists treat a small group of clients together as a group. This may be more cost effective than individual therapy, and possibly even more effective.
Sexual abuse	Sexual abuse is a term used to describe non- consentual sexual relations between two or more parties which are considered criminally and/or morally offensive.
Puberty	Puberty refers to the process of physical changes by which a child's body becomes an adult body capable of reproduction.
Mood disorder	A mood disorder is a condition where the prevailing emotional mood is distorted or inappropriate to the circumstances.
Alcoholism	A disorder that involves long-term, repeated, uncontrolled, compulsive, and excessive use of alcoholic beverages and that impairs the drinker's health and work and social relationships

Go to **Cram101.com** for the Practice Tests for this Chapter.

	is called alcoholism.
Pathology	Pathology is the study of the processes underlying disease and other forms of illness, harmful abnormality, or dysfunction.
Cognitive-behavioral therapy	Cognitive-behavioral therapy refers to group of treatment procedures aimed at identifying and modifying faulty thought processes, attitudes and attributions, and problem behaviors.
Body mass index	The body mass index is a calculated number, used to compare and analyse the health effects of body weight on human bodies of all heights. It is equal to the weight, divided by the square of the height.
Cholesterol	Cholesterol is a steroid, a lipid, and an alcohol, found in the cell membranes of all body tissues, and transported in the blood plasma of all animals. Cholesterol is an important component of the membranes of cells, providing stability; it makes the membrane's fluidity stable over a bigger temperature interval.
Fluoxetine	Fluoxetine is an antidepressant drug used medically in the treatment of depression, obsessive-compulsive disorder, bulimia nervosa, premenstrual dysphoric disorder and panic disorder. It is sold under the brand names Prozac®, and others.
Relaxation training	Relaxation training is an intervention technique used for tics. The person is taught to relax the muscles involved in the tics.
Self-efficacy	Self-efficacy is the belief that one has the capabilities to execute the courses of actions required to manage prospective situations.
Antecedents	In behavior modification, events that typically precede the target response are called antecedents.
Binge eating disorder	Binge eating disorder is a syndrome in which people feel their eating is out of control; eat what most would think is an unusually large amount of food; eat much more quickly than usual; eat until so full they are uncomfortable; eat large amounts of food, even when they are not really hungry; eat alone because they are embarrassed about the amount of food they eat; feel disgusted, depressed, or guilty after overeating.
Guilt	Guilt describes many concepts related to a negative emotion or condition caused by actions which are believed to be, morally wrong. According to Freud, the avoidance of guilt is the basis for moral behavior.
Psychophysio-ogical disorder	Any physical disorder that has a strong psychological basis or component is called a psychophysiological disorder.
Neurotransmitter	A neurotransmitter is a chemical that is used to relay, amplify and modulate electrical signals between a neurons and another cell.
Neuron	The neuron is the primary cell of the nervous system. They are found in the brain, the spinal cord, in the nerves and ganglia of the peripheral nervous system. It is a specialized cell that conducts impulses through the nervous system and contains three major parts: cell body, dendrites, and an axon. It can have many dendrites but only one axon.
Nerve	A nerve is an enclosed, cable-like bundle of nerve fibers or axons, which includes the glia that ensheath the axons in myelin. Neurons are sometimes called nerve cells, though this term is technically imprecise since many neurons do not form nerves.
Norepinephrine	Norepinephrine is released from the adrenal glands as a hormone into the blood, but it is also a neurotransmitter in the nervous system. As a stress hormone, it affects parts of the human brain where attention and impulsivity are controlled. Along with epinephrine, this compound effects the fight-or-flight response, activating the sympathetic nervous system to

	directly increase heart rate, release energy from fat, and increase muscle readiness.
Spinal cord	The spinal cord is a part of the vertebrate nervous system that is enclosed in and protected by the vertebral column (it passes through the spinal canal). It consists of nerve cells. The spinal cord carries sensory signals and motor innervation to most of the skeletal muscles in the body.
Serotonin	Serotonin, a neurotransmitter, is believed to play an important part of the biochemistry of depression, bipolar disorder and anxiety. It is also believed to be influential on sexuality and appetite.
Rapid Eye Movement	Rapid eye movement is the stage of sleep during which the most vivid (though not all) dreams occur. During this stage, the eyes move rapidly, and the activity of the brain's neurons is quite similar to that during waking hours. It is the lightest form of sleep in that people awakened during REM usually feel alert and refreshed.
Stages	Stages represent relatively discrete periods of time in which functioning is qualitatively different from functioning at other periods.
Stage 2 sleep	A sleep deeper than that of stage 1, characterized by a slower, more regular wave pattern, along with momentary interruptions of 'sleep spindles' is called stage 2 sleep.
Rem sleep	Sleep characterized by rapid eye movements, paralysis of large muscles, fast and irregular heart rate and respiration rate, increased brain-wave activity, and vivid dreams is referred to as REM sleep. An infant spends about half the time in REM sleep when sleeping.
Light sleep	Stage 1 sleep, marked by small irregular brain waves and some alpha waves, is called light sleep.
Stage 1 sleep	The state of transition between wakefulness and sleep, characterized by relatively rapid, low-voltage brain waves is called stage 1 sleep.
Sleep spindles	Sleep spindles refer to distinctive bursts of brain-wave activity that indicate a person is asleep.
Electrode	Any device used to electrically stimulate nerve tissue or to record its activity is an electrode.
Delta wave	A delta wave is a large, slow brain wave associated with deep sleep. They are present only in stage-three sleep, stage -four sleep, and coma.
Deep sleep	Deep sleep refers to stage 4 sleep; the deepest form of normal sleep.
Night terror	A night terror is a parasomnia sleep disorder characterized by extreme terror and a temporary inability to regain full consciousness. The subject wakes abruptly from the fourth stage of sleep, with waking usually accompanied by gasping, moaning, or screaming. It is often impossible to fully awaken the person, and after the episode the subject normally settles back to sleep without waking.
Sleep cycle	Sleep cycle refers to a cycle of sleep lasting about 90 minutes and including one or more stages of NREM sleep followed by a period of REM sleep.
Deprivation	Deprivation, is the loss or withholding of normal stimulation, nutrition, comfort, love, and so forth; a condition of lacking. The level of stimulation is less than what is required.
Epilepsy	Epilepsy is a chronic neurological condition characterized by recurrent unprovoked neural discharges. It is commonly controlled with medication, although surgical methods are used as well.
Mental disorder	Mental disorder refers to a disturbance in a person's emotions, drives, thought processes, or behavior that involves serious and relatively prolonged distress and/or impairment in ability

Go to Cram101.com for the Practice Tests for this Chapter.

	to function, is not simply a normal response to some event or set of events in the person's environment.
Schizophrenia	Schizophrenia is characterized by persistent defects in the perception or expression of reality. A person suffering from untreated schizophrenia typically demonstrates grossly disorganized thinking, and may also experience delusions or auditory hallucinations
Pineal gland	The pineal gland is a small endocrine gland. It is located near the center of the brain, between the two hemispheres and near the central switching point of the thalamic bodies. It is responsible for the production of melatonin, which has a role in regulating circadian rhythms.
Melatonin	Melatonin produced in the pineal gland acts as an endocrine hormone since it is released into the blood. Melatonin helps regulate sleep-wake or circadian rhythms.
Circadian rhythm	The circadian rhythm is a name given to the "internal body clock" that regulates the (roughly) 24 hour cycle of biological processes in animals and plants.
Neuroscience	A field that combines the work of psychologists, biologists, biochemists, medical researchers, and others in the study of the structure and function of the nervous system is neuroscience.
Dyssomnias	Dyssomnias are a broad classification of sleeping disorder that make it difficult to get to sleep, or to stay sleeping.
Parasomnia	A parasomnia is any sleep disorder such as sleepwalking, night terrors, rhythmic movement disorder, REM behavior disorder, restless leg syndrome, and sleep talking or somniloquy, characterized by partial arousals during sleep or during transitions between wakefulness and sleep.
Sleep stages	Levels of sleep identified by brain-wave patterns and behavioral changes are called sleep stages.
Substance abuse	Substance abuse refers to the overindulgence in and dependence on a stimulant, depressant, or other chemical substance, leading to effects that are detrimental to the individual's physical or mental health, or the welfare of others.
DSM-IV TR	The current Diagnostic and Statistical Manual of Mental Disorders of the American Psychiatric Association is called DSM-IV TR.
Hypersomnia	Hypersomnia is an excessive amount of sleepiness, resulting in an inability to stay awake. A person is considered to have hypersomnia if he or she sleeps more than 10 hours per day on a regular basis for at least two weeks.
Insomnia	Insomnia is a sleep disorder characterized by an inability to sleep and/or to remain asleep for a reasonable period during the night.
Syndrome	The term syndrome is the association of several clinically recognizable features, signs, symptoms, phenomena or characteristics which often occur together, so that the presence of one feature indicates the presence of the others.
Maladaptive	In psychology, a behavior or trait is adaptive when it helps an individual adjust and function well within their social environment. A maladaptive behavior or trait is counterproductive to the individual.
Sympathetic	The sympathetic nervous system activates what is often termed the "fight or flight response". It is an automatic regulation system, that is, one that operates without the intervention of conscious thought.
Sleep apnea	Sleep apnea refers to a sleep disorder involving periods during sleep when breathing stops and the person must awaken briefly in order to breathe; major symptoms are excessive daytime

	sleepiness and loud snoring.
Apnea	Apnea is the absence of external breathing. During apnea there is no movement of the muscles of respiration and the volume of the lungs initially remains unchanged. .
Antianxiety drugs	Drugs that can reduce a person's level of excitability while increasing feelings of well-being are called antianxiety drugs.
Meditation	Meditation usually refers to a state in which the body is consciously relaxed and the mind is allowed to become calm and focused.
Nightmare	Nightmare was the original term for the state later known as waking dream, and more currently as sleep paralysis, associated with rapid eye movement (REM) periods of sleep.
Sleep terror	A sleep terror is a parasomnia sleep disorder characterized by extreme terror and a temporary inability to regain full consciousness. The subject wakes abruptly from the fourth stage of sleep, with waking usually accompanied by gasping, moaning, or screaming. It is often impossible to fully awaken the person, and after the episode the subject normally settles back to sleep without waking. Sometimes the sleep terror can be recalled by the subject.
Generalization	In conditioning, the tendency for a conditioned response to be evoked by stimuli that are similar to the stimulus to which the response was conditioned is a generalization. The greater the similarity among the stimuli, the greater the probability of generalization.
Variability	Statistically, variability refers to how much the scores in a distribution spread out, away from the mean.
Activating effect	The arousal-producing effects of sex hormones that increase the likelihood of sexual behavior is called the activating effect.
Central nervous system	The vertebrate central nervous system consists of the brain and spinal cord.
Coronary heart disease	Coronary heart disease is the end result of the accumulation of atheromatous plaques within the walls of the arteries that supply the myocardium (the muscle of the heart).
Lesion	A lesion is a non-specific term referring to abnormal tissue in the body. It can be caused by any disease process including trauma (physical, chemical, electrical), infection, neoplasm, metabolic and autoimmune.
Plaques	Plaques refer to small, round areas composed of remnants of lost neurons and beta-amyloid, a waxy protein deposit; present in the brains of patients with Alzheimer's disease.
Atherosclerosis	Process by which a fatty substance or plaque builds up inside arteries to form obstructions is called atherosclerosis.
Myocardial infarction	Acute myocardial infarction, commonly known as a heart attack, is a serious, sudden heart condition usually characterized by varying degrees of chest pain or discomfort, weakness, sweating, nausea, vomiting, and arrhythmias, sometimes causing loss of consciousness. It occurs when a part of the heart muscle is injured, and this part may die because of sudden total interruption of blood flow to the area.
Cardiovascular system	The human cardiovascular system comprises the blood, the heart, and a dual-circuit system of blood vessels that serve as conduits between the heart, the lungs, and the peripheral tissues of the body.
Temperament	Temperament refers to a basic, innate disposition to change behavior. The activity level is an important dimension of temperament.
Stress hormones	Group of hormones including cortico steroids, that are involved in the body's physiological stress response are referred to as stress hormones.

Go to **Cram101.com** for the Practice Tests for this Chapter.

Catecholamines	Catecholamines are chemical compounds derived from the amino acid tyrosine that act as hormones or neurotransmitters. High catecholamine levels in blood are associated with stress.
Epinephrine	Epinephrine is a hormone and a neurotransmitter. Epinephrine plays a central role in the short-term stress reaction—the physiological response to threatening or exciting conditions. It is secreted by the adrenal medulla. When released into the bloodstream, epinephrine binds to multiple receptors and has numerous effects throughout the body.
Social isolation	Social isolation refers to a type of loneliness that occurs when a person lacks a sense of integrated involvement. Being deprived of participation in a group or community involving companionship, shared interests, organized activities, and meaningful roles causes a person to feel alone.
Autonomic nervous system	A division of the peripheral nervous system, the autonomic nervous system, regulates glands and activities such as heartbeat, respiration, digestion, and dilation of the pupils. It is responsible for homeostasis, maintaining a relatively constant internal environment .
Electrocardi-gram	An electrocardiogram is a graphic produced by an electrocardiograph, which records the electrical voltage in the heart in the form of a continuous strip graph. It is the prime tool in cardiac electrophysiology, and has a prime function in screening and diagnosis of cardiovascular diseases..
Creativity	Creativity is the ability to think about something in novel and unusual ways and come up with unique solutions to problems. It involves divergent thinking, having many solutions or views to a problem.
Diastolic blood pressure	Blood pressure level when the heart is at rest or between heartbeats is called diastolic blood pressure.
Protein	A protein is a complex, high-molecular-weight organic compound that consists of amino acids joined by peptide bonds. It is essential to the structure and function of all living cells and viruses. Many are enzymes or subunits of enzymes.
Assertiveness	Assertiveness basically means the ability to express your thoughts and feelings in a way that clearly states your needs and keeps the lines of communication open with the other.
Role-playing	Role-playing refers to a technique that teaches people to behave in a certain way by encouraging them to pretend that they are in a particular situation; it helps people acquire complex behaviors in an efficient way.
Cardiovascular disease	Cardiovascular disease refers to afflictions in the mechanisms, including the heart, blood vessels, and their controllers, that are responsible for transporting blood to the body's tissues and organs. Psychological factors may play important roles in such diseases and their treatments.
Biofeedback	Biofeedback is the process of measuring and quantifying an aspect of a subject's physiology, analyzing the data, and then feeding back the information to the subject in a form that allows the subject to enact physiological change.
Denial	Denial is a psychological defense mechanism in which a person faced with a fact that is uncomfortable or painful to accept rejects it instead, insisting that it is not true despite what may be overwhelming evidence.
Motivation	In psychology, motivation is the driving force (desire) behind all actions of an organism.
Ambivalence	The simultaneous holding of strong positive and negative emotional attitudes toward the same situation or person is called ambivalence.
Socioeconomic Status	A family's socioeconomic status is based on family income, parental education level, parental occupation, and social status in the community. Those with high status often have more

Go to **Cram101.com** for the Practice Tests for this Chapter.

	success in preparing their children for school because they have access to a wide range of resources.
Ethnicity	Ethnicity refers to a characteristic based on cultural heritage, nationality characteristics, race, religion, and language.
Chronic fatigue syndrome	Chronic fatigue syndrome is incapacitating exhaustion following only minimal exertion, accompanied by fever, headaches, muscle and joint pain, depression, and anxiety.
Acute onset	Acute onset refers to the sudden beginning of a disease or disorder.
Neurasthenia	Neurasthenia was a term first coined by George Miller Beard in 1869. Beard described a condition with symptoms of fatigue, anxiety, headache, impotence, neuralgia and depression. It was explained as being a result of exhaustion of the central nervous system's energy reserves, which Beard attributed to civilization. This disorder is similar to present-day chronic fatigue syndrome.
Sensation	Sensation is the first stage in the chain of biochemical and neurologic events that begins with the impinging of a stimulus upon the receptor cells of a sensory organ, which then leads to perception, the mental state that is reflected in statements like "I see a uniformly blue wall."
Migraine	Migraine is a form of headache, usually very intense and disabling. It is a neurologic disease.
Heredity	Heredity is the transfer of characteristics from parent to offspring through their genes.
Cluster headache	Cluster headache sufferers typically experience very severe headaches of a piercing quality near one eye or temple that last for between 15 minutes and three hours. The headaches are unilateral and occasionally change sides.
Narcolepsy	A serious sleep disorder characterized by excessive daytime sleepiness and sudden, uncontrollable attacks of REM sleep is called narcolepsy.
Hallucination	A hallucination is a sensory perception experienced in the absence of an external stimulus, as distinct from an illusion, which is a misperception of an external stimulus. They may occur in any sensory modality - visual, auditory, olfactory, gustatory, tactile, or mixed.
Assertiveness training	In behavior therapy, a direct method of training people to express their own desires and feelings and to maintain their own rights in interactions with others, while at the same time respecting the others' rights is called assertiveness training.

130

Go to **Cram101.com** for the Practice Tests for this Chapter.

Personality	Personality refers to the pattern of enduring characteristics that differentiates a person, the patterns of behaviors that make each individual unique.
Pathology	Pathology is the study of the processes underlying disease and other forms of illness, harmful abnormality, or dysfunction.
Attention	Attention is the cognitive process of selectively concentrating on one thing while ignoring other things. Psychologists have labeled three types of attention: sustained attention, selective attention, and divided attention.
Somatization disorder	With somatization disorder a patient manifests a psychological condition as a physical complaint. One prevalent general etiological explanation is that internal psychological conflicts are unconsciously expressed as physical signs.
Conversion disorder	A disorder in which anxiety or unconscious conflicts are converted into physical symptoms that often have the effect of helping the person cope with anxiety or conflict is referred to as a conversion disorder.
Hypochondriasis	The persistent beliefs that one has a medical disorder despite lack of medical findings are called hypochondriasis.
Pain disorder	Pain disorder is when a patient experiences chronic and constant pain in one or more areas, and is thought to be caused by psychological stress. The pain is often so severe that it disables the patient from proper functioning. It can last as short as a few days, to as long as many years.
Clinician	A health professional authorized to provide services to people suffering from one or more pathologies is a clinician.
Chronic	Chronic refers to a relatively long duration, usually more than a few months.
Acute	Acute means sudden, sharp, and abrupt. Usually short in duration.
Nervous system	The body's electrochemical communication circuitry, made up of billions of neurons is a nervous system.
Descartes	Descartes was concerned with the sharp contrast between the certainty of mathematics and the controversial nature of philosophy, and came to believe that the sciences could be made to yield results as certain as those of mathematics. He introduced the method of rationalism for arriving at knowledge. He also saw the human condition as a competition between the body and soul, introducing the concept of dualism.
Theories	Theories are logically self-consistent models or frameworks describing the behavior of a certain natural or social phenomenon. They are broad explanations and predictions concerning phenomena of interest.
Sensory receptor	A sensory receptor is a structure that recognizes a stimulus in the environment of an organism. In response to stimuli the sensory receptor initiates sensory transduction by creating graded potentials or action potentials in the same cell or in an adjacent one.
Sensation	Sensation is the first stage in the chain of biochemical and neurologic events that begins with the impinging of a stimulus upon the receptor cells of a sensory organ, which then leads to perception, the mental state that is reflected in statements like "I see a uniformly blue wall."
Scientific research	Research that is objective, systematic, and testable is called scientific research.
Biopsychosocial	The biopsychosocial model is a way of looking at the mind and body of a patient as two important systems that are interlinked. The biopsychosocial model draws a distinction between the actual pathological processes that cause disease, and the patient's perception of their

Go to **Cram101.com** for the Practice Tests for this Chapter.

health and the effects on it, called the illness.

Depression	In everyday language depression refers to any downturn in mood, which may be relatively transitory and perhaps due to something trivial. This is differentiated from Clinical depression which is marked by symptoms that last two weeks or more and are so severe that they interfere with daily living.
Anxiety	Anxiety is a complex combination of the feeling of fear, apprehension and worry often accompanied by physical sensations such as palpitations, chest pain and/or shortness of breath.
Operant Conditioning	A simple form of learning in which an organism learns to engage in behavior because it is reinforced is referred to as operant conditioning. The consequences of a behavior produce changes in the probability of the behavior's occurence.
Cognitive-behavioral therapy	Cognitive-behavioral therapy refers to group of treatment procedures aimed at identifying and modifying faulty thought processes, attitudes and attributions, and problem behaviors.
Observational learning	The acquisition of knowledge and skills through the observation of others rather than by means of direct experience is observational learning. Four major processes are thought to influence the observational learning: attentional, retentional, behavioral production, and motivational.
Acquisition	Acquisition is the process of adapting to the environment, learning or becoming conditioned. In classical conditoning terms, it is the initial learning of the stimulus response link, which involves a neutral stimulus being associated with a unconditioned stimulus and becoming a conditioned stimulus.
Catastrophizing	Catastrophizing refers to interpreting negative life events in pessimistic, global terms. People who consistently explain bad events as catastrophes are found to have a shortened life span.
Maladaptive	In psychology, a behavior or trait is adaptive when it helps an individual adjust and function well within their social environment. A maladaptive behavior or trait is counterproductive to the individual.
Attitude	An enduring mental representation of a person, place, or thing that evokes an emotional response and related behavior is called attitude.
Acute pain	Acute pain refers to pain that typically follows an injury and that disappears once the injury heals or is effectively treated.
Self-esteem	Self-esteem refers to a person's subjective appraisal of himself or herself as intrinsically positive or negative to some degree.
Individual differences	Individual differences psychology studies the ways in which individual people differ in their behavior. This is distinguished from other aspects of psychology in that although psychology is ostensibly a study of individuals, modern psychologists invariably study groups.
Variable	A variable refers to a measurable factor, characteristic, or attribute of an individual or a system.
Perception	Perception is the process of acquiring, interpreting, selecting, and organizing sensory information.
Psychopathology	Psychopathology refers to the field concerned with the nature and development of mental disorders.
Social support	Social Support is the physical and emotional comfort given by family, friends, co-workers and others. Research has identified three main types of social support: emotional, practical,

sharing points of view.

Arthritis	Arthritis is a group of conditions that affect the health of the bone joints in the body. Arthritis can be caused from strains and injuries caused by repetitive motion, sports, overexertion, and falls. Unlike the autoimmune diseases, it largely affects older people and results from the degeneration of joint cartilage.
Biofeedback	Biofeedback is the process of measuring and quantifying an aspect of a subject's physiology, analyzing the data, and then feeding back the information to the subject in a form that allows the subject to enact physiological change.
Behavioral medicine	Behavioral medicine refers to an interdisciplinary field that focuses on developing and integrating behavioral and biomedical knowledge to promote health and reduce illness.
Self-Regulatory	Bandura proposes that self-regulatory systems mediate external influences and provide a basis for purposeful action, allowing people to have personal control over their own thoughts, feelings, motivations, and actions.
Hypertension	Hypertension is a medical condition where the blood pressure in the arteries is chronically elevated. Persistent hypertension is one of the risk factors for strokes, heart attacks, heart failure and arterial aneurysm, and is a leading cause of chronic renal failure.
Learning	Learning is a relatively permanent change in behavior that results from experience. Thus, to attribute a behavioral change to learning, the change must be relatively permanent and must result from experience.
Epilepsy	Epilepsy is a chronic neurological condition characterized by recurrent unprovoked neural discharges. It is commonly controlled with medication, although surgical methods are used as well.
Brain	The brain controls and coordinates most movement, behavior and homeostatic body functions such as heartbeat, blood pressure, fluid balance and body temperature. Functions of the brain are responsible for cognition, emotion, memory, motor learning and other sorts of learning. The brain is primarily made up of two types of cells: glia and neurons.
Cognitive restructuring	Cognitive restructuring refers to any behavior therapy procedure that attempts to alter the manner in which a client thinks about life so that he or she changes overt behavior and emotions.
Script	A schema, or behavioral sequence, for an event is called a script. It is a form of schematic organization, with real-world events organized in terms of temporal and causal relations between component acts.
Neurotransmitter	A neurotransmitter is a chemical that is used to relay, amplify and modulate electrical signals between a neurons and another cell.
Self-efficacy	Self-efficacy is the belief that one has the capabilities to execute the courses of actions required to manage prospective situations.
Feedback	Feedback refers to information returned to a person about the effects a response has had.
Physiological changes	Alterations in heart rate, blood pressure, perspiration, and other involuntary responses are physiological changes.
Reinforcer	In operant conditioning, a reinforcer is any stimulus that increases the probability that a preceding behavior will occur again. In Classical Conditioning, the unconditioned stimulus (US) is the reinforcer.
Psychotherapy	Psychotherapy is a set of techniques based on psychological principles intended to improve mental health, emotional or behavioral issues.

Go to **Cram101.com** for the Practice Tests for this Chapter.

Insight	Insight refers to a sudden awareness of the relationships among various elements that had previously appeared to be independent of one another.
Anxiety disorder	Anxiety disorder is a blanket term covering several different forms of abnormal anxiety, fear, phobia and nervous condition, that come on suddenly and prevent pursuing normal daily routines.
Trauma	Trauma refers to a severe physical injury or wound to the body caused by an external force, or a psychological shock having a lasting effect on mental life.
Motivation	In psychology, motivation is the driving force (desire) behind all actions of an organism.
Affect	A subjective feeling or emotional tone often accompanied by bodily expressions noticeable to others is called affect.
Emotion	An emotion is a mental states that arise spontaneously, rather than through conscious effort. They are often accompanied by physiological changes.
Suicide	Suicide behavior is rare in childhood but escalates in adolescence. The suicide rate increases in a linear fashion from adolescence through late adulthood.
Rationalization	Rationalization is the process of constructing a logical justification for a decision that was originally arrived at through a different mental process. It is one of Freud's defense mechanisms.
Psychological disorder	Mental processes and/or behavior patterns that cause emotional distress and/or substantial impairment in functioning is a psychological disorder.
Heredity	Heredity is the transfer of characteristics from parent to offspring through their genes.
Psychodynamic	Most psychodynamic approaches are centered around the idea of a maladapted function developed early in life (usually childhood) which are at least in part unconscious. This maladapted function (a.k.a. defense mechanism) does not do well in place of a normal/healthy one.
Anatomy	Anatomy is the branch of biology that deals with the structure and organization of living things. It can be divided into animal anatomy (zootomy) and plant anatomy (phytonomy). Major branches of anatomy include comparative anatomy, histology, and human anatomy.
Anesthesia	Anesthesia is the process of blocking the perception of pain and other sensations. This allows patients to undergo surgery and other procedures without the distress and pain they would otherwise experience.
La belle indifference	French term that describes a lack of concern, la belle indifference, is used to characterize people with conversion disorders.
Hysteria	Hysteria is a diagnostic label applied to a state of mind, one of unmanageable fear or emotional excesses. The fear is often centered on a body part, most often on an imagined problem with that body part.
Uterus	The uterus or womb is the major female reproductive organ. The main function of the uterus is to accept a fertilized ovum which becomes implanted into the endometrium, and derives nourishment from blood vessels which develop exclusively for this purpose.
Affective	Affective is the way people react emotionally, their ability to feel another living thing's pain or joy.
Trait	An enduring personality characteristic that tends to lead to certain behaviors is called a trait. The term trait also means a genetically inherited feature of an organism.
Mass hysteria	Mass hysteria is the sociopsychological phenomenon of the manifestation of the same hysterical symptoms by more than one person. It may begin when a group witness an individual becoming hysterical during a traumatic or extremely stressful event. A potential symptom is

	group nausea, in which a person becoming violently ill triggers a similar reaction in other group members.
Population	Population refers to all members of a well-defined group of organisms, events, or things.
Social psychologists	Social psychologists study the nature and causes of human social behavior, emphasizing on how people think and relate towards each other.
Antecedents	In behavior modification, events that typically precede the target response are called antecedents.
Body dysmorphic disorder	Body dysmorphic disorder is a disorder which involves a disturbed body image. The central feature is that persons who are afflicted with it are excessively dissatisfied with their body because of a perceived physical defect.
Substance abuse	Substance abuse refers to the overindulgence in and dependence on a stimulant, depressant, or other chemical substance, leading to effects that are detrimental to the individual's physical or mental health, or the welfare of others.
Body image	A person's body image is their perception of their physical appearance. It is more than what a person thinks they will see in a mirror, it is inextricably tied to their self-esteem and acceptance by peers.
Adolescence	The period of life bounded by puberty and the assumption of adult responsibilities is adolescence.
Eating disorders	Psychological disorders characterized by distortion of the body image and gross disturbances in eating patterns are called eating disorders.
Anorexia	Anorexia nervosa is an eating disorder characterized by voluntary starvation and exercise stress.
Anabolic steroid	Anabolic steroids are a class of natural and synthetic steroid hormones that promote cell growth and division, resulting in growth of muscle tissue and sometimes bone size and strength. Testosterone is the best known natural anabolic steroid, as well as the best known natural androgen.
Cognition	The intellectual processes through which information is obtained, transformed, stored, retrieved, and otherwise used is cognition.
Exposure therapy	An exposure therapy is any method of treating fears, including flooding and systematic desensitization, that involves exposing the client to the feared object or situation so that the process of extinction or habituation of the fear response can occur.
Factitious disorder	A factitious disorder is an illness whose symptoms are either self-induced or falsified by the patient.
Somatoform disorder	Psychological difficulty that take on a physical form, but for which there is no medical cause is referred to as a somatoform disorder.
Malingering	Malingering is a medical and psychological term that refers to an individual faking the symptoms of mental or physical disorders for a myriad of reasons such as fraud, dereliction of responsibilities, attempting to obtain medications or to lighten criminal sentences.
Syndrome	The term syndrome is the association of several clinically recognizable features, signs, symptoms, phenomena or characteristics which often occur together, so that the presence of one feature indicates the presence of the others.
Munchausen syndrome	As an adult disorder, Munchausen SYNDROME refers to an intentional fabrication of illness.
Compensation	In personaility, compensation, according to Adler, is an effort to overcome imagined or real

inferiorities by developing one's abilities.

Schema

Schema refers to a way of mentally representing the world, such as a belief or an expectation, that can influence perception of persons, objects, and situations.

Control group

A group that does not receive the treatment effect in an experiment is referred to as the control group or sometimes as the comparison group.

Go to **Cram101.com** for the Practice Tests for this Chapter.

143

Anxiety disorder	Anxiety disorder is a blanket term covering several different forms of abnormal anxiety, fear, phobia and nervous condition, that come on suddenly and prevent pursuing normal daily routines.
Anxiety	Anxiety is a complex combination of the feeling of fear, apprehension and worry often accompanied by physical sensations such as palpitations, chest pain and/or shortness of breath.
Chronic	Chronic refers to a relatively long duration, usually more than a few months.
Panic attack	An attack of overwhelming anxiety, fear, or terror is called panic attack.
Obsessive-compulsive disorder	Obsessive-compulsive disorder is an anxiety disorder manifested in a variety of forms, but is most commonly characterized by a subject's obsessive drive to perform a particular task or set of tasks, compulsions commonly termed rituals.
Catastrophic thinking	Unrealistically pessimistic appraisals of stress that exaggerate the magnitude of one's problems are called catastrophic thinking.
Scientific research	Research that is objective, systematic, and testable is called scientific research.
Anxiety neurosis	Anxiety neurosis is the DSM-II term for what are now called panic disorders and generalized anxiety disorders.
Benjamin Rush	Benjamin Rush was far ahead of his time in the treatment of mental illness. In fact, he is considered the Father of American Psychiatry, publishing the first textbook on the subject in the United States, Medical Inquiries and Observations upon the Diseases of the Mind (1812).
Sigmund Freud	Sigmund Freud was the founder of the psychoanalytic school, based on his theory that unconscious motives control much behavior, that particular kinds of unconscious thoughts and memories are the source of neurosis, and that neurosis could be treated through bringing these unconscious thoughts and memories to consciousness in psychoanalytic treatment.
Conditioning	Conditioning describes the process by which behaviors can be learned or modified through interaction with the environment.
Maladaptive	In psychology, a behavior or trait is adaptive when it helps an individual adjust and function well within their social environment. A maladaptive behavior or trait is counterproductive to the individual.
Antianxiety drugs	Drugs that can reduce a person's level of excitability while increasing feelings of well-being are called antianxiety drugs.
Stress disorder	A significant emotional disturbance caused by stresses outside the range of normal human experience is referred to as stress disorder.
Panic disorder	A panic attack is a period of intense fear or discomfort, typically with an abrupt onset and usually lasting no more than thirty minutes. The disorder is strikingly different from other types of anxiety, in that panic attacks are very sudden, appear to be unprovoked, and are often disabling. People who have repeated attacks, or feel severe anxiety about having another attack are said to have panic disorder.
Stimulus	A change in an environmental condition that elicits a response is a stimulus.
Psychodynamic	Most psychodynamic approaches are centered around the idea of a maladapted function developed early in life (usually childhood) which are at least in part unconscious. This maladapted function (a.k.a. defense mechanism) does not do well in place of a normal/healthy one.
Neurosis	Neurosis, any mental disorder that, although may cause distress, does not interfere with rational thought or the persons' ability to function.

Specific phobia	A specific phobia is a generic term for anxiety disorders that amount to unreasonable or irrational fear or anxiety related with exposure to specific objects or situations. As a result, the affected persons tend to actively avoid these objects or situations.
Social phobia	An irrational, excessive fear of public scrutiny is referred to as social phobia.
Statistics	Statistics is a type of data analysis which practice includes the planning, summarizing, and interpreting of observations of a system possibly followed by predicting or forecasting of future events based on a mathematical model of the system being observed.
Statistic	A statistic is an observable random variable of a sample.
Survey	A method of scientific investigation in which a large sample of people answer questions about their attitudes or behavior is referred to as a survey.
Depression	In everyday language depression refers to any downturn in mood, which may be relatively transitory and perhaps due to something trivial. This is differentiated from Clinical depression which is marked by symptoms that last two weeks or more and are so severe that they interfere with daily living.
Scheme	According to Piaget, a hypothetical mental structure that permits the classification and organization of new information is called a scheme.
Parasympathetic	The parasympathetic nervous system is one of two divisions of the autonomic nervous system. It conserves energy as it slows the heart rate, increases intestinal and gland activity, and relaxes sphincter muscles. In another words, it acts to reverse the effects of the Sympathetic nervous system.
Nervous system	The body's electrochemical communication circuitry, made up of billions of neurons is a nervous system.
Sympathetic	The sympathetic nervous system activates what is often termed the "fight or flight response". It is an automatic regulation system, that is, one that operates without the intervention of conscious thought.
Population	Population refers to all members of a well-defined group of organisms, events, or things.
Psychotherapy	Psychotherapy is a set of techniques based on psychological principles intended to improve mental health, emotional or behavioral issues.
Amygdala	Located in the brain's medial temporal lobe, the almond-shaped amygdala is believed to play a key role in the emotions. It forms part of the limbic system and is linked to both fear responses and pleasure. Its size is positively correlated with aggressive behavior across species.
Brain	The brain controls and coordinates most movement, behavior and homeostatic body functions such as heartbeat, blood pressure, fluid balance and body temperature. Functions of the brain are responsible for cognition, emotion, memory, motor learning and other sorts of learning. The brain is primarily made up of two types of cells: glia and neurons.
Phobia	A persistent, irrational fear of an object, situation, or activity that the person feels compelled to avoid is referred to as a phobia.
Affect	A subjective feeling or emotional tone often accompanied by bodily expressions noticeable to others is called affect.
Personality disorder	A mental disorder characterized by a set of inflexible, maladaptive personality traits that keep a person from functioning properly in society is referred to as a personality disorder.
Performance anxiety	Anxiety concerning one's ability to perform, especially when performance may be evaluated by other people is performance anxiety.

Nocturnal	A person who exhibits nocturnal habits is referred to as a night owl.
Nightmare	Nightmare was the original term for the state later known as waking dream, and more currently as sleep paralysis, associated with rapid eye movement (REM) periods of sleep.
Asthma	Asthma is a complex disease characterized by bronchial hyperresponsiveness (BHR), inflammation, mucus production and intermittent airway obstruction.
Personality	Personality refers to the pattern of enduring characteristics that differentiates a person, the patterns of behaviors that make each individual unique.
Clinician	A health professional authorized to provide services to people suffering from one or more pathologies is a clinician.
Compulsion	An apparently irresistible urge to repeat an act or engage in ritualistic behavior such as hand washing is referred to as a compulsion.
Obsession	An obsession is a thought or idea that the sufferer cannot stop thinking about. Common examples include fears of acquiring disease, getting hurt, or causing harm to someone. They are typically automatic, frequent, distressing, and difficult to control or put an end to by themselves.
Cognition	The intellectual processes through which information is obtained, transformed, stored, retrieved, and otherwise used is cognition.
Imipramine	Imipramine is the first antidepressant to be developed in the late 1950s. The drug became a prototypical drug for the development of the later released tricyclics. It is not as commonly used today but sometimes used to treat major depression as a second-line treatment.
Heredity	Heredity is the transfer of characteristics from parent to offspring through their genes.
Attention	Attention is the cognitive process of selectively concentrating on one thing while ignoring other things. Psychologists have labeled three types of attention: sustained attention, selective attention, and divided attention.
Evolution	Commonly used to refer to gradual change, evolution is the change in the frequency of alleles within a population from one generation to the next. This change may be caused by different mechanisms, including natural selection, genetic drift, or changes in population (gene flow).
Stages	Stages represent relatively discrete periods of time in which functioning is qualitatively different from functioning at other periods.
Threshold	In general, a threshold is a fixed location or value where an abrupt change is observed. In the sensory modalities, it is the minimum amount of stimulus energy necessary to elicit a sensory response.
Agoraphobia	An irrational fear of open, crowded places is called agoraphobia. Many people suffering from agoraphobia, however, are not afraid of the open spaces themselves, but of situations often associated with these spaces, such as social gatherings.
Motivation	In psychology, motivation is the driving force (desire) behind all actions of an organism.
Social support	Social Support is the physical and emotional comfort given by family, friends, co-workers and others. Research has identified three main types of social support: emotional, practical, sharing points of view.
Tremor	Tremor is the rhythmic, oscillating shaking movement of the whole body or just a certain part of it, caused by problems of the neurons responsible from muscle action.
Extinction	In operant extinction, if no reinforcement is delivered after the response, gradually the behavior will no longer occur in the presence of the stimulus. The process is more rapid following continuous reinforcement rather than after partial reinforcement. In Classical

	Conditioning, repeated presentations of the CS without being followed by the US results in the extinction of the CS.
Shyness	A tendency to avoid others plus uneasiness and strain when socializing is called shyness.
Sensation	Sensation is the first stage in the chain of biochemical and neurologic events that begins with the impinging of a stimulus upon the receptor cells of a sensory organ, which then leads to perception, the mental state that is reflected in statements like "I see a uniformly blue wall."
Antidepressants	Antidepressants are medications used primarily in the treatment of clinical depression. Antidepressants create little if any immediate change in mood and require between several days and several weeks to take effect.
Antidepressant	An antidepressant is a medication used primarily in the treatment of clinical depression. They are not thought to produce tolerance, although sudden withdrawal may produce adverse effects. They create little if any immediate change in mood and require between several days and several weeks to take effect.
Exposure therapy	An exposure therapy is any method of treating fears, including flooding and systematic desensitization, that involves exposing the client to the feared object or situation so that the process of extinction or habituation of the fear response can occur.
Separation anxiety	Separation anxiety is a psychological condition in which an individual has excessive anxiety regarding separation from home, or from those with whom the individual has a strong attachment.
Brain imaging	Brain imaging is a fairly recent discipline within medicine and neuroscience. Brain imaging falls into two broad categories -- structural imaging and functional imaging.
Guilt	Guilt describes many concepts related to a negative emotion or condition caused by actions which are believed to be, morally wrong. According to Freud, the avoidance of guilt is the basis for moral behavior.
Late adolescence	Late adolescence refers to approximately the latter half of the second decade of life. Career interests, dating, and identity exploration are often more pronounced in late adolescence than in early adolescence.
Early adulthood	The developmental period beginning in the late teens or early twenties and lasting into the thirties is called early adulthood; characterized by an increasing self-awareness.
Psychiatrist	A psychiatrist is a physician who specializes in the diagnosis and treatment of psychological disorders.
Conscientiou-ness	Conscientiousness is one of the dimensions of the five-factor model of personality and individual differences involving being organized, thorough, and reliable as opposed to careless, negligent, and unreliable.
Psychotic behavior	A psychotic behavior is a severe psychological disorder characterized by hallucinations and loss of contact with reality.
Psychosis	Psychosis is a generic term for mental states in which the components of rational thought and perception are severely impaired. Persons experiencing a psychosis may experience hallucinations, hold paranoid or delusional beliefs, demonstrate personality changes and exhibit disorganized thinking. This is usually accompanied by features such as a lack of insight into the unusual or bizarre nature of their behavior, difficulties with social interaction and impairments in carrying out the activities of daily living.
Hypochondriasis	The persistent beliefs that one has a medical disorder despite lack of medical findings are called hypochondriasis.

Anorexia	Anorexia nervosa is an eating disorder characterized by voluntary starvation and exercise stress.
Acute stress disorder	Acute stress disorder is a psychological condition arising in response to a terrifying event.
Trauma	Trauma refers to a severe physical injury or wound to the body caused by an external force, or a psychological shock having a lasting effect on mental life.
Acute	Acute means sudden, sharp, and abrupt. Usually short in duration.
Depersonaliz- tion	Depersonalization is the experience of feelings of loss of a sense of reality. A sufferer feels that they have changed and the world has become less real — it is vague, dreamlike, or lacking in significance.
Derealization	Derealization is a loss of the sense that the surroundings are real. The effect is present in several psychological disorders, such as panic disorder, depersonalization disorder, and schizophrenia.
Amnesia	Amnesia is a condition in which memory is disturbed. The causes of amnesia are organic or functional. Organic causes include damage to the brain, through trauma or disease, or use of certain (generally sedative) drugs.
Psychological disorder	Mental processes and/or behavior patterns that cause emotional distress and/or substantial impairment in functioning is a psychological disorder.
Dissociation	Dissociation is a psychological state or condition in which certain thoughts, emotions, sensations, or memories are separated from the rest.
Hypothesis	A specific statement about behavior or mental processes that is testable through research is a hypothesis.
Reexperiencing	Careful and systematic visualizing and reliving of traumatic life events in order to diminish their power and emotional effects as a means of treating dissociative identity disorder or posttraumatic stress disorder is called reexperiencing.
Denial	Denial is a psychological defense mechanism in which a person faced with a fact that is uncomfortable or painful to accept rejects it instead, insisting that it is not true despite what may be overwhelming evidence.
Tranquilizer	A sedative, or tranquilizer, is a drug that depresses the central nervous system (CNS), which causes calmness, relaxation, reduction of anxiety, sleepiness, slowed breathing, slurred speech, staggering gait, poor judgment, and slow, uncertain reflexes.
Emotion	An emotion is a mental states that arise spontaneously, rather than through conscious effort. They are often accompanied by physiological changes.
Cognitive- behavioral therapy	Cognitive-behavioral therapy refers to group of treatment procedures aimed at identifying and modifying faulty thought processes, attitudes and attributions, and problem behaviors.
Cognitive skills	Cognitive skills such as reasoning, attention, and memory can be advanced and sustained through practice and training.
Debriefing	Process of informing a participant after the experiment about the nature of the experiment, clarifying any misunderstanding, and answering any questions that the participant may have concerning the experiment is called debriefing.
Life satisfaction	A person's attitudes about his or her overall life are referred to as life satisfaction.
Comorbidity	Comorbidity refers to the presence of more than one mental disorder occurring in an

Go to **Cram101.com** for the Practice Tests for this Chapter.

individual at the same time.

Suicide	Suicide behavior is rare in childhood but escalates in adolescence. The suicide rate increases in a linear fashion from adolescence through late adulthood.
Mood disorder	A mood disorder is a condition where the prevailing emotional mood is distorted or inappropriate to the circumstances.
Trait	An enduring personality characteristic that tends to lead to certain behaviors is called a trait. The term trait also means a genetically inherited feature of an organism.
Depressive disorders	Depressive disorders are mood disorders in which the individual suffers depression without ever experiencing mania.
Mental disorder	Mental disorder refers to a disturbance in a person's emotions, drives, thought processes, or behavior that involves serious and relatively prolonged distress and/or impairment in ability to function, is not simply a normal response to some event or set of events in the person's environment.
Defense mechanism	A Defense mechanism is a set of unconscious ways to protect one's personality from unpleasant thoughts and realities which may otherwise cause anxiety. The notion is an integral part of the psychoanalytic theory.
Reaction formation	In Freud's psychoanalytic theory, reaction formation is a defense mechanism in which anxiety-producing or unacceptable emotions are replaced by their direct opposites.
Reinforcement	In operant conditioning, reinforcement is any change in an environment that (a) occurs after the behavior, (b) seems to make that behavior re-occur more often in the future and (c) that reoccurence of behavior must be the result of the change.
Learning	Learning is a relatively permanent change in behavior that results from experience. Thus, to attribute a behavioral change to learning, the change must be relatively permanent and must result from experience.
Behavior therapy	Behavior therapy refers to the systematic application of the principles of learning to direct modification of a client's problem behaviors.
Variable	A variable refers to a measurable factor, characteristic, or attribute of an individual or a system.
Systematic desensitization	Systematic desensitization refers to Wolpe's behavioral fear-reduction technique in which a hierarchy of fear-evoking stimuli are presented while the person remains relaxed. The fear-evoking stimuli thereby become associated with muscle relaxation.
In vivo	In vivo is used to indicate the presence of a whole/living organism, in distinction to a partial or dead organism, or a computer model. In vivo research is more suited to observe an overall effect than in vitro research, which is better suited to deduce mechanisms of action.
Implosion	A behavioral treatment that attempts to extinguish a fear by having the client imagine the anxiety siituation at its maximum intensity is called implosion.
Theories	Theories are logically self-consistent models or frameworks describing the behavior of a certain natural or social phenomenon. They are broad explanations and predictions concerning phenomena of interest.
Desensitization	Desensitization refers to the type of sensory or behavioral adaptation in which we become less sensitive to constant stimuli.
Flooding	Flooding is a behavioral fear-reduction technique based on principles of classical conditioning. Fear-evoking stimuli are presented continuously in the absence of harm so that fear responses are extinguished. However, subjects tend to avoid the stimulus, making

extinction difficult.

Exposure treatment	An exposure treatment is any method of treating fears, including flooding and systematic desensitization, that involves exposing the client to the feared object or situation so that the process of extinction or habituation of the fear response can occur.
Exposure and response prevention	Exposure and response prevention is a form of behavior therapy that exposes patients with obsessive compulsive disorder to stimuli generating increasing anxiety. Patients must agree not to carry out their normal rituals for a specified period of time after exposure.
Acquisition	Acquisition is the process of adapting to the environment, learning or becoming conditioned. In classical conditoning terms, it is the initial learning of the stimulus response link, which involves a neutral stimulus being associated with a unconditioned stimulus and becoming a conditioned stimulus.
Self-efficacy	Self-efficacy is the belief that one has the capabilities to execute the courses of actions required to manage prospective situations.
Participant modeling	A behavior therapy in which an appropriate response is modeled in graduated steps and the client attempts each step, encouraged and supported by the therapist is participant modeling.
Behavioral therapy	The treatment of a mental disorder through the application of basic principles of conditioning and learning is called behavioral therapy.
Attitude	An enduring mental representation of a person, place, or thing that evokes an emotional response and related behavior is called attitude.
Cognitive restructuring	Cognitive restructuring refers to any behavior therapy procedure that attempts to alter the manner in which a client thinks about life so that he or she changes overt behavior and emotions.
Albert Ellis	Albert Ellis is a psychologist whose Rational Emotive Behavior Therapy (REBT), is the foundation of all cognitive and cognitive behavior therapies.
Thought stopping	Thought stopping is a behavioral approach that uses aversive stimuli to interrupt or prevent upsetting thoughts.
Cognitive therapy	Cognitive therapy is a kind of psychotherapy used to treat depression, anxiety disorders, phobias, and other forms of mental disorder. It involves recognizing distorted thinking and learning how to replace it with more realistic thoughts and actions.
Aaron Beck	Aaron Beck was initially trained as a psychoanalyst and conducted research on the psychoanalytic treatment of depression. With out the strong ability to collect data to this end, he began exploring cognitive approaches to treatment and originated cognitive behavior therapy.
Empathy	Empathy is the recognition and understanding of the states of mind, including beliefs, desires and particularly emotions of others without injecting your own.
Causation	Causation concerns the time order relationship between two or more objects such that if a specific antecendent condition occurs the same consequent must always follow.
Fear response	In the Mowrer-Miller theory, a response to a threatening or noxious situation that is covert but that is assumed to function as a stimulus to produce measurable physiological changes in the body and observable overt behavior is referred to as the fear response.
Hippocampus	The hippocampus is a part of the brain located inside the temporal lobe. It forms a part of the limbic system and plays a part in memory and navigation.
Cortisol	Cortisol is a corticosteroid hormone that is involved in the response to stress; it increases blood pressure and blood sugar levels and suppresses the immune system. Synthetic cortisol,

also known as hydrocortisone, is used as a drug mainly to fight allergies and inflammation.

Hormone	A hormone is a chemical messenger from one cell (or group of cells) to another. The best known are those produced by endocrine glands, but they are produced by nearly every organ system. The function of hormones is to serve as a signal to the target cells; the action of the hormone is determined by the pattern of secretion and the signal transduction of the receiving tissue.
Gland	A gland is an organ in an animal's body that synthesizes a substance for release such as hormones, often into the bloodstream or into cavities inside the body or its outer surface.
Benzodiazepines	The benzodiazepines are a class of drugs with hypnotic, anxiolytic, anticonvulsant, amnestic and muscle relaxant properties. Benzodiazepines are often used for short-term relief of severe, disabling anxiety or insomnia.
Somatic therapy	Any bodily therapy, such as drug therapy, electroconvulsive therapy, or psychosurgery is a somatic therapy.
Placebo	Placebo refers to a bogus treatment that has the appearance of being genuine.
Punishment	Punishment is the addtion of a stimulus that reduces the frequency of a response, or the removal of a stimulus that results in a reduction of the response.
Psychological dependence	Psychological dependence may lead to psychological withdrawal symptoms. Addictions can theoretically form for any rewarding behavior, or as a habitual means to avoid undesired activity, but typically they only do so to a clinical level in individuals who have emotional, social, or psychological dysfunctions, taking the place of normal positive stimuli not otherwise attained
Alprazolam	Alprazolam has a calming effect, with potential side effects of drowsiness, clumsiness, fatigue, and headache. The drug can also have more severe side effects, such as blurred vision, slurred speech, and changes in normal behavior. The drug is habituating, and users develop a tolerance.
Withdrawal symptoms	Withdrawal symptoms are physiological changes that occur when the use of a drug is stopped or dosage decreased.
Tricyclic	Tricyclic antidepressants are a class of antidepressant drugs first used in the 1950s. They are named after the drugs' molecular structure, which contains three rings of atoms.
Seizure	A seizure is a temporary alteration in brain function expressed as a changed mental state, tonic or clonic movements and various other symptoms. They are due to temporary abnormal electrical activity of a group of brain cells.
Fluoxetine	Fluoxetine is an antidepressant drug used medically in the treatment of depression, obsessive-compulsive disorder, bulimia nervosa, premenstrual dysphoric disorder and panic disorder. It is sold under the brand names Prozac®, and others.
Reliability	Reliability means the extent to which a test produces a consistent , reproducible score .
Classical conditioning	Classical conditioning is a simple form of learning in which an organism comes to associate or anticipate events. A neutral stimulus comes to evoke the response usually evoked by a natural or unconditioned stimulus by being paired repeatedly with the unconditioned stimulus.
Insight	Insight refers to a sudden awareness of the relationships among various elements that had previously appeared to be independent of one another.

Transsexual	A transsexual person establishes a permanent identity with the opposite gender to their assigned sex. They make or desire to make a transition from their birth sex to that of the opposite sex, with some type of medical alteration to their body.
Homosexual	Homosexual refers to a sexual orientation characterized by aesthetic attraction, romantic love, and sexual desire exclusively for members of the same sex or gender identity.
Sexual dysfunction	Sexual dysfunction or sexual malfunction is difficulty during any stage of the sexual act (which includes desire, arousal, orgasm, and resolution) that prevents the individual or couple from enjoying sexual activity.
Gender identity	Gender identity describes the gender with which a person identifies, but can also be used to refer to the gender that other people attribute to the individual on the basis of what they know from gender role indications.
Paraphilia	Paraphilia is a sexual disorder in which sexual urges, fantasies, and behavior generally involve children, other nonconsenting partners, nonhuman objects, or the suffering and humiliation of oneself or one's partner .
Sigmund Freud	Sigmund Freud was the founder of the psychoanalytic school, based on his theory that unconscious motives control much behavior, that particular kinds of unconscious thoughts and memories are the source of neurosis, and that neurosis could be treated through bringing these unconscious thoughts and memories to consciousness in psychoanalytic treatment.
Theories	Theories are logically self-consistent models or frameworks describing the behavior of a certain natural or social phenomenon. They are broad explanations and predictions concerning phenomena of interest.
Homosexuality	Homosexuality refers to a sexual orientation characterized by aesthetic attraction, romantic love, and sexual desire exclusively for members of the same sex or gender identity.
Alfred Kinsey	Alfred Kinsey researched human sexuality and profoundly influenced social and cultural values in the United States especially in the 1960s and was an important influence on the sexual revolution
Reliability	Reliability means the extent to which a test produces a consistent , reproducible score .
Validity	The extent to which a test measures what it is intended to measure is called validity.
Survey	A method of scientific investigation in which a large sample of people answer questions about their attitudes or behavior is referred to as a survey.
Population	Population refers to all members of a well-defined group of organisms, events, or things.
Peer pressure	Peer pressure comprises a set of group dynamics whereby a group of people in which one feels comfortable may override the sexual personal habits, individual moral inhibitions or idiosyncratic desires to impose a group norm of attitudes or behaviors.
Clitoris	Clitoris refers to an external female sex organ that is highly sensitive to sexual stimulation.
American Psychological Association	The American Psychological Association is a professional organization representing psychology in the US. The mission statement is to "advance psychology as a science and profession and as a means of promoting health, education , and human welfare".
Mental illness	Mental illness is the term formerly used to mean psychological disorder but less preferred because it implies that the causes of the disorder can be found in a medical disease process.
Variance	The degree to which scores differ among individuals in a distribution of scores is the variance.
Sexual	Sexual orientation refers to the sex or gender of people who are the focus of a person's

Go to **Cram101.com** for the Practice Tests for this Chapter.

orientation	amorous or erotic desires, fantasies, and spontaneous feelings, the gender(s) toward which one is primarily "oriented".
Guilt	Guilt describes many concepts related to a negative emotion or condition caused by actions which are believed to be, morally wrong. According to Freud, the avoidance of guilt is the basis for moral behavior.
Attitude	An enduring mental representation of a person, place, or thing that evokes an emotional response and related behavior is called attitude.
Discrimination	In Learning theory, discrimination refers the ability to distinguish between a conditioned stimulus and other stimuli. It can be brought about by extensive training or differential reinforcement. In social terms, it is the denial of privileges to a person or a group on the basis of prejudice.
Role model	A person who serves as a positive example of desirable behavior is referred to as a role model.
Ambivalence	The simultaneous holding of strong positive and negative emotional attitudes toward the same situation or person is called ambivalence.
Lesbian	A lesbian is a homosexual woman. They are women who are sexually and romantically attracted to other women.
Adolescence	The period of life bounded by puberty and the assumption of adult responsibilities is adolescence.
Bisexuality	Bisexuality is a sexual orientation characterized by aesthetic attraction, romantic love and sexual desire for both males and females.
Attention	Attention is the cognitive process of selectively concentrating on one thing while ignoring other things. Psychologists have labeled three types of attention: sustained attention, selective attention, and divided attention.
Variable	A variable refers to a measurable factor, characteristic, or attribute of an individual or a system.
Learning	Learning is a relatively permanent change in behavior that results from experience. Thus, to attribute a behavioral change to learning, the change must be relatively permanent and must result from experience.
Fraternal twins	Fraternal twins usually occur when two fertilized eggs are implanted in the uterine wall at the same time. The two eggs form two zygotes, and these twins are therefore also known as dizygotic. Dizygotic twins are no more similar genetically than any siblings.
Monozygotic	Identical twins occur when a single egg is fertilized to form one zygote, calld monozygotic, but the zygote then divides into two separate embryos. The two embryos develop into foetuses sharing the same womb. Monozygotic twins are genetically identical unless there has been a mutation in development, and they are almost always the same gender.
Dizygotic	Fraternal twins (commonly known as "non-identical twins") usually occur when two fertilized eggs are implanted in the uterine wall at the same time. The two eggs form two zygotes, and these twins are therefore also known as dizygotic.
Identical twins	Identical twins occur when a single egg is fertilized to form one zygote (monozygotic) but the zygote then divides into two separate embryos. The two embryos develop into foetuses sharing the same womb. Monozygotic twins are genetically identical unless there has been a mutation in development, and they are almost always the same gender.
Sexual response cycle	Masters and Johnson's model of the sexual response cycle consists of four stages or phases: excitement, plateau, orgasmic, resolution.

Psychological disorder	Mental processes and/or behavior patterns that cause emotional distress and/or substantial impairment in functioning is a psychological disorder.
Predisposition	Predisposition refers to an inclination or diathesis to respond in a certain way, either inborn or acquired. In abnormal psychology, it is a factor that lowers the ability to withstand stress and inclines the individual toward pathology.
Personality	Personality refers to the pattern of enduring characteristics that differentiates a person, the patterns of behaviors that make each individual unique.
Trauma	Trauma refers to a severe physical injury or wound to the body caused by an external force, or a psychological shock having a lasting effect on mental life.
Depression	In everyday language depression refers to any downturn in mood, which may be relatively transitory and perhaps due to something trivial. This is differentiated from Clinical depression which is marked by symptoms that last two weeks or more and are so severe that they interfere with daily living.
Anxiety	Anxiety is a complex combination of the feeling of fear, apprehension and worry often accompanied by physical sensations such as palpitations, chest pain and/or shortness of breath.
Clinician	A health professional authorized to provide services to people suffering from one or more pathologies is a clinician.
Premature ejaculation	Premature ejaculation is the most common sexual problem in men, characterized by a lack of voluntary control over ejaculation
Resolution phase	The resolution phase refers to the fourth phase of the sexual response cycle. The resolution phase occurs after orgasm and allows the muscles to relax, blood pressure to drop and the body to slow down from its excited state.
Diabetes	Diabetes is a medical disorder characterized by varying or persistent elevated blood sugar levels, especially after eating. All types of diabetes share similar symptoms and complications at advanced stages: dehydration and ketoacidosis, cardiovascular disease, chronic renal failure, retinal damage which can lead to blindness, nerve damage which can lead to erectile dysfunction, gangrene with risk of amputation of toes, feet, and even legs.
Sexual aversion disorder	A sexual desire disorder characterized by an aversion to or a desire to avoid genital contact with a sexual partner is referred to as a sexual aversion disorder.
Panic attack	An attack of overwhelming anxiety, fear, or terror is called panic attack.
Arousal stage	The arousal stage is the phase of sexual activity that include sensations of pleasure with physiological changes, including the erection of the penis in males and the nipples in females. Females also experience vaginal lubrication and blood pooling in the pelvic region.
Penis	The penis is the external male copulatory organ and the external male organ of urination. In humans, the penis is homologous to the female clitoris, as it develops from the same embryonic structure. It is capable of erection for use in copulation.
Hypoactive sexual desire disorder	A sexual dysfunction in which people lack sexual desire is referred to as hypoactive sexual desire disorder.
Psychotherapy	Psychotherapy is a set of techniques based on psychological principles intended to improve mental health, emotional or behavioral issues.
Ejaculation	Ejaculation is the process of ejecting semen from the penis, and is usually accompanied by orgasm as a result of sexual stimulation.

Erectile dysfunction	Erectile dysfunction, also known as impotence, is the inability to develop or maintain an erection of the penis for satisfactory sexual intercourse regardless of the capability of ejaculation. There are various underlying causes, many of which are medically reversible.
Masturbation	Masturbation is the manual excitation of the sexual organs, most often to the point of orgasm. It can refer to excitation either by oneself or by another, but commonly refers to such activities performed alone.
Psychophysio- ogical disorder	Any physical disorder that has a strong psychological basis or component is called a psychophysiological disorder.
Reinforcement	In operant conditioning, reinforcement is any change in an environment that (a) occurs after the behavior, (b) seems to make that behavior re-occur more often in the future and (c) that reoccurence of behavior must be the result of the change.
Nocturnal	A person who exhibits nocturnal habits is referred to as a night owl.
Narcotic	The term narcotic originally referred to a variety of substances that induced sleep (such state is narcosis). In legal context, narcotic refers to opium, opium derivatives, and their semisynthetic or totally synthetic substitutes.
Psychopathology	Psychopathology refers to the field concerned with the nature and development of mental disorders.
Psychodynamic	Most psychodynamic approaches are centered around the idea of a maladapted function developed early in life (usually childhood) which are at least in part unconscious. This maladapted function (a.k.a. defense mechanism) does not do well in place of a normal/healthy one.
Performance anxiety	Anxiety concerning one's ability to perform, especially when performance may be evaluated by other people is performance anxiety.
Orgasm phase	The orgasm phase is the stage of sexual activity involving ejaculation in men and vaginal wall contractions in women. Women are able to experience orgasm again immediately while men are unable to form an erection for a time interval called a refractory period.
Excitement phase	The excitement phase refers to the first phase of the sexual response cycle, characterized by muscle tension, increases in the heart rate, and erection in the male and vaginal lubrication in the female.
Sex therapy	Sex therapy is the treatment of sexual dysfunction, such as non-consumation, premature ejaculation or erectile dysfunction, problems commonly caused by stress, tiredness and other environmental and relationship factors.
Retarded ejaculation	Retarded ejaculation is a male orgasmic disorder in which ejaculation is delayed so the patient is unable to reach orgasm with his partner, though he is able to ejaculate during masturbation.
Major depressive disorder	The diagnosis of a major depressive disorder occurs when an individual experiences a major depressive episode and depressed characteristics, such as lethargy and depression, last for 2 weeks or longer and daily functioning becomes impaired.
Chronic	Chronic refers to a relatively long duration, usually more than a few months.
Rape	Rape is a crime where the victim is forced into sexual activity, in particular sexual penetration, against his or her will.
Female orgasmic disorder	The persistent inability of a woman to reach orgasm, or a delay in reaching orgasm despite adequate sexual stimulation is called the female orgasmic disorder.
Couples therapy	Therapy with married or unmarried couples whose major problem is within their relationship is referred to as couples therapy.

Personality trait	According to the Diagnostic and Statistical Manual of the American Psychiatric Association, a personality trait is a "prominent aspect of personality that is exhibited in a wide range of important social and personal contexts. ...".
Self-esteem	Self-esteem refers to a person's subjective appraisal of himself or herself as intrinsically positive or negative to some degree.
Body image	A person's body image is their perception of their physical appearance. It is more than what a person thinks they will see in a mirror, it is inextricably tied to their self-esteem and acceptance by peers.
Affect	A subjective feeling or emotional tone often accompanied by bodily expressions noticeable to others is called affect.
Dyspareunia	Dyspareunia is painful sexual intercourse, due to medical or psychological causes. The term is used almost exclusively in women, although the problem may occur in men.
Substance abuse	Substance abuse refers to the overindulgence in and dependence on a stimulant, depressant, or other chemical substance, leading to effects that are detrimental to the individual's physical or mental health, or the welfare of others.
Antidepressant	An antidepressant is a medication used primarily in the treatment of clinical depression. They are not thought to produce tolerance, although sudden withdrawal may produce adverse effects. They create little if any immediate change in mood and require between several days and several weeks to take effect.
Antipsychotic	The term antipsychotic is applied to a group of drugs used to treat psychosis.
Estrogen	Estrogen is a group of steroid compounds that function as the primary female sex hormone. They are produced primarily by developing follicles in the ovaries, the corpus luteum and the placenta.
Cocaine	Cocaine is a crystalline tropane alkaloid that is obtained from the leaves of the coca plant. It is a stimulant of the central nervous system and an appetite suppressant, creating what has been described as a euphoric sense of happiness and increased energy.
Opiates	A group of narcotics derived from the opium poppy that provide a euphoric rush and depress the nervous system are referred to as opiates.
Steroid	A steroid is a lipid characterized by a carbon skeleton with four fused rings. Different steroids vary in the functional groups attached to these rings. Hundreds of distinct steroids have been identified in plants and animals. Their most important role in most living systems is as hormones.
Emotion	An emotion is a mental states that arise spontaneously, rather than through conscious effort. They are often accompanied by physiological changes.
Masters and Johnson	Masters and Johnson produced the four stage model of sexual response, which they described as the human sexual response cycle. They defined the four stages of this cycle as: excitement phase, plateau phase, orgasm, and resolution phase.
Laboratory study	Any research study in which the subjects are brought to a specially designated area that has been set up to facilitate the researcher's ability to control the environment or collect data is referred to as a laboratory study.
Sensation	Sensation is the first stage in the chain of biochemical and neurologic events that begins with the impinging of a stimulus upon the receptor cells of a sensory organ, which then leads to perception, the mental state that is reflected in statements like "I see a uniformly blue wall."
Physiology	The study of the functions and activities of living cells, tissues, and organs and of the

physical and chemical phenomena involved is referred to as physiology.

Sensate focus	Sensate focus are a set of exercises prescribed at the beginning of the Masters and Johnson sex therapy program. Partners are instructed to fondle each other to give pleasure but to refrain from intercourse, thus reducing anxiety about sexual performance.
Stages	Stages represent relatively discrete periods of time in which functioning is qualitatively different from functioning at other periods.
Reflex	A simple, involuntary response to a stimulus is referred to as reflex. Reflex actions originate at the spinal cord rather than the brain.
Denial	Denial is a psychological defense mechanism in which a person faced with a fact that is uncomfortable or painful to accept rejects it instead, insisting that it is not true despite what may be overwhelming evidence.
Tactile	Pertaining to the sense of touch is referred to as tactile.
Systematic desensitization	Systematic desensitization refers to Wolpe's behavioral fear-reduction technique in which a hierarchy of fear-evoking stimuli are presented while the person remains relaxed. The fear-evoking stimuli thereby become associated with muscle relaxation.
Genitals	Genitals refers to the internal and external reproductive organs.
Hormone	A hormone is a chemical messenger from one cell (or group of cells) to another. The best known are those produced by endocrine glands, but they are produced by nearly every organ system. The function of hormones is to serve as a signal to the target cells; the action of the hormone is determined by the pattern of secretion and the signal transduction of the receiving tissue.
Vaginismus	Vaginismus is a condition where the muscles at the entrance to vagina contract, preventing successful sexual intercourse. It is most commonly caused by a psychological reaction but it may sometimes be due to vaginal inflammation or damage.
Motivation	In psychology, motivation is the driving force (desire) behind all actions of an organism.
Insight	Insight refers to a sudden awareness of the relationships among various elements that had previously appeared to be independent of one another.
Gender identity disorder	Gender identity disorder is a condition where a person who has been assigned one gender but identifies as belonging to another gender, or does not conform with the gender role their respective society prescribes to them.
Chromosome	The DNA which carries genetic information in biological cells is normally packaged in the form of one or more large macromolecules called a chromosome. Humans normally have 46.
Gene	A gene is an ultramicroscopic area of the chromosome. It is the smallest physical unit of the DNA molecule that carries a piece of hereditary information.
Self-concept	Self-concept refers to domain-specific evaluations of the self where a domain may be academics, athletics, etc.
Puberty	Puberty refers to the process of physical changes by which a child's body becomes an adult body capable of reproduction.
Gender role	A cluster of behaviors that characterizes traditional female or male behaviors within a cultural setting is a gender role.
Sex-reassignment surgery	Sex-reassignment surgery is an operation removing the existing genitalia and constructing a substitute for the genitals of the opposite sex.

Secondary sex characteristics	Secondary sex characteristics are traits that distinguish the two sexes of a species, but that are not directly part of the reproductive system.
Anatomy	Anatomy is the branch of biology that deals with the structure and organization of living things. It can be divided into animal anatomy (zootomy) and plant anatomy (phytonomy). Major branches of anatomy include comparative anatomy, histology, and human anatomy.
Hypothalamus	The hypothalamus is a region of the brain located below the thalamus, forming the major portion of the ventral region of the diencephalon and functioning to regulate certain metabolic processes and other autonomic activities.
Brain	The brain controls and coordinates most movement, behavior and homeostatic body functions such as heartbeat, blood pressure, fluid balance and body temperature. Functions of the brain are responsible for cognition, emotion, memory, motor learning and other sorts of learning. The brain is primarily made up of two types of cells: glia and neurons.
Testosterone	Testosterone is a steroid hormone from the androgen group. It is the principal male sex hormone and the "original" anabolic steroid.
Uterus	The uterus or womb is the major female reproductive organ. The main function of the uterus is to accept a fertilized ovum which becomes implanted into the endometrium, and derives nourishment from blood vessels which develop exclusively for this purpose.
Infancy	The developmental period that extends from birth to 18 or 24 months is called infancy.
Reinforcer	In operant conditioning, a reinforcer is any stimulus that increases the probability that a preceding behavior will occur again. In Classical Conditioning, the unconditioned stimulus (US) is the reinforcer.
Maladaptive	In psychology, a behavior or trait is adaptive when it helps an individual adjust and function well within their social environment. A maladaptive behavior or trait is counterproductive to the individual.
Control group	A group that does not receive the treatment effect in an experiment is referred to as the control group or sometimes as the comparison group.
Gender identification	The process of identifying oneself as male or female and adopting the roles and values of that gender is called gender identification.
DSM-IV TR	The current Diagnostic and Statistical Manual of Mental Disorders of the American Psychiatric Association is called DSM-IV TR.
Fetishism	Sexual fetishism, first described as such by Alfred Binet in his Le fétichisme dans l'amour, though the concept and certainly the activity is quite ancient, is a form of paraphilia where the object of affection is a specific inanimate object or part of a person's body.
Transvestic fetishism	Transvestic fetishism is a sexual fetish for the clothing of the opposite gender. It is one of a number of cross-dressing behaviors.
Masochism	The counterpart of sadism is masochism, the sexual pleasure or gratification of having pain or suffering inflicted upon the self, often consisting of sexual fantasies or urges for being beaten, humiliated, bound, tortured, or otherwise made to suffer, either as an enhancement to or a substitute for sexual pleasure.
Sadism	Sadism is the sexual pleasure or gratification in the infliction of pain and suffering upon another person. It is considered to be a paraphilia. The word is derived from the name of the Marquis de Sade, a prolific French writer of sadistic novels.
Hermaphrodite	Hermaphrodite refers to a person with parts of both male and female genitalia.
Construct	A generalized concept, such as anxiety or gravity, is a construct.

Scrotum	The scrotum is an external sack of skin that holds the testes.
Suicide	Suicide behavior is rare in childhood but escalates in adolescence. The suicide rate increases in a linear fashion from adolescence through late adulthood.
Schizophrenia	Schizophrenia is characterized by persistent defects in the perception or expression of reality. A person suffering from untreated schizophrenia typically demonstrates grossly disorganized thinking, and may also experience delusions or auditory hallucinations
Attachment	Attachment is the tendency to seek closeness to another person and feel secure when that person is present.
Stimulant	A stimulant is a drug which increases the activity of the sympathetic nervous system and produces a sense of euphoria or awakeness.
Subculture	As understood in sociology, anthropology and cultural studies, a subculture is a set of people with a distinct set of behavior and beliefs that differentiate them from a larger culture of which they are a part.
Society	The social sciences use the term society to mean a group of people that form a semi-closed (or semi-open) social system, in which most interactions are with other individuals belonging to the group.
Biological predisposition	The genetic readiness of animals and humans to perform certain behaviors is a biological predisposition.
Conditioning	Conditioning describes the process by which behaviors can be learned or modified through interaction with the environment.
Conditioned response	A conditioned response is the response to a stimulus that occurs when an animal has learned to associate the stimulus with a certain positive or negative effect.
Aversive stimulus	A stimulus that elicits pain, fear, or avoidance is an aversive stimulus.
Aversion therapy	Aversion therapy is a now largely discredited form of treatment in which the patient is exposed to a stimulus while simultaneously being hurt or made ill. The theory is that the patient will come to associate the stimulus with unpleasant sensations and will no longer seek it out.
Covert sensitization	A form of aversion therapy in which the person is told to imagine undesirably attractive situations and activities while unpleasant feelings are being induced by imagery is covert sensitization.
Sexual sadism	A preference for obtaining or increasing sexual gratification by inflicting pain or humiliation on another person is referred to as sexual sadism.
Sexual masochism	Sexual masochism is a preference for obtaining or increasing sexual gratification through subjection of the self to pain or humiliation.
Hypermasculinity	Hypermasculinity is to an extreme gender-role identification with an exaggerated version of the traditional male role; includes callous sexual attitudes toward women, the belief that violence is manly, and the enjoyment of danger as a source of excitement.
Voyeurism	Voyeurism is a practice in which an individual derives sexual pleasure from observing other people. Such people may be engaged in sexual acts, or be nude or in underwear, or dressed in whatever other way the "voyeur" finds appealing.
Early childhood	Early childhood refers to the developmental period extending from the end of infancy to about 5 or 6 years of age; sometimes called the preschool years.
Mental disorder	Mental disorder refers to a disturbance in a person's emotions, drives, thought processes, or

	behavior that involves serious and relatively prolonged distress and/or impairment in ability to function, is not simply a normal response to some event or set of events in the person's environment.
Frotteurism	Disorder characterized by recurrent and intense sexual urges, acts, or fantasies or touching or rubbing against a nonconsenting person is referred to as frotteurism.
Exhibitionism	Marked preference for obtaining sexual gratification by exposing one's genitals to an unwilling observer is called exhibitionism.
Pedophilia	Pedophilia is the condition of being sexually attracted primarily or exclusively to prepubescent children.
Socialization	Social rules and social relations are created, communicated, and changed in verbal and nonverbal ways creating social complexity useful in identifying outsiders and intelligent breeding partners. The process of learning these skills is called socialization.
Psychosexual development	In psychodynamic theory, the process by which libidinal energy is expressed through different erogenous zones during different stages of development is called psychosexual development.
Reflection	Reflection is the process of rephrasing or repeating thoughts and feelings expressed, making the person more aware of what they are saying or thinking.
Overt behavior	An action or response that is directly observable and measurable is an overt behavior.
Generalization	In conditioning, the tendency for a conditioned response to be evoked by stimuli that are similar to the stimulus to which the response was conditioned is a generalization. The greater the similarity among the stimuli, the greater the probability of generalization.
Punishment	Punishment is the addtion of a stimulus that reduces the frequency of a response, or the removal of a stimulus that results in a reduction of the response.
Antecedents	In behavior modification, events that typically precede the target response are called antecedents.
Prenatal	Prenatal period refers to the time from conception to birth.
Heredity	Heredity is the transfer of characteristics from parent to offspring through their genes.
Control subjects	Control subjects are participants in an experiment who do not receive the treatment effect but for whom all other conditions are held comparable to those of experimental subjects.
Mood disorder	A mood disorder is a condition where the prevailing emotional mood is distorted or inappropriate to the circumstances.
Psychosis	Psychosis is a generic term for mental states in which the components of rational thought and perception are severely impaired. Persons experiencing a psychosis may experience hallucinations, hold paranoid or delusional beliefs, demonstrate personality changes and exhibit disorganized thinking. This is usually accompanied by features such as a lack of insight into the unusual or bizarre nature of their behavior, difficulties with social interaction and impairments in carrying out the activities of daily living.
Reinforcement contingencies	The circumstances or rules that determine whether responses lead to the presentation of reinforcers are referred to as reinforcement contingencies. Skinner defined culture as a set of reinforcement contingencies.
Social skills training	Social skills training refers to a behavior therapy designed to improve interpersonal skills that emphasizes shaping, modeling, and behavioral rehearsal.
Cognition	The intellectual processes through which information is obtained, transformed, stored, retrieved, and otherwise used is cognition.

Empathy	Empathy is the recognition and understanding of the states of mind, including beliefs, desires and particularly emotions of others without injecting your own.
Sexual harassment	Deliberate or repeated verbal comments, gestures, or physical contact of a sexual nature that is unwanted by the recipient is called sexual harassment.
Representative sample	Representative sample refers to a sample of participants selected from the larger population in such a way that important subgroups within the population are included in the sample in the same proportions as they are found in the larger population.
Behavioral therapy	The treatment of a mental disorder through the application of basic principles of conditioning and learning is called behavioral therapy.
Desensitization	Desensitization refers to the type of sensory or behavioral adaptation in which we become less sensitive to constant stimuli.
Child sexual abuse	Child sexual abuse denotes sex between prepubescent minors and adults. It has a special status among forms of abuse, because it includes not only what is considered sexual abuse between adults, but also all forms of sexual activity involving children and adults as partners

Go to **Cram101.com** for the Practice Tests for this Chapter.
And, **NEVER** highlight a book again!

Personality disorder	A mental disorder characterized by a set of inflexible, maladaptive personality traits that keep a person from functioning properly in society is referred to as a personality disorder.
Adjustment disorder	An emotional disturbance caused by ongoing stressors within the range of common experience is called an adjustment disorder.
Personality	Personality refers to the pattern of enduring characteristics that differentiates a person, the patterns of behaviors that make each individual unique.
Emotion	An emotion is a mental states that arise spontaneously, rather than through conscious effort. They are often accompanied by physiological changes.
Personality type	A persistent style of complex behaviors defined by a group of related traits is referred to as a personality type. Myer Friedman and his co-workers first defined personality types in the 1950s. Friedman classified people into 2 categories, Type A and Type B.
Maladaptive	In psychology, a behavior or trait is adaptive when it helps an individual adjust and function well within their social environment. A maladaptive behavior or trait is counterproductive to the individual.
Clinician	A health professional authorized to provide services to people suffering from one or more pathologies is a clinician.
Mental disorder	Mental disorder refers to a disturbance in a person's emotions, drives, thought processes, or behavior that involves serious and relatively prolonged distress and/or impairment in ability to function, is not simply a normal response to some event or set of events in the person's environment.
Affect	A subjective feeling or emotional tone often accompanied by bodily expressions noticeable to others is called affect.
Trait	An enduring personality characteristic that tends to lead to certain behaviors is called a trait. The term trait also means a genetically inherited feature of an organism.
Anxiety	Anxiety is a complex combination of the feeling of fear, apprehension and worry often accompanied by physical sensations such as palpitations, chest pain and/or shortness of breath.
Individual differences	Individual differences psychology studies the ways in which individual people differ in their behavior. This is distinguished from other aspects of psychology in that although psychology is ostensibly a study of individuals, modern psychologists invariably study groups.
Population	Population refers to all members of a well-defined group of organisms, events, or things.
Heterogeneous	A heterogeneous compound, mixture, or other such object is one that consists of many different items, which are often not easily sorted or separated, though they are clearly distinct.
Mental retardation	Mental retardation refers to having significantly below-average intellectual functioning and limitations in at least two areas of adaptive functioning. Many categorize retardation as mild, moderate, severe, or profound.
Late adolescence	Late adolescence refers to approximately the latter half of the second decade of life. Career interests, dating, and identity exploration are often more pronounced in late adolescence than in early adolescence.
Schizophrenia	Schizophrenia is characterized by persistent defects in the perception or expression of reality. A person suffering from untreated schizophrenia typically demonstrates grossly disorganized thinking, and may also experience delusions or auditory hallucinations
Social isolation	Social isolation refers to a type of loneliness that occurs when a person lacks a sense of

integrated involvement. Being deprived of participation in a group or community involving companionship, shared interests, organized activities, and meaningful roles causes a person to feel alone.

Premorbid	Premorbid refers to individual's level of functioning prior to the development of a disorder.
Paranoid	The term paranoid is typically used in a general sense to signify any self-referential delusion, or more specifically, to signify a delusion involving the fear of persecution.
Chronic	Chronic refers to a relatively long duration, usually more than a few months.
Prototypal approach	A prototypal approach for categorizing disorders using both the essential defining characteristics and a range of other nonessential characteristics commonly observed.
Attention	Attention is the cognitive process of selectively concentrating on one thing while ignoring other things. Psychologists have labeled three types of attention: sustained attention, selective attention, and divided attention.
Depression	In everyday language depression refers to any downturn in mood, which may be relatively transitory and perhaps due to something trivial. This is differentiated from Clinical depression which is marked by symptoms that last two weeks or more and are so severe that they interfere with daily living.
Psychosis	Psychosis is a generic term for mental states in which the components of rational thought and perception are severely impaired. Persons experiencing a psychosis may experience hallucinations, hold paranoid or delusional beliefs, demonstrate personality changes and exhibit disorganized thinking. This is usually accompanied by features such as a lack of insight into the unusual or bizarre nature of their behavior, difficulties with social interaction and impairments in carrying out the activities of daily living.
Social skills	Social skills are skills used to interact and communicate with others to assist status in the social structure and other motivations.
Empathy	Empathy is the recognition and understanding of the states of mind, including beliefs, desires and particularly emotions of others without injecting your own.
Social anxiety	A feeling of apprehension in the presence of others is social anxiety.
Perception	Perception is the process of acquiring, interpreting, selecting, and organizing sensory information.
Cognition	The intellectual processes through which information is obtained, transformed, stored, retrieved, and otherwise used is cognition.
Reflection	Reflection is the process of rephrasing or repeating thoughts and feelings expressed, making the person more aware of what they are saying or thinking.
Narcissism	Narcissism is the pattern of thinking and behaving which involves infatuation and obsession with one's self to the exclusion of others.
Self-esteem	Self-esteem refers to a person's subjective appraisal of himself or herself as intrinsically positive or negative to some degree.
Graham	Graham has conducted a number of studies that reveal stronger socioeconomic-status influences rather than ethnic influences in achievement.
Psychoanalyst	A psychoanalyst is a specially trained therapist who attempts to treat the individual by uncovering and revealing to the individual otherwise subconscious factors that are contributing to some undesirable behavor.
Attitude	An enduring mental representation of a person, place, or thing that evokes an emotional response and related behavior is called attitude.

Denial	Denial is a psychological defense mechanism in which a person faced with a fact that is uncomfortable or painful to accept rejects it instead, insisting that it is not true despite what may be overwhelming evidence.
Suicide	Suicide behavior is rare in childhood but escalates in adolescence. The suicide rate increases in a linear fashion from adolescence through late adulthood.
Gender identity	Gender identity describes the gender with which a person identifies, but can also be used to refer to the gender that other people attribute to the individual on the basis of what they know from gender role indications.
Self-image	A person's self-image is the mental picture, generally of a kind that is quite resistant to change, that depicts not only details that are potentially available to objective investigation by others, but also items that have been learned by that person about himself or herself.
Sedative	A sedative is a drug that depresses the central nervous system (CNS), which causes calmness, relaxation, reduction of anxiety, sleepiness, slowed breathing, slurred speech, staggering gait, poor judgment, and slow, uncertain reflexes.
Mood disorder	A mood disorder is a condition where the prevailing emotional mood is distorted or inappropriate to the circumstances.
Affective	Affective is the way people react emotionally, their ability to feel another living thing's pain or joy.
Comorbidity	Comorbidity refers to the presence of more than one mental disorder occurring in an individual at the same time.
Theories	Theories are logically self-consistent models or frameworks describing the behavior of a certain natural or social phenomenon. They are broad explanations and predictions concerning phenomena of interest.
Early childhood	Early childhood refers to the developmental period extending from the end of infancy to about 5 or 6 years of age; sometimes called the preschool years.
Attachment	Attachment is the tendency to seek closeness to another person and feel secure when that person is present.
Adolescence	The period of life bounded by puberty and the assumption of adult responsibilities is adolescence.
Alcoholism	A disorder that involves long-term, repeated, uncontrolled, compulsive, and excessive use of alcoholic beverages and that impairs the drinker's health and work and social relationships is called alcoholism.
Guilt	Guilt describes many concepts related to a negative emotion or condition caused by actions which are believed to be, morally wrong. According to Freud, the avoidance of guilt is the basis for moral behavior.
Psychological deficit	The term used to indicate that performance of a pertinent psychological process is below that expected of a normal person is psychological deficit.
Distinctive features	The characteristics of an object that differentiate it from other objects are distinctive features.
Psychotherapy	Psychotherapy is a set of techniques based on psychological principles intended to improve mental health, emotional or behavioral issues.
Psychoanalysis	Psychoanalysis refers to the school of psychology that emphasizes the importance of unconscious motives and conflicts as determinants of human behavior. It was Freud's method of

exploring human personality.

Trauma	Trauma refers to a severe physical injury or wound to the body caused by an external force, or a psychological shock having a lasting effect on mental life.
Variable	A variable refers to a measurable factor, characteristic, or attribute of an individual or a system.
Prognosis	A forecast about the probable course of an illess is referred to as prognosis.
Antidepressants	Antidepressants are medications used primarily in the treatment of clinical depression. Antidepressants create little if any immediate change in mood and require between several days and several weeks to take effect.
Antidepressant	An antidepressant is a medication used primarily in the treatment of clinical depression. They are not thought to produce tolerance, although sudden withdrawal may produce adverse effects. They create little if any immediate change in mood and require between several days and several weeks to take effect.
Abnormal psychology	The scientific study whose objectives are to describe, explain, predict, and control behaviors that are considered strange or unusual is referred to as abnormal psychology.
Anti-social	Anti-social behavior is lacking in judgement and consideration for others, ranging from careless negligence to deliberately damaging activity, vandalism and graffiti for example.
Super-ego	The Super-ego stands in opposition to the desires of the Id. The Super-ego is based upon the internalization of the world view, norms and mores a child absorbs from parents and the surrounding environment at a young age. As the conscience, it includes our sense of right and wrong, maintaining taboos specific to a child's internalization of parental culture.
Survey	A method of scientific investigation in which a large sample of people answer questions about their attitudes or behavior is referred to as a survey.
Dialectical behavior therapy	Dialectical behavior therapy refers to a therapeutic approach to borderline personality disorder that combines client-centered empathy and acceptance with behavioral problem solving, social-skills training, and limit setting.
Psychodynamic	Most psychodynamic approaches are centered around the idea of a maladapted function developed early in life (usually childhood) which are at least in part unconscious. This maladapted function (a.k.a. defense mechanism) does not do well in place of a normal/healthy one.
Acquisition	Acquisition is the process of adapting to the environment, learning or becoming conditioned. In classical conditoning terms, it is the initial learning of the stimulus response link, which involves a neutral stimulus being associated with a unconditioned stimulus and becoming a conditioned stimulus.
Learning	Learning is a relatively permanent change in behavior that results from experience. Thus, to attribute a behavioral change to learning, the change must be relatively permanent and must result from experience.
Stages	Stages represent relatively discrete periods of time in which functioning is qualitatively different from functioning at other periods.
Psychological test	Psychological test refers to a standardized measure of a sample of a person's behavior.
Binge	Binge refers to relatively brief episode of uncontrolled, excessive consumption.
Control subjects	Control subjects are participants in an experiment who do not receive the treatment effect but for whom all other conditions are held comparable to those of experimental subjects.
Heredity	Heredity is the transfer of characteristics from parent to offspring through their genes.

Neurochemistry	Neurochemistry is a branch of neuroscience that is heavily devoted to the study of neurochemicals. A neurochemical is an organic molecule that participates in neural activity. This term is often used to refer to neurotransmitters and other molecules such as neuro-active drugs that influence neuron function.
Neurotransmitter	A neurotransmitter is a chemical that is used to relay, amplify and modulate electrical signals between a neurons and another cell.
Metabolites	Metabolites are the intermediates and products of metabolism.
Serotonin	Serotonin, a neurotransmitter, is believed to play an important part of the biochemistry of depression, bipolar disorder and anxiety. It is also believed to be influential on sexuality and appetite.
Brain	The brain controls and coordinates most movement, behavior and homeostatic body functions such as heartbeat, blood pressure, fluid balance and body temperature. Functions of the brain are responsible for cognition, emotion, memory, motor learning and other sorts of learning. The brain is primarily made up of two types of cells: glia and neurons.
Child abuse	Child abuse is the physical or psychological maltreatment of a child.
Punishment	Punishment is the addtion of a stimulus that reduces the frequency of a response, or the removal of a stimulus that results in a reduction of the response.
Amphetamine	Amphetamine is a synthetic stimulant used to suppress the appetite, control weight, and treat disorders including narcolepsy and ADHD. It is also used recreationally and for performance enhancement.
Cocaine	Cocaine is a crystalline tropane alkaloid that is obtained from the leaves of the coca plant. It is a stimulant of the central nervous system and an appetite suppressant, creating what has been described as a euphoric sense of happiness and increased energy.
Personality test	A personality test aims to describe aspects of a person's character that remain stable across situations.
Moral development	Development regarding rules and conventions about what people should do in their interactions with other people is called moral development.
Early adulthood	The developmental period beginning in the late teens or early twenties and lasting into the thirties is called early adulthood; characterized by an increasing self-awareness.
Hypothesis	A specific statement about behavior or mental processes that is testable through research is a hypothesis.
Norms	In testing, standards of test performance that permit the comparison of one person's score on the test to the scores of others who have taken the same test are referred to as norms.
Self-worth	In psychology, self-esteem or self-worth refers to a person's subjective appraisal of himself or herself as intrinsically positive or negative to some degree.
Friendship	The essentials of friendship are reciprocity and commitment between individuals who see themselves more or less as equals. Interaction between friends rests on a more equal power base than the interaction between children and adults.
Self-efficacy	Self-efficacy is the belief that one has the capabilities to execute the courses of actions required to manage prospective situations.
Insight	Insight refers to a sudden awareness of the relationships among various elements that had previously appeared to be independent of one another.
Ingratiation	Ingratiation is a technique for gaining compliance in which a requester first induces the target person to like them, then attempts to change their behavior in some desired manner.

Go to **Cram101.com** for the Practice Tests for this Chapter.

Empirical	Empirical means the use of working hypotheses which are capable of being disproved using observation or experiment.
Anxiety disorder	Anxiety disorder is a blanket term covering several different forms of abnormal anxiety, fear, phobia and nervous condition, that come on suddenly and prevent pursuing normal daily routines.
Consciousness	The awareness of the sensations, thoughts, and feelings being experienced at a given moment is called consciousness.
Exposure therapy	An exposure therapy is any method of treating fears, including flooding and systematic desensitization, that involves exposing the client to the feared object or situation so that the process of extinction or habituation of the fear response can occur.
Group therapy	Group therapy is a form of psychotherapy during which one or several therapists treat a small group of clients together as a group. This may be more cost effective than individual therapy, and possibly even more effective.
Psychoactive drug	A psychoactive drug or psychotropic substance is a chemical that alters brain function, resulting in temporary changes in perception, mood, consciousness, or behavior. Such drugs are often used for recreational and spiritual purposes, as well as in medicine, especially for treating neurological and psychological illnesses.
Antipsychotic	The term antipsychotic is applied to a group of drugs used to treat psychosis.
Lithium	Lithium salts are used as mood stabilizing drugs primarily in the treatment of bipolar disorder, depression, and mania; but also in treating schizophrenia. Lithium is widely distributed in the central nervous system and interacts with a number of neurotransmitters and receptors, decreasing noradrenaline release and increasing serotonin synthesis.
Systematic desensitization	Systematic desensitization refers to Wolpe's behavioral fear-reduction technique in which a hierarchy of fear-evoking stimuli are presented while the person remains relaxed. The fear-evoking stimuli thereby become associated with muscle relaxation.
Assertiveness training	In behavior therapy, a direct method of training people to express their own desires and feelings and to maintain their own rights in interactions with others, while at the same time respecting the others' rights is called assertiveness training.
Family therapy	Family therapy is a branch of psychotherapy that treats family problems. Family therapists consider the family as a system of interacting members; as such, the problems in the family are seen to arise as an emergent property of the interactions in the system, rather than ascribed exclusively to the "faults" or psychological problems of individual members.
Ethnic group	An ethnic group is a culture or subculture whose members are readily distinguishable by outsiders based on traits originating from a common racial, national, linguistic, or religious source. Members of an ethnic group are often presumed to be culturally or biologically similar, although this is not in fact necessarily the case.
Personality trait	According to the Diagnostic and Statistical Manual of the American Psychiatric Association, a personality trait is a "prominent aspect of personality that is exhibited in a wide range of important social and personal contexts. ...".
Shaping	The concept of reinforcing successive, increasingly accurate approximations to a target behavior is called shaping. The target behavior is broken down into a hierarchy of elemental steps, each step more sophisticated then the last. By successively reinforcing each of the the elemental steps, a form of differential reinforcement, until that step is learned while extinguishing the step below, the target behavior is gradually achieved.
Acculturation	Acculturation is the obtainment of culture by an individual or a group of people.

Go to **Cram101.com** for the Practice Tests for this Chapter.

Inference	Inference is the act or process of drawing a conclusion based solely on what one already knows.
Threshold	In general, a threshold is a fixed location or value where an abrupt change is observed. In the sensory modalities, it is the minimum amount of stimulus energy necessary to elicit a sensory response.
Conscientiou-ness	Conscientiousness is one of the dimensions of the five-factor model of personality and individual differences involving being organized, thorough, and reliable as opposed to careless, negligent, and unreliable.
Agreeableness	Agreeableness, one of the big-five personality traits, reflects individual differences in concern with cooperation and social harmony. It is the degree individuals value getting along with others.
Assertiveness	Assertiveness basically means the ability to express your thoughts and feelings in a way that clearly states your needs and keeps the lines of communication open with the other.
Extraversion	Extraversion, one of the big-five personailty traits, is marked by pronounced engagement with the external world. They are people who enjoy being with people, are full of energy, and often experience positive emotions.
Neuroticism	Eysenck's use of the term neuroticism (or Emotional Stability) was proposed as the dimension describing individual differences in the predisposition towards neurotic disorder.
Protective factors	Protective factors are influences that reduce the impact of early stress and tend to lead to positive outcomes.
Social influence	Social influence is when the actions or thoughts of individual(s) are changed by other individual(s). Peer pressure is an example of social influence.
Psychiatrist	A psychiatrist is a physician who specializes in the diagnosis and treatment of psychological disorders.

Mood disorder	A mood disorder is a condition where the prevailing emotional mood is distorted or inappropriate to the circumstances.
Depression	In everyday language depression refers to any downturn in mood, which may be relatively transitory and perhaps due to something trivial. This is differentiated from Clinical depression which is marked by symptoms that last two weeks or more and are so severe that they interfere with daily living.
Mania	Mania is a medical condition characterized by severely elevated mood. Mania is most usually associated with bipolar disorder, where episodes of mania may cyclically alternate with episodes of depression.
Bipolar disorder	Bipolar Disorder is a mood disorder typically characterized by fluctuations between manic and depressive states; and, more generally, atypical mood regulation and mood instability.
Attention	Attention is the cognitive process of selectively concentrating on one thing while ignoring other things. Psychologists have labeled three types of attention: sustained attention, selective attention, and divided attention.
Antidepressant	An antidepressant is a medication used primarily in the treatment of clinical depression. They are not thought to produce tolerance, although sudden withdrawal may produce adverse effects. They create little if any immediate change in mood and require between several days and several weeks to take effect.
Psychiatrist	A psychiatrist is a physician who specializes in the diagnosis and treatment of psychological disorders.
Lithium	Lithium salts are used as mood stabilizing drugs primarily in the treatment of bipolar disorder, depression, and mania; but also in treating schizophrenia. Lithium is widely distributed in the central nervous system and interacts with a number of neurotransmitters and receptors, decreasing noradrenaline release and increasing serotonin synthesis.
Clinician	A health professional authorized to provide services to people suffering from one or more pathologies is a clinician.
Guilt	Guilt describes many concepts related to a negative emotion or condition caused by actions which are believed to be, morally wrong. According to Freud, the avoidance of guilt is the basis for moral behavior.
Empathy	Empathy is the recognition and understanding of the states of mind, including beliefs, desires and particularly emotions of others without injecting your own.
Melancholia	Melancholia was described as a distinct disease as early as the fifth and fourth centuries BC in the Hippocratic writings. It was characterized by "aversion to food, despondency, sleeplessness, irritability, restlessness," as well as the statement that "Grief and fear, when lingering, provoke melancholia". It is now generally believed that melancholia was the same phenomenon as what is now called clinical depression.
Perception	Perception is the process of acquiring, interpreting, selecting, and organizing sensory information.
Adjustment disorder	An emotional disturbance caused by ongoing stressors within the range of common experience is called an adjustment disorder.
Psychotherapy	Psychotherapy is a set of techniques based on psychological principles intended to improve mental health, emotional or behavioral issues.
Electroshock	First introduced as a treatment for schizophrenia, Electroconvulsive therapy, also known as electroshock or ECT, is a controversial type of psychiatric shock therapy involving the induction of an artificial seizure in a patient by passing electricity through the brain.

Nightmare	Nightmare was the original term for the state later known as waking dream, and more currently as sleep paralysis, associated with rapid eye movement (REM) periods of sleep.
Diabetes	Diabetes is a medical disorder characterized by varying or persistent elevated blood sugar levels, especially after eating. All types of diabetes share similar symptoms and complications at advanced stages: dehydration and ketoacidosis, cardiovascular disease, chronic renal failure, retinal damage which can lead to blindness, nerve damage which can lead to erectile dysfunction, gangrene with risk of amputation of toes, feet, and even legs.
Suicide	Suicide behavior is rare in childhood but escalates in adolescence. The suicide rate increases in a linear fashion from adolescence through late adulthood.
Major depression	Major depression is characterized by a severely depressed mood that persists for at least two weeks. Episodes of depression may start suddenly or slowly and can occur several times through a person's life. The disorder may be categorized as "single episode" or "recurrent" depending on whether previous episodes have been experienced before.
Personality disorder	A mental disorder characterized by a set of inflexible, maladaptive personality traits that keep a person from functioning properly in society is referred to as a personality disorder.
Population	Population refers to all members of a well-defined group of organisms, events, or things.
Affect	A subjective feeling or emotional tone often accompanied by bodily expressions noticeable to others is called affect.
Migraine	Migraine is a form of headache, usually very intense and disabling. It is a neurologic disease.
Anxiety	Anxiety is a complex combination of the feeling of fear, apprehension and worry often accompanied by physical sensations such as palpitations, chest pain and/or shortness of breath.
Social support	Social Support is the physical and emotional comfort given by family, friends, co-workers and others. Research has identified three main types of social support: emotional, practical, sharing points of view.
Heredity	Heredity is the transfer of characteristics from parent to offspring through their genes.
Family studies	Scientific studies in which researchers assess hereditary influence by examining blood relatives to see how much they resemble each other on a specific trait are called family studies.
Monozygotic	Identical twins occur when a single egg is fertilized to form one zygote, calld monozygotic, but the zygote then divides into two separate embryos. The two embryos develop into foetuses sharing the same womb. Monozygotic twins are genetically identical unless there has been a mutation in development, and they are almost always the same gender.
Dizygotic	Fraternal twins (commonly known as "non-identical twins") usually occur when two fertilized eggs are implanted in the uterine wall at the same time. The two eggs form two zygotes, and these twins are therefore also known as dizygotic.
Cohort	A cohort is a group of individuals defined by their date of birth.
Psychological view	The belief or theory that mental disorders are caused by psychological and emotional factors, rather than organic or biological factors is called the psychological view.
Friendship	The essentials of friendship are reciprocity and commitment between individuals who see themselves more or less as equals. Interaction between friends rests on a more equal power base than the interaction between children and adults.
Depressive	Depressive disorders are mood disorders in which the individual suffers depression without

Go to **Cram101.com** for the Practice Tests for this Chapter.

disorders	ever experiencing mania.
Dysthymic disorder	A dysthymic disorder is a form of the mood disorder of depression characterized by a lack of enjoyment/pleasure in life that continues for at least two years. It differs from clinical depression in the severity of the symptoms.
Dysthymia	Dysthymia or dysthymic disorder is a form of the mood disorder of depression characterized by a lack of enjoyment/pleasure in life that continues for at least two years. It differs from clinical depression in the severity of the symptoms.
Chronic	Chronic refers to a relatively long duration, usually more than a few months.
Major depressive episode	A major depressive episode is a common and severe experience of depression. It includes feelings of worthlessness, disturbances in bodily activities such as sleep, loss of interest, and the inability to experience pleasure. It lasts for at least two weeks.
Hypomanic episode	A hypomanic episode is a less severe and less disruptive version of a manic episode that is one of the criteria for several mood disorders.
Self-esteem	Self-esteem refers to a person's subjective appraisal of himself or herself as intrinsically positive or negative to some degree.
Major depressive disorder	The diagnosis of a major depressive disorder occurs when an individual experiences a major depressive episode and depressed characteristics, such as lethargy and depression, last for 2 weeks or longer and daily functioning becomes impaired.
Comorbidity	Comorbidity refers to the presence of more than one mental disorder occurring in an individual at the same time.
Substance abuse	Substance abuse refers to the overindulgence in and dependence on a stimulant, depressant, or other chemical substance, leading to effects that are detrimental to the individual's physical or mental health, or the welfare of others.
Manic episode	A manic episode is a period of unusually high energy, sometimes including uncontrollable excitement. Such episodes most commonly occur as part of bipolar disorder. In extreme cases, the person may need to be hospitalized.
Hallucination	A hallucination is a sensory perception experienced in the absence of an external stimulus, as distinct from an illusion, which is a misperception of an external stimulus. They may occur in any sensory modality - visual, auditory, olfactory, gustatory, tactile, or mixed.
Delusion	A false belief, not generally shared by others, and that cannot be changed despite strong evidence to the contrary is a delusion.
Sullivan	Sullivan developed the Self System, a configuration of the personality traits developed in childhood and reinforced by positive affirmation and the security operations developed in childhood to avoid anxiety and threats to self-esteem.
Neurotransmitter	A neurotransmitter is a chemical that is used to relay, amplify and modulate electrical signals between a neurons and another cell.
Brain	The brain controls and coordinates most movement, behavior and homeostatic body functions such as heartbeat, blood pressure, fluid balance and body temperature. Functions of the brain are responsible for cognition, emotion, memory, motor learning and other sorts of learning. The brain is primarily made up of two types of cells: glia and neurons.
Norepinephrine	Norepinephrine is released from the adrenal glands as a hormone into the blood, but it is also a neurotransmitter in the nervous system. As a stress hormone, it affects parts of the human brain where attention and impulsivity are controlled. Along with epinephrine, this compound effects the fight-or-flight response, activating the sympathetic nervous system to directly increase heart rate, release energy from fat, and increase muscle readiness.

Go to **Cram101.com** for the Practice Tests for this Chapter.

Epinephrine	Epinephrine is a hormone and a neurotransmitter. Epinephrine plays a central role in the short-term stress reaction—the physiological response to threatening or exciting conditions. It is secreted by the adrenal medulla. When released into the bloodstream, epinephrine binds to multiple receptors and has numerous effects throughout the body.
Gamma-aminobutyric acid	Gamma-aminobutyric acid is a neurotransmitter that reduces activity across the synapse and thus inhibits a range of behaviors and emotions, especially generalized anxiety.
Acetylcholine	The chemical compound acetylcholine was the first neurotransmitter to be identified. It plays a role in learning, memory, and rapid eye movement sleep and causes the skeletal muscle fibers to contract.
Neuron	The neuron is the primary cell of the nervous system. They are found in the brain, the spinal cord, in the nerves and ganglia of the peripheral nervous system. It is a specialized cell that conducts impulses through the nervous system and contains three major parts: cell body, dendrites, and an axon. It can have many dendrites but only one axon.
Synaptic cleft	Synaptic cleft refers to a microscopic gap between the terminal button of a neuron and the cell membrane of another neuron.
Receptor	A sensory receptor is a structure that recognizes a stimulus in the internal or external environment of an organism. In response to stimuli the sensory receptor initiates sensory transduction by creating graded potentials or action potentials in the same cell or in an adjacent one.
Action potential	The electrical impulse that provides the basis for the conduction of a neural impulse along an axon of a neuron is the action potential. When a biological cell or patch of membrane undergoes an action potential, or electrical excitation, the polarity of the transmembrane voltage swings rapidly from negative to positive and back.
Amino acid	Amino acid is the basic structural building unit of proteins. They form short polymer chains called peptides or polypeptides which in turn form structures called proteins.
Tryptophan	Tryptophan is a sleep-promoting amino acid and a precursor for serotonin (a neurotransmitter) and melatonin (a neurohormone). Tryptophan has been implicated as a possible cause of schizophrenia in people who cannot metabolize it properly.
Serotonin	Serotonin, a neurotransmitter, is believed to play an important part of the biochemistry of depression, bipolar disorder and anxiety. It is also believed to be influential on sexuality and appetite.
Synapse	A synapse is specialized junction through which cells of the nervous system signal to one another and to non-neuronal cells such as muscles or glands.
Reuptake	Reuptake is the reabsorption of a neurotransmitter by the molecular transporter of a pre-synaptic neuron after it has performed its function of transmitting a neural impulse.
Monoamine oxidase	Monoamine oxidase is an enzyme that catalyzes the oxidation of monoamines. They are found bound to the outer membrane of mitochondria in most cell types in the body. Because of the vital role that it play in the inactivation of neurotransmitters, dysfunction (too much/too little MAO activity) is thought to be responsible for a number of neurological disorders.
Enzyme	An enzyme is a protein that catalyzes, or speeds up, a chemical reaction. Enzymes are essential to sustain life because most chemical reactions in biological cells would occur too slowly, or would lead to different products, without enzymes.
Antidepressants	Antidepressants are medications used primarily in the treatment of clinical depression. Antidepressants create little if any immediate change in mood and require between several days and several weeks to take effect.

Tricyclic antidepressant	A tricyclic antidepressant is of a class of antidepressant drugs first used in the 1950s. They are named after the drugs' molecular structure, which contains three rings of atoms.
Blocking	If the one of the two members of a compound stimulus fails to produce the CR due to an earlier conditioning of the other member of the compound stimulus, blocking has occurred.
Dopamine	Dopamine is critical to the way the brain controls our movements and is a crucial part of the basal ganglia motor loop. It is commonly associated with the 'pleasure system' of the brain, providing feelings of enjoyment and reinforcement to motivate us to do, or continue doing, certain activities.
Positron emission tomography	Positron Emission Tomography measures emissions from radioactively labeled chemicals that have been injected into the bloodstream. The greatest benefit is that different compounds can show blood flow and oxygen and glucose metabolism in the tissues of the working brain.
Magnetic resonance imaging	Magnetic resonance imaging is a method of creating images of the inside of opaque organs in living organisms as well as detecting the amount of bound water in geological structures. It is primarily used to demonstrate pathological or other physiological alterations of living tissues and is a commonly used form of medical imaging.
Photon	A photon is a quantum of the electromagnetic field, for instance light. In some respects a photon acts as a particle, for instance when registered by the light sensitive device in a camera. It also acts like a wave, as when passing through the optics in a camera.
Metabolism	Metabolism is the biochemical modification of chemical compounds in living organisms and cells.
Cerebrum	The cerebrum (the portion of the brain that performs motor and sensory functions and a variety of mental activities) is divided into four lobes - the frontal, temporal, parietal and occipital lobes.
Biological rhythm	A biological rhythm is a hypothetical cyclic pattern of alterations in physiology, emotions, and/or intellect
Circadian rhythm	The circadian rhythm is a name given to the "internal body clock" that regulates the (roughly) 24 hour cycle of biological processes in animals and plants.
Affective	Affective is the way people react emotionally, their ability to feel another living thing's pain or joy.
Synchrony	In child development, synchrony is the carefully coordinated interaction between the parent and the child or adolescent in which, often unknowingly, they are attuned to each other's behavior.
Basic research	Basic research has as its primary objective the advancement of knowledge and the theoretical understanding of the relations among variables . It is exploratory and often driven by the researcher's curiosity, interest or hunch.
Monoamine oxidase inhibitors	Monoamine oxidase inhibitors are a group of antidepressant drugs that prevent the enzyme monoamine oxidase from deactivating neurotransmitters of the central nervous system.
Stroke	A stroke occurs when the blood supply to a part of the brain is suddenly interrupted by occlusion, by hemorrhage, or other causes
Schizophrenia	Schizophrenia is characterized by persistent defects in the perception or expression of reality. A person suffering from untreated schizophrenia typically demonstrates grossly disorganized thinking, and may also experience delusions or auditory hallucinations
Imipramine	Imipramine is the first antidepressant to be developed in the late 1950s. The drug became a prototypical drug for the development of the later released tricyclics. It is not as commonly

used today but sometimes used to treat major depression as a second-line treatment.

Fluoxetine	Fluoxetine is an antidepressant drug used medically in the treatment of depression, obsessive-compulsive disorder, bulimia nervosa, premenstrual dysphoric disorder and panic disorder. It is sold under the brand names Prozac®, and others.
Hypomania	Hypomania is a state involving combinations of: elevated mood, irritability, racing thoughts, people-seeking, hypersexuality, grandiose thinking, religiosity, and pressured speech.
Early adulthood	The developmental period beginning in the late teens or early twenties and lasting into the thirties is called early adulthood; characterized by an increasing self-awareness.
Theories	Theories are logically self-consistent models or frameworks describing the behavior of a certain natural or social phenomenon. They are broad explanations and predictions concerning phenomena of interest.
Noradrenaline	Noradrenaline is released from the adrenal glands as a hormone into the blood, but it is also a neurotransmitter in the nervous system. As a stress hormone, it affects parts of the human brain where attention and impulsivity are controlled. Along with epinephrine, this compound effects the fight-or-flight response, activating the sympathetic nervous system to directly increase heart rate, release energy from fat, and increase muscle readiness.
Phototherapy	Phototherapy consists of exposure to specific wavelengths of light using lasers, LEDs, fluorescent lamps, or very bright, full-spectrum light, for a prescribed amount of time. It has proven effective in treating Acne vulgaris, seasonal affective disorder (SAD), and for some people it has ameliorated delayed sleep phase syndrome.
Simulation	A simulation is an imitation of some real device or state of affairs. Simulation attempts to represent certain features of the behavior of a physical or abstract system by the behavior of another system.
Electrode	Any device used to electrically stimulate nerve tissue or to record its activity is an electrode.
Seizure	A seizure is a temporary alteration in brain function expressed as a changed mental state, tonic or clonic movements and various other symptoms. They are due to temporary abnormal electrical activity of a group of brain cells.
Hypothalamus	The hypothalamus is a region of the brain located below the thalamus, forming the major portion of the ventral region of the diencephalon and functioning to regulate certain metabolic processes and other autonomic activities.
Acute	Acute means sudden, sharp, and abrupt. Usually short in duration.
Learning	Learning is a relatively permanent change in behavior that results from experience. Thus, to attribute a behavioral change to learning, the change must be relatively permanent and must result from experience.
Tricyclic	Tricyclic antidepressants are a class of antidepressant drugs first used in the 1950s. They are named after the drugs' molecular structure, which contains three rings of atoms.
Clinical depression	Although nearly any mood with some element of sadness may colloquially be termed a depression, clinical depression is more than just a temporary state of sadness. Symptoms lasting two weeks or longer in duration, and of a severity that they begin to interfere with daily living.
Variable	A variable refers to a measurable factor, characteristic, or attribute of an individual or a system.
Relapse prevention	Extending therapeutic progress by teaching the client how to cope with future troubling situations is a relapse prevention technique.

Biological therapies	Treatments to reduce or eliminate the symptoms of psychological disorders by altering the way an individual's body functions are called biological therapies.
Psychodynamic	Most psychodynamic approaches are centered around the idea of a maladapted function developed early in life (usually childhood) which are at least in part unconscious. This maladapted function (a.k.a. defense mechanism) does not do well in place of a normal/healthy one.
Interpersonal therapy	A brief psychotherapy designed to help depressed people better understand and cope with problems relating to their interpersonal relationships is referred to as interpersonal therapy.
Psychoanalytic	Freud's theory that unconscious forces act as determinants of personality is called psychoanalytic theory. The theory is a developmental theory characterized by critical stages of development.
Psychoanalyst	A psychoanalyst is a specially trained therapist who attempts to treat the individual by uncovering and revealing to the individual otherwise subconscious factors that are contributing to some undesirable behavior.
Bowlby	Bowlby, a developmental psychologist of the psychoanalytic tradition, was responsible for much of the early research conducted on attachment in humans. He identified three stages of separation: protest, despair, and detachment.
Interpersonal psychotherapy	A brief treatment approach that emphasizes resolution of interpersonal problems and stressors such as role disputes in marital conflict, or forming relationships in marriage or a new job is referred to as interpersonal psychotherapy.
Psychodynamic therapy	Psychodynamic therapy uses a range of different techniques, applied to the client considering his or her needs. Most approaches are centered around the idea of a maladapted function developed early in life which are at least in part unconscious.
Cognitive-behavioral therapy	Cognitive-behavioral therapy refers to group of treatment procedures aimed at identifying and modifying faulty thought processes, attitudes and attributions, and problem behaviors.
Humanistic	Humanistic refers to any system of thought focused on subjective experience and human problems and potentials.
Self-concept	Self-concept refers to domain-specific evaluations of the self where a domain may be academics, athletics, etc.
Carl Rogers	Carl Rogers was instrumental in the development of non-directive psychotherapy, also known as "client-centered" psychotherapy. Rogers' basic tenets were unconditional positive regard, genuineness, and empathic understanding, with each demonstrated by the counselor.
Social reinforcement	Praise, attention, approval, and/or affection from others is referred to as social reinforcement.
Social skills	Social skills are skills used to interact and communicate with others to assist status in the social structure and other motivations.
Social skills training	Social skills training refers to a behavior therapy designed to improve interpersonal skills that emphasizes shaping, modeling, and behavioral rehearsal.
Habit	A habit is a response that has become completely separated from its eliciting stimulus. Early learning theorists used the term to describe S-R associations, however not all S-R associations become a habit, rather many are extinguished after reinforcement is withdrawn.
Schemata	Cognitive categories or frames of reference are called schemata.
Coding	In senation, coding is the process by which information about the quality and quantity of a

Go to Cram101.com for the Practice Tests for this Chapter.

	stimulus is preserved in the pattern of action potentials sent through sensory neurons to the central nervous system.
Aaron Beck	Aaron Beck was initially trained as a psychoanalyst and conducted research on the psychoanalytic treatment of depression. With out the strong ability to collect data to this end, he began exploring cognitive approaches to treatment and originated cognitive behavior therapy.
Cognition	The intellectual processes through which information is obtained, transformed, stored, retrieved, and otherwise used is cognition.
Attributional style	One's tendency to attribute one's behavior to internal or external factors, stable or unstable factors, and so on is their attributional style.
Attribution process	The process by which people draw inferences about the motives and traits of others is the attribution process.
Persona	In Jungian archetypal psychology, the Persona is the mask or appearance one presents to the world. It may appear in dreams under various guises.
Learned helplessness	Learned helplessness is a description of the effect of inescapable positive punishment (such as electrical shock) on animal (and by extension, human) behavior.
Cognitive therapy	Cognitive therapy is a kind of psychotherapy used to treat depression, anxiety disorders, phobias, and other forms of mental disorder. It involves recognizing distorted thinking and learning how to replace it with more realistic thoughts and actions.
Motivation	In psychology, motivation is the driving force (desire) behind all actions of an organism.
Role-play	A training technique that involves having the trainee pretend to perform a task is called role-play.
Emotion	An emotion is a mental states that arise spontaneously, rather than through conscious effort. They are often accompanied by physiological changes.
Maladaptive	In psychology, a behavior or trait is adaptive when it helps an individual adjust and function well within their social environment. A maladaptive behavior or trait is counterproductive to the individual.
Society	The social sciences use the term society to mean a group of people that form a semi-closed (or semi-open) social system, in which most interactions are with other individuals belonging to the group.
Placebo	Placebo refers to a bogus treatment that has the appearance of being genuine.
Comparative research	Comparative research is a research methodology that aims to make comparisons across different countries or cultures. A major problem is that the data sets in different countries may not use the same categories, or define categories differently.
Managed health care	A term that refers to the industrialization of health care, whereby large organizations in the private sector control the delivery of services is called managed health care.
Clinical psychologist	A psychologist, usually with a Ph.D, whose training is in the diagnosis, treatment, or research of psychological and behavioral disorders is a clinical psychologist.
Mental illness	Mental illness is the term formerly used to mean psychological disorder but less preferred because it implies that the causes of the disorder can be found in a medical disease process.
Insomnia	Insomnia is a sleep disorder characterized by an inability to sleep and/or to remain asleep for a reasonable period during the night.
Personality	Personality refers to the pattern of enduring characteristics that differentiates a person,

	the patterns of behaviors that make each individual unique.
Creativity	Creativity is the ability to think about something in novel and unusual ways and come up with unique solutions to problems. It involves divergent thinking, having many solutions or views to a problem.
Adolescence	The period of life bounded by puberty and the assumption of adult responsibilities is adolescence.
Bipolar ii disorder	A mood disorder in which a person is mostly depressed but has also had one or more episodes of mild mania is called bipolar II disorder.
DSM-IV TR	The current Diagnostic and Statistical Manual of Mental Disorders of the American Psychiatric Association is called DSM-IV TR.
Chlorpromazine	Chlorpromazine was the first antipsychotic drug, used during the 1950s and 1960s. Used as chlorpromazine hydrochloride and sold under the tradenames Largactil (the "liquid cosh") and Thorazine, it has sedative, hypotensive and antiemetic properties as well as anticholinergic and antidopaminergic effects. Today, Chlorpromazine is considered a typical antipsychotic.
Antipsychotic	The term antipsychotic is applied to a group of drugs used to treat psychosis.
Flight of ideas	Flight of ideas is a symptom of mania that involves a rapid shift in conversation from one subject to another with only superficial associative connections.
Sanity	Sanity considered as a legal term denotes that an individual is of sound mind and therefore can bear legal responsibility for his or her actions.
Insanity	A legal status indicating that a person cannot be held responsible for his or her actions because of mental illness is called insanity.
Steroid	A steroid is a lipid characterized by a carbon skeleton with four fused rings. Different steroids vary in the functional groups attached to these rings. Hundreds of distinct steroids have been identified in plants and animals. Their most important role in most living systems is as hormones.
Tumor	A tumor is an abnormal growth that when located in the brain can either be malignant and directly destroy brain tissue, or be benign and disrupt functioning by increasing intracranial pressure.
Scheme	According to Piaget, a hypothetical mental structure that permits the classification and organization of new information is called a scheme.
Cyclothymia	Cyclothymia is a chronic mood disturbance generally lasting at least two years and characterized by mood swings including periods of hypomania and depression.
Predisposition	Predisposition refers to an inclination or diathesis to respond in a certain way, either inborn or acquired. In abnormal psychology, it is a factor that lowers the ability to withstand stress and inclines the individual toward pathology.
Genetics	Genetics is the science of genes, heredity, and the variation of organisms.
Unipolar mood disorder	Unipolar mood disorder refers to a mood disorder characterized by depression or mania, but not both.
Control group	A group that does not receive the treatment effect in an experiment is referred to as the control group or sometimes as the comparison group.
Chromosome	The DNA which carries genetic information in biological cells is normally packaged in the form of one or more large macromolecules called a chromosome. Humans normally have 46.
Gene	A gene is an ultramicroscopic area of the chromosome. It is the smallest physical unit of the

Go to **Cram101.com** for the Practice Tests for this Chapter.

	DNA molecule that carries a piece of hereditary information.
Unipolar depression	Unipolar depression refers to a term applied to the disorder of individuals who have experienced episodes of depression but not of mania. It is referred to as major depression in DSM-IV-TR.
Panic disorder	A panic attack is a period of intense fear or discomfort, typically with an abrupt onset and usually lasting no more than thirty minutes. The disorder is strikingly different from other types of anxiety, in that panic attacks are very sudden, appear to be unprovoked, and are often disabling. People who have repeated attacks, or feel severe anxiety about having another attack are said to have panic disorder.
Phobia	A persistent, irrational fear of an object, situation, or activity that the person feels compelled to avoid is referred to as a phobia.
Pharmacotherapy	The use of drugs to alleviate the symptoms of emotional disturbance is referred to as pharmacotherapy.
Family therapy	Family therapy is a branch of psychotherapy that treats family problems. Family therapists consider the family as a system of interacting members; as such, the problems in the family are seen to arise as an emergent property of the interactions in the system, rather than ascribed exclusively to the "faults" or psychological problems of individual members.
Negative feedback	In negative feedback, the output of a system is added back into the input, so as to reverse the direction of change. This tends to keep the output from changing, so it is stabilizing and attempts to maintain homeostasis.
Lethality	The probability that a person will choose to end his or her life is their lethality.
Lesbian	A lesbian is a homosexual woman. They are women who are sexually and romantically attracted to other women.
Ethnic group	An ethnic group is a culture or subculture whose members are readily distinguishable by outsiders based on traits originating from a common racial, national, linguistic, or religious source. Members of an ethnic group are often presumed to be culturally or biologically similar, although this is not in fact necessarily the case.
Ethnicity	Ethnicity refers to a characteristic based on cultural heritage, nationality characteristics, race, religion, and language.
Attitude	An enduring mental representation of a person, place, or thing that evokes an emotional response and related behavior is called attitude.
Statistics	Statistics is a type of data analysis which practice includes the planning, summarizing, and interpreting of observations of a system possibly followed by predicting or forecasting of future events based on a mathematical model of the system being observed.
Statistic	A statistic is an observable random variable of a sample.
Insight	Insight refers to a sudden awareness of the relationships among various elements that had previously appeared to be independent of one another.
Self-awareness	Realization that one's existence and functioning are separate from those of other people and things is called self-awareness.
Subculture	As understood in sociology, anthropology and cultural studies, a subculture is a set of people with a distinct set of behavior and beliefs that differentiate them from a larger culture of which they are a part.
Social stigma	A social stigma a distinctive characteristic in a person which can cause or be the result of marginalization when used as an insult by individuals or groups.

Go to **Cram101.com** for the Practice Tests for this Chapter.

Clinical study	An intensive investigation of a single person, especially one suffering from some injury or disease is referred to as a clinical study.
Etiology	Etiology is the study of causation. The term is used in philosophy, physics and biology in reference to the causes of various phenomena. It is generally the study of why things occur, or even the reasons behind the way that things act.
Anxiety disorder	Anxiety disorder is a blanket term covering several different forms of abnormal anxiety, fear, phobia and nervous condition, that come on suddenly and prevent pursuing normal daily routines.
Catecholamines	Catecholamines are chemical compounds derived from the amino acid tyrosine that act as hormones or neurotransmitters. High catecholamine levels in blood are associated with stress.
Hypothesis	A specific statement about behavior or mental processes that is testable through research is a hypothesis.
Receptor site	A location on the dendrite of a receiving neuron that is tailored to receive a specific neurotransmitter is a receptor site.
Schema	Schema refers to a way of mentally representing the world, such as a belief or an expectation, that can influence perception of persons, objects, and situations.

Go to **Cram101.com** for the Practice Tests for this Chapter.

Mental processes	The thoughts, feelings, and motives that each of us experiences privately but that cannot be observed directly are called mental processes.
Hallucination	A hallucination is a sensory perception experienced in the absence of an external stimulus, as distinct from an illusion, which is a misperception of an external stimulus. They may occur in any sensory modality - visual, auditory, olfactory, gustatory, tactile, or mixed.
Schizophrenia	Schizophrenia is characterized by persistent defects in the perception or expression of reality. A person suffering from untreated schizophrenia typically demonstrates grossly disorganized thinking, and may also experience delusions or auditory hallucinations
Delusion	A false belief, not generally shared by others, and that cannot be changed despite strong evidence to the contrary is a delusion.
Theories	Theories are logically self-consistent models or frameworks describing the behavior of a certain natural or social phenomenon. They are broad explanations and predictions concerning phenomena of interest.
Mental illness	Mental illness is the term formerly used to mean psychological disorder but less preferred because it implies that the causes of the disorder can be found in a medical disease process.
Consciousness	The awareness of the sensations, thoughts, and feelings being experienced at a given moment is called consciousness.
Perception	Perception is the process of acquiring, interpreting, selecting, and organizing sensory information.
Inference	Inference is the act or process of drawing a conclusion based solely on what one already knows.
Psychosis	Psychosis is a generic term for mental states in which the components of rational thought and perception are severely impaired. Persons experiencing a psychosis may experience hallucinations, hold paranoid or delusional beliefs, demonstrate personality changes and exhibit disorganized thinking. This is usually accompanied by features such as a lack of insight into the unusual or bizarre nature of their behavior, difficulties with social interaction and impairments in carrying out the activities of daily living.
IQ test	An IQ test is a standardized test developed to measure a person's cognitive abilities ("intelligence") in relation to their age group.
Mood disorder	A mood disorder is a condition where the prevailing emotional mood is distorted or inappropriate to the circumstances.
Psychological disorder	Mental processes and/or behavior patterns that cause emotional distress and/or substantial impairment in functioning is a psychological disorder.
Brain	The brain controls and coordinates most movement, behavior and homeostatic body functions such as heartbeat, blood pressure, fluid balance and body temperature. Functions of the brain are responsible for cognition, emotion, memory, motor learning and other sorts of learning. The brain is primarily made up of two types of cells: glia and neurons.
Syphilis	Syphilis is a sexually transmitted disease that is caused by a spirochaete bacterium, Treponema pallidum. If not treated, syphilis can cause serious effects such as damage to the nervous system, heart, or brain. Untreated syphilis can be ultimately fatal.
Major depressive disorder	The diagnosis of a major depressive disorder occurs when an individual experiences a major depressive episode and depressed characteristics, such as lethargy and depression, last for 2 weeks or longer and daily functioning becomes impaired.
Population	Population refers to all members of a well-defined group of organisms, events, or things.

217

Sperling	Sperling has studied cognitive psychology and was a prominent researcher in memory. He is responsible for the concept of iconic memory.
Chronic	Chronic refers to a relatively long duration, usually more than a few months.
Society	The social sciences use the term society to mean a group of people that form a semi-closed (or semi-open) social system, in which most interactions are with other individuals belonging to the group.
Suicide	Suicide behavior is rare in childhood but escalates in adolescence. The suicide rate increases in a linear fashion from adolescence through late adulthood.
Paranoid	The term paranoid is typically used in a general sense to signify any self-referential delusion, or more specifically, to signify a delusion involving the fear of persecution.
Paranoid schizophrenia	Paranoid schizophrenia is a type of schizophrenia characterized primarily by delusions-commonly of persecution-and by vivid hallucinations .
Affect	A subjective feeling or emotional tone often accompanied by bodily expressions noticeable to others is called affect.
Waxy flexibility	A feature of catatonic schizophrenia in which persons maintain postures into which they are placed is referred to as waxy flexibility.
Catatonic behavior	Catatonic behavior is a symptom of schizophrenia in which the person is unresponsive to the environment. It may take the form of active resistance, excited motor activity, or a complete lack of movement or awareness of the environment.
Flat affect	A deviation in emotional response wherein virtually no emotion is expressed whatever the stimulus, emotional expressiveness is blunted, or a lack of expression and muscle tone is noted in the face, is called flat affect.
Dementia praecox	An older term for schizophrenia, chosen to describe what was believed to be an incurable and progressive deterioration of mental functioning beginning in adolescence is called dementia praecox.
Kraepelin	Kraepelin postulated that there is a specific brain or other biological pathology underlying each of the major psychiatric disorders. Just as his laboratory discovered the pathologic basis of what is now known as Alzheimers disease, Kraepelin was confident that it would someday be possible to identify the pathologic basis of each of the major psychiatric disorders.
Adolescence	The period of life bounded by puberty and the assumption of adult responsibilities is adolescence.
Personality	Personality refers to the pattern of enduring characteristics that differentiates a person, the patterns of behaviors that make each individual unique.
Bleuler	Bleuler is particularly notable for naming schizophrenia, a disorder which was previously known as dementia praecox. Bleuler realised the condition was neither a dementia, nor did it always occur in young people (praecox meaning early) and so gave the condition the name from the Greek for split (schizo) and mind (phrene).
Motivation	In psychology, motivation is the driving force (desire) behind all actions of an organism.
Emotion	An emotion is a mental states that arise spontaneously, rather than through conscious effort. They are often accompanied by physiological changes.
Mental disorder	Mental disorder refers to a disturbance in a person's emotions, drives, thought processes, or behavior that involves serious and relatively prolonged distress and/or impairment in ability to function, is not simply a normal response to some event or set of events in the person's

	environment.
Depression	In everyday language depression refers to any downturn in mood, which may be relatively transitory and perhaps due to something trivial. This is differentiated from Clinical depression which is marked by symptoms that last two weeks or more and are so severe that they interfere with daily living.
Mania	Mania is a medical condition characterized by severely elevated mood. Mania is most usually associated with bipolar disorder, where episodes of mania may cyclically alternate with episodes of depression.
Clinician	A health professional authorized to provide services to people suffering from one or more pathologies is a clinician.
Abnormal psychology	The scientific study whose objectives are to describe, explain, predict, and control behaviors that are considered strange or unusual is referred to as abnormal psychology.
Bipolar disorder	Bipolar Disorder is a mood disorder typically characterized by fluctuations between manic and depressive states; and, more generally, atypical mood regulation and mood instability.
Anatomy	Anatomy is the branch of biology that deals with the structure and organization of living things. It can be divided into animal anatomy (zootomy) and plant anatomy (phytonomy). Major branches of anatomy include comparative anatomy, histology, and human anatomy.
Disorganized schizophrenia	Disorganized schizophrenia is characterized by prominent disorganized behavior and speech, and flat or inappropriate emotion and affect. Furthermore, the criteria for the catatonic subtype of schizophrenia must not have been met.
Undifferentited type of schizophrenia	Category for individuals who meet the criteria for schizophrenia but not for any one of the defined subtypes is called undifferentiated type of schizophrenia.
Stages	Stages represent relatively discrete periods of time in which functioning is qualitatively different from functioning at other periods.
Poverty of speech	Poverty of speech is a general lack of additional, unprompted content seen in normal speech. As a symptom, it is commonly seen in patients suffering from Schizophrenia. It can complicate psychotherapy severely because of the considerable difficulty in holding a fluent conversation.
Acute	Acute means sudden, sharp, and abrupt. Usually short in duration.
DSM-IV TR	The current Diagnostic and Statistical Manual of Mental Disorders of the American Psychiatric Association is called DSM-IV TR.
Anchor	An anchor is a sample of work or performance used to set the specific performance standard for a rubric level .
Psychiatrist	A psychiatrist is a physician who specializes in the diagnosis and treatment of psychological disorders.
Insanity	A legal status indicating that a person cannot be held responsible for his or her actions because of mental illness is called insanity.
Projection	Attributing one's own undesirable thoughts, impulses, traits, or behaviors to others is referred to as projection.
Nervous system	The body's electrochemical communication circuitry, made up of billions of neurons is a nervous system.
Delirium	Delirium is a medical term used to describe an acute decline in attention and cognition. Delirium is probably the single most common acute disorder affecting adults in general

hospitals. It affects 10-20% of all adults in hospital, and 30-40% of older patients.

Senses	The senses are systems that consist of a sensory cell type that respond to a specific kind of physical energy, and that correspond to a defined region within the brain where the signals are received and interpreted.
Cerebral cortex	The cerebral cortex is the outermost layer of the cerebrum and has a grey color. It is made up of four lobes and it is involved in many complex brain functions including memory, perceptual awareness, "thinking", language and consciousness. The cerebral cortex receives sensory information from many different sensory organs eg: eyes, ears, etc. and processes the information.
Gray matter	Gray matter is a category of nervous tissue with many nerve cell bodies and few myelinated axons. Generally, gray matter can be understood as the parts of the brain responsible for information processing; whereas, white matter is responsible for information transmission. In addition, gray matter does not have a myelin sheath and does not regenerate after injury unlike white matter.
Control subjects	Control subjects are participants in an experiment who do not receive the treatment effect but for whom all other conditions are held comparable to those of experimental subjects.
Neuron	The neuron is the primary cell of the nervous system. They are found in the brain, the spinal cord, in the nerves and ganglia of the peripheral nervous system. It is a specialized cell that conducts impulses through the nervous system and contains three major parts: cell body, dendrites, and an axon. It can have many dendrites but only one axon.
Loosening of associations	Continual shifting from topic to topic without any apparent logical or meaningful connection between thoughts is referred to as a loosening of associations.
Seizure	A seizure is a temporary alteration in brain function expressed as a changed mental state, tonic or clonic movements and various other symptoms. They are due to temporary abnormal electrical activity of a group of brain cells.
Substance abuse	Substance abuse refers to the overindulgence in and dependence on a stimulant, depressant, or other chemical substance, leading to effects that are detrimental to the individual's physical or mental health, or the welfare of others.
Prognosis	A forecast about the probable course of an illess is referred to as prognosis.
Antipsychotic	The term antipsychotic is applied to a group of drugs used to treat psychosis.
Personality disorder	A mental disorder characterized by a set of inflexible, maladaptive personality traits that keep a person from functioning properly in society is referred to as a personality disorder.
Social anxiety	A feeling of apprehension in the presence of others is social anxiety.
Thought disorder	Thought disorder describes a persistent underlying disturbance to conscious thought and is classified largely by its effects on speech and writing. Affected persons may show pressure of speech, derailment or flight of ideas, thought blocking, rhyming, punning, or word salad.
Threshold	In general, a threshold is a fixed location or value where an abrupt change is observed. In the sensory modalities, it is the minimum amount of stimulus energy necessary to elicit a sensory response.
Variable	A variable refers to a measurable factor, characteristic, or attribute of an individual or a system.
Case study	A carefully drawn biography that may be obtained through interviews, questionnaires, and psychological tests is called a case study.
Adoption studies	Research studies that assess hereditary influence by examining the resemblance between

Go to **Cram101.com** for the Practice Tests for this Chapter.

	adopted children and both their biological and their adoptive parents are referred to as adoption studies. The studies have been inconclusive about the relative importance of heredity in intelligence.
Index case	The index case refers to the person who in an investigation bears the diagnosis or trait in which the investigator is interested.
Identical twins	Identical twins occur when a single egg is fertilized to form one zygote (monozygotic) but the zygote then divides into two separate embryos. The two embryos develop into foetuses sharing the same womb. Monozygotic twins are genetically identical unless there has been a mutation in development, and they are almost always the same gender.
Gene	A gene is an ultramicroscopic area of the chromosome. It is the smallest physical unit of the DNA molecule that carries a piece of hereditary information.
Trait	An enduring personality characteristic that tends to lead to certain behaviors is called a trait. The term trait also means a genetically inherited feature of an organism.
Recessive gene	Recessive gene refers to an allele that causes a phenotype (visible or detectable characteristic) that is only seen in a homozygous genotype (an organism that has two copies of the same allele). Thus, both parents have to be carriers of a recessive trait in order for a child to express that trait.
Chromosome	The DNA which carries genetic information in biological cells is normally packaged in the form of one or more large macromolecules called a chromosome. Humans normally have 46.
Predisposition	Predisposition refers to an inclination or diathesis to respond in a certain way, either inborn or acquired. In abnormal psychology, it is a factor that lowers the ability to withstand stress and inclines the individual toward pathology.
DNA sequence	A DNA sequence is a succession of letters representing the primary structure of a real or hypothetical DNA molecule or strand.
Prenatal	Prenatal period refers to the time from conception to birth.
Hypothesis	A specific statement about behavior or mental processes that is testable through research is a hypothesis.
Heredity	Heredity is the transfer of characteristics from parent to offspring through their genes.
Iris	The iris is the most visible part of the eye. The iris is an annulus (or flattened ring) consisting of pigmented fibrovascular tissue known as a stroma. The stroma connects a sphincter muscle, which contracts the pupil, and a set of dialator muscles which open it.
Nervous breakdown	Nervous breakdown is often used by laymen to describe a sudden and acute attack of mental illness—for instance, clinical depression or anxiety disorder—in a previously outwardly healthy person. Breakdowns are the result of chronic and unrelenting nervous strain, and not a sign of weakness.
Alpha wave	The brain wave associated with deep relaxation is referred to as the alpha wave. Recorded by electroencephalography (EEG) , they are synchronous and coherent (regular like sawtooth) and in the frequency range of 8 - 12 Hz. It is also called Berger's wave in memory of the founder of EEG.
Frontal lobe	The frontal lobe comprises four major folds of cortical tissue: the precentral gyrus, superior gyrus and the middle gyrus of the frontal gyri, the inferior frontal gyrus. It has been found to play a part in impulse control, judgement, language, memory, motor function, problem solving, sexual behavior, socialization and spontaneity.
Control group	A group that does not receive the treatment effect in an experiment is referred to as the control group or sometimes as the comparison group.

Go to **Cram101.com** for the Practice Tests for this Chapter.

Displacement	An unconscious defense mechanism in which the individual directs aggressive or sexual feelings away from the primary object to someone or something safe is referred to as displacement. Displacement in linguistics is simply the ability to talk about things not present.
Dendrite	A dendrite is a slender, typically branched projection of a nerve cell, or "neuron," which conducts the electrical stimulation received from other cells to the body or soma of the cell from which it projects. This stimulation arrives through synapses, which typically are located near the tips of the dendrites and away from the soma.
Synapse	A synapse is specialized junction through which cells of the nervous system signal to one another and to non-neuronal cells such as muscles or glands.
Prefrontal cortex	The prefrontal cortex is the anterior part of the frontal lobes of the brain, lying in front of the motor and associative areas. It has been implicated in planning complex cognitive behaviors, personality expression and moderating correct social behavior. The prefrontal cortex continues to develop until around age 6.
Working Memory	Working memory is the collection of structures and processes in the brain used for temporarily storing and manipulating information. Working memory consists of both memory for items that are currently being processed, and components governing attention and directing the processing itself.
Maturation	The orderly unfolding of traits, as regulated by the genetic code is called maturation.
Temporal lobe	The temporal lobe is part of the cerebrum. It lies at the side of the brain, beneath the lateral or Sylvian fissure. Adjacent areas in the superior, posterior and lateral parts of the temporal lobe are involved in high-level auditory processing.
Hippocampus	The hippocampus is a part of the brain located inside the temporal lobe. It forms a part of the limbic system and plays a part in memory and navigation.
Attention	Attention is the cognitive process of selectively concentrating on one thing while ignoring other things. Psychologists have labeled three types of attention: sustained attention, selective attention, and divided attention.
Cognition	The intellectual processes through which information is obtained, transformed, stored, retrieved, and otherwise used is cognition.
Thalamus	An area near the center of the brain involved in the relay of sensory information to the cortex and in the functions of sleep and attention is the thalamus.
Cerebrospinal fluid	A solution that fills the hollow cavities of the brain and circulates around the brain and spinal cord is called cerebrospinal fluid.
Alcoholism	A disorder that involves long-term, repeated, uncontrolled, compulsive, and excessive use of alcoholic beverages and that impairs the drinker's health and work and social relationships is called alcoholism.
Ultrasound	Ultrasound is sound with a frequency greater than the upper limit of human hearing, approximately 20 kilohertz. Medical use can visualise muscle and soft tissue, making them useful for scanning the organs, and obstetric ultrasonography is commonly used during pregnancy.
Fetus	A fetus develops from the end of the 8th week of pregnancy (when the major structures have formed), until birth.
Dopamine	Dopamine is critical to the way the brain controls our movements and is a crucial part of the basal ganglia motor loop. It is commonly associated with the 'pleasure system' of the brain, providing feelings of enjoyment and reinforcement to motivate us to do, or continue doing,

certain activities.

Infancy	The developmental period that extends from birth to 18 or 24 months is called infancy.
Dopamine hypothesis	The suggestion that schizophrenia may result from excess dopamine activity at certain synaptic sites is referred to as the dopamine hypothesis.
Neurotransmitter	A neurotransmitter is a chemical that is used to relay, amplify and modulate electrical signals between a neurons and another cell.
Chlorpromazine	Chlorpromazine was the first antipsychotic drug, used during the 1950s and 1960s. Used as chlorpromazine hydrochloride and sold under the tradenames Largactil (the "liquid cosh") and Thorazine, it has sedative, hypotensive and antiemetic properties as well as anticholinergic and antidopaminergic effects. Today, Chlorpromazine is considered a typical antipsychotic.
Receptor	A sensory receptor is a structure that recognizes a stimulus in the internal or external environment of an organism. In response to stimuli the sensory receptor initiates sensory transduction by creating graded potentials or action potentials in the same cell or in an adjacent one.
Serotonin	Serotonin, a neurotransmitter, is believed to play an important part of the biochemistry of depression, bipolar disorder and anxiety. It is also believed to be influential on sexuality and appetite.
Glutamate	Glutamate is one of the 20 standard amino acids used by all organisms in their proteins. It is critical for proper cell function, but it is not an essential nutrient in humans because it can be manufactured from other compounds.
Metabolism	Metabolism is the biochemical modification of chemical compounds in living organisms and cells.
Genetics	Genetics is the science of genes, heredity, and the variation of organisms.
Family studies	Scientific studies in which researchers assess hereditary influence by examining blood relatives to see how much they resemble each other on a specific trait are called family studies.
Construct	A generalized concept, such as anxiety or gravity, is a construct.
Monozygotic	Identical twins occur when a single egg is fertilized to form one zygote, calld monozygotic, but the zygote then divides into two separate embryos. The two embryos develop into foetuses sharing the same womb. Monozygotic twins are genetically identical unless there has been a mutation in development, and they are almost always the same gender.
Mutation	Mutation is a permanent, sometimes transmissible (if the change is to a germ cell) change to the genetic material (usually DNA or RNA) of a cell. They can be caused by copying errors in the genetic material during cell division and by exposure to radiation, chemicals, or viruses, or can occur deliberately under cellular control during the processes such as meiosis or hypermutation.
Longitudinal study	Longitudinal study is a type of developmental study in which the same group of participants is followed and measured for an extended period of time, often years.
Wechsler Intelligence Scale for Children	The Wechsler Intelligence Scale for Children is an intelligence test that can be completed without reading or writing. It generates an IQ score. It also generates four composite scores; Verbal Comprehension, Perceptual Reasoning, Processing Speed and Working Memory.
Stimulus	A change in an environmental condition that elicits a response is a stimulus.
Psychoanalyst	A psychoanalyst is a specially trained therapist who attempts to treat the individual by

Go to **Cram101.com** for the Practice Tests for this Chapter.

uncovering and revealing to the individual otherwise subconscious factors that are contributing to some undesirable behavior.

Ambivalence	The simultaneous holding of strong positive and negative emotional attitudes toward the same situation or person is called ambivalence.
Halfway house	A halfway house is a term for a drug rehabilitation or sex offender center, where drug users or sex offenders respectively are allowed to move more freely than in a prison but are still monitored by staff and/or law enforcement. There is often opposition from neighborhoods where halfway houses attempt to locate.
Informed consent	The term used by psychologists to indicate that a person has agreed to participate in research after receiving information about the purposes of the study and the nature of the treatments is informed consent. Even with informed consent, subjects may withdraw from any experiment at any time.
Insight	Insight refers to a sudden awareness of the relationships among various elements that had previously appeared to be independent of one another.
Cognitive skills	Cognitive skills such as reasoning, attention, and memory can be advanced and sustained through practice and training.
Psychosocial treatment	Psychosocial treatment focuses on social and cultural factors as well as psychological influences. These approaches include cognitive, behavioral, and interpersonal methods.
Therapeutic alliance	A therapeutic alliance refers to a caring relationship that unites a therapist and a client in working to solve the client's problems.
Reality testing	Reality testing is the capacity to perceive one's environment and oneself according to accurate sensory impressions.
Problem solving	An attempt to find an appropriate way of attaining a goal when the goal is not readily available is called problem solving.
Psychotherapy	Psychotherapy is a set of techniques based on psychological principles intended to improve mental health, emotional or behavioral issues.
Learning	Learning is a relatively permanent change in behavior that results from experience. Thus, to attribute a behavioral change to learning, the change must be relatively permanent and must result from experience.
Social skills	Social skills are skills used to interact and communicate with others to assist status in the social structure and other motivations.
Self-esteem	Self-esteem refers to a person's subjective appraisal of himself or herself as intrinsically positive or negative to some degree.
Social perception	A subfield of social psychology that studies the ways in which we form and modify impressions of others is social perception.
Assertiveness	Assertiveness basically means the ability to express your thoughts and feelings in a way that clearly states your needs and keeps the lines of communication open with the other.
Social skills training	Social skills training refers to a behavior therapy designed to improve interpersonal skills that emphasizes shaping, modeling, and behavioral rehearsal.
Reinforcement	In operant conditioning, reinforcement is any change in an environment that (a) occurs after the behavior, (b) seems to make that behavior re-occur more often in the future and (c) that reoccurence of behavior must be the result of the change.
Incentive	An incentive is what is expected once a behavior is performed. An incentive acts as a reinforcer.

Go to **Cram101.com** for the Practice Tests for this Chapter.

231

Task analysis	The procedure of identifying the component elements of a behavior chain is called task analysis.
Extraneous variables	Variables that are not directly related to the hypothesis under study and that the experimenter does not actively attempt to control are called extraneous variables.
Feedback	Feedback refers to information returned to a person about the effects a response has had.
Overlearning	Continued rehearsal of material after one first appears to have mastered it is called overlearning.
Reinforcer	In operant conditioning, a reinforcer is any stimulus that increases the probability that a preceding behavior will occur again. In Classical Conditioning, the unconditioned stimulus (US) is the reinforcer.
Cognitive approach	A cognitive approach focuses on the mental processes involved in knowing: how we direct our attention, perceive, remember, think, and solve problems.
Cognitive therapy	Cognitive therapy is a kind of psychotherapy used to treat depression, anxiety disorders, phobias, and other forms of mental disorder. It involves recognizing distorted thinking and learning how to replace it with more realistic thoughts and actions.
Psychotic behavior	A psychotic behavior is a severe psychological disorder characterized by hallucinations and loss of contact with reality.
Affective	Affective is the way people react emotionally, their ability to feel another living thing's pain or joy.
Twin study	A twin study is a kind of genetic study done to determine heritability. The premise is that since identical twins (especially identical twins raised apart) have identical genotypes, differences between them are solely due to environmental factors. By examining the degree to which twins are differentiated, a study may determine the extent to which a particular trait is influenced by genes or the environment.
Guilt	Guilt describes many concepts related to a negative emotion or condition caused by actions which are believed to be, morally wrong. According to Freud, the avoidance of guilt is the basis for moral behavior.
Empathy	Empathy is the recognition and understanding of the states of mind, including beliefs, desires and particularly emotions of others without injecting your own.
Attitude	An enduring mental representation of a person, place, or thing that evokes an emotional response and related behavior is called attitude.
Adaptive behavior	An adaptive behavior increases the probability of the individual or organism to survive or exist within its environment.
Schizoaffective disorder	Schizoaffective disorder is a psychiatric diagnosis describing a situation where both the symptoms of mood disorder and psychosis are present. The disorder usually begins in early adulthood, and is more common in women.
Major mood disorder	A major mood disorder is characterized by a severely depressed mood that persists for at least two weeks. Episodes may start suddenly or slowly and can occur several times through a person's life. The disorder may be categorized as "single episode" or "recurrent" depending on whether previous episodes have been experienced before.
Major depressive episode	A major depressive episode is a common and severe experience of depression. It includes feelings of worthlessness, disturbances in bodily activities such as sleep, loss of interest, and the inability to experience pleasure. It lasts for at least two weeks.
Manic episode	A manic episode is a period of unusually high energy, sometimes including uncontrollable

Go to **Cram101.com** for the Practice Tests for this Chapter.

excitement. Such episodes most commonly occur as part of bipolar disorder. In extreme cases, the person may need to be hospitalized.

Late adolescence	Late adolescence refers to approximately the latter half of the second decade of life. Career interests, dating, and identity exploration are often more pronounced in late adolescence than in early adolescence.
Early adulthood	The developmental period beginning in the late teens or early twenties and lasting into the thirties is called early adulthood; characterized by an increasing self-awareness.
Lithium	Lithium salts are used as mood stabilizing drugs primarily in the treatment of bipolar disorder, depression, and mania; but also in treating schizophrenia. Lithium is widely distributed in the central nervous system and interacts with a number of neurotransmitters and receptors, decreasing noradrenaline release and increasing serotonin synthesis.
Antidepressants	Antidepressants are medications used primarily in the treatment of clinical depression. Antidepressants create little if any immediate change in mood and require between several days and several weeks to take effect.
Antidepressant	An antidepressant is a medication used primarily in the treatment of clinical depression. They are not thought to produce tolerance, although sudden withdrawal may produce adverse effects. They create little if any immediate change in mood and require between several days and several weeks to take effect.
Delusional disorder	Delusional disorder is a mental illness that involves holding one or more non-bizarre delusions in the absence of any other significant psychopathology. In particular a person with delusional disorder has never met any other criteria for schizophrenia and does not have any marked hallucinations.
Paranoia	In popular culture, the term paranoia is usually used to describe excessive concern about one's own well-being, sometimes suggesting a person holds persecutory beliefs concerning a threat to themselves or their property and is often linked to a belief in conspiracy theories.
Psychopathology	Psychopathology refers to the field concerned with the nature and development of mental disorders.
Social isolation	Social isolation refers to a type of loneliness that occurs when a person lacks a sense of integrated involvement. Being deprived of participation in a group or community involving companionship, shared interests, organized activities, and meaningful roles causes a person to feel alone.
Parietal lobe	The parietal lobe is positioned above (superior to) the occipital lobe and behind (posterior to) the frontal lobe. It plays important roles in integrating sensory information from various senses, and in the manipulation of objects.
Tricyclic antidepressant	A tricyclic antidepressant is of a class of antidepressant drugs first used in the 1950s. They are named after the drugs' molecular structure, which contains three rings of atoms.
Anxiety	Anxiety is a complex combination of the feeling of fear, apprehension and worry often accompanied by physical sensations such as palpitations, chest pain and/or shortness of breath.
Tardive dyskinesia	Tardive dyskinesia is a serious neurological disorder caused by the long-term use of traditional antipsychotic drugs.
Clozapine	Clozapine (trade names Clozaril), was the first of the atypical antipsychotic drugs. Clozapine is the only FDA-approved medication indicated for treatment-resistant schizophrenia and for reducing the risk of suicidal behavior in patients with schizophrenia.

Go to **Cram101.com** for the Practice Tests for this Chapter.

Residual schizophrenia	Residual schizophrenia is a diagnosis given to patients who have had an episode of schizophrenia but who currently do not show psychotic symptoms, but do show signs of the disorder.
Statistics	Statistics is a type of data analysis which practice includes the planning, summarizing, and interpreting of observations of a system possibly followed by predicting or forecasting of future events based on a mathematical model of the system being observed.
Statistic	A statistic is an observable random variable of a sample.

Neuropsychological test	A neuropsychological test use specifically designed tasks used to measure a psychological function known to be linked to a particular brain structure or pathway. They usually involve the systematic administration of clearly defined procedures in a formal environment.
Behavioral observation	A form of behavioral assessment that entails careful observation of a person's overt behavior in a particular situation is behavioral observation.
Brain	The brain controls and coordinates most movement, behavior and homeostatic body functions such as heartbeat, blood pressure, fluid balance and body temperature. Functions of the brain are responsible for cognition, emotion, memory, motor learning and other sorts of learning. The brain is primarily made up of two types of cells: glia and neurons.
Nervous system	The body's electrochemical communication circuitry, made up of billions of neurons is a nervous system.
Delirium	Delirium is a medical term used to describe an acute decline in attention and cognition. Delirium is probably the single most common acute disorder affecting adults in general hospitals. It affects 10-20% of all adults in hospital, and 30-40% of older patients.
Frontal lobe	The frontal lobe comprises four major folds of cortical tissue: the precentral gyrus, superior gyrus and the middle gyrus of the frontal gyri, the inferior frontal gyrus. It has been found to play a part in impulse control, judgement, language, memory, motor function, problem solving, sexual behavior, socialization and spontaneity.
Aphasia	Aphasia is a loss or impairment of the ability to produce or comprehend language, due to brain damage. It is usually a result of damage to the language centers of the brain.
Mental disorder	Mental disorder refers to a disturbance in a person's emotions, drives, thought processes, or behavior that involves serious and relatively prolonged distress and/or impairment in ability to function, is not simply a normal response to some event or set of events in the person's environment.
Consciousness	The awareness of the sensations, thoughts, and feelings being experienced at a given moment is called consciousness.
Adolescence	The period of life bounded by puberty and the assumption of adult responsibilities is adolescence.
Abnormal behavior	An action, thought, or feeling that is harmful to the person or to others is called abnormal behavior.
Molecular level	Molecular level is research at the physiological or biochemical level. It investigates the whole through analysis of the parts that make up the whole.
Maladaptive	In psychology, a behavior or trait is adaptive when it helps an individual adjust and function well within their social environment. A maladaptive behavior or trait is counterproductive to the individual.
Stroke	A stroke occurs when the blood supply to a part of the brain is suddenly interrupted by occlusion, by hemorrhage, or other causes
Clinician	A health professional authorized to provide services to people suffering from one or more pathologies is a clinician.
Variable	A variable refers to a measurable factor, characteristic, or attribute of an individual or a system.
Individual differences	Individual differences psychology studies the ways in which individual people differ in their behavior. This is distinguished from other aspects of psychology in that although psychology is ostensibly a study of individuals, modern psychologists invariably study groups.

Social support	Social Support is the physical and emotional comfort given by family, friends, co-workers and others. Research has identified three main types of social support: emotional, practical, sharing points of view.
Personality	Personality refers to the pattern of enduring characteristics that differentiates a person, the patterns of behaviors that make each individual unique.
Infancy	The developmental period that extends from birth to 18 or 24 months is called infancy.
Social isolation	Social isolation refers to a type of loneliness that occurs when a person lacks a sense of integrated involvement. Being deprived of participation in a group or community involving companionship, shared interests, organized activities, and meaningful roles causes a person to feel alone.
Insight	Insight refers to a sudden awareness of the relationships among various elements that had previously appeared to be independent of one another.
Depersonaliz-tion	Depersonalization is the experience of feelings of loss of a sense of reality. A sufferer feels that they have changed and the world has become less real — it is vague, dreamlike, or lacking in significance.
Hallucination	A hallucination is a sensory perception experienced in the absence of an external stimulus, as distinct from an illusion, which is a misperception of an external stimulus. They may occur in any sensory modality - visual, auditory, olfactory, gustatory, tactile, or mixed.
Paranoid	The term paranoid is typically used in a general sense to signify any self-referential delusion, or more specifically, to signify a delusion involving the fear of persecution.
Anxiety	Anxiety is a complex combination of the feeling of fear, apprehension and worry often accompanied by physical sensations such as palpitations, chest pain and/or shortness of breath.
Psychological testing	Psychological testing is a field characterized by the use of small samples of behavior in order to infer larger generalizations about a given individual. The technical term for psychological testing is psychometrics.
Inference	Inference is the act or process of drawing a conclusion based solely on what one already knows.
Attention	Attention is the cognitive process of selectively concentrating on one thing while ignoring other things. Psychologists have labeled three types of attention: sustained attention, selective attention, and divided attention.
Neuropsychol-gist	A psychologist concerned with the relationships among cognition, affect, behavior, and brain function is a neuropsychologist.
Neuropsychology	Neuropsychology is a branch of psychology that aims to understand how the structure and function of the brain relates to specific psychological processes.
Lesion	A lesion is a non-specific term referring to abnormal tissue in the body. It can be caused by any disease process including trauma (physical, chemical, electrical), infection, neoplasm, metabolic and autoimmune.
Emotion	An emotion is a mental states that arise spontaneously, rather than through conscious effort. They are often accompanied by physiological changes.
Brain imaging	Brain imaging is a fairly recent discipline within medicine and neuroscience. Brain imaging falls into two broad categories -- structural imaging and functional imaging.
Metabolism	Metabolism is the biochemical modification of chemical compounds in living organisms and cells.

Glucose	Glucose, a simple monosaccharide sugar, is one of the most important carbohydrates and is used as a source of energy in animals and plants. Glucose is one of the main products of photosynthesis and starts respiration.
Neurotransmitter	A neurotransmitter is a chemical that is used to relay, amplify and modulate electrical signals between a neurons and another cell.
Magnetic resonance imaging	Magnetic resonance imaging is a method of creating images of the inside of opaque organs in living organisms as well as detecting the amount of bound water in geological structures. It is primarily used to demonstrate pathological or other physiological alterations of living tissues and is a commonly used form of medical imaging.
Anatomy	Anatomy is the branch of biology that deals with the structure and organization of living things. It can be divided into animal anatomy (zootomy) and plant anatomy (phytonomy). Major branches of anatomy include comparative anatomy, histology, and human anatomy.
Positron emission tomography	Positron Emission Tomography measures emissions from radioactively labeled chemicals that have been injected into the bloodstream. The greatest benefit is that different compounds can show blood flow and oxygen and glucose metabolism in the tissues of the working brain.
White matter	White matter is one of the two main solid components of the central nervous system. It is composed of axons which connect various grey matter areas of the brain to each other and carry nerve impulses between neurons.
Tumor	A tumor is an abnormal growth that when located in the brain can either be malignant and directly destroy brain tissue, or be benign and disrupt functioning by increasing intracranial pressure.
Visual illusion	Visual illusion refers to a discrepancy or incongruency between reality and the perceptual representation of it.
Perception	Perception is the process of acquiring, interpreting, selecting, and organizing sensory information.
Affect	A subjective feeling or emotional tone often accompanied by bodily expressions noticeable to others is called affect.
Sensory deprivation	Sensory deprivation is the deliberate reduction or removal of stimuli from one or more of the senses. Though short periods of sensory deprivation can be relaxing, extended deprivation can result in extreme anxiety, hallucinations, bizarre thoughts, depression, and antisocial behavior.
Drug addiction	Drug addiction, or substance dependence is the compulsive use of drugs, to the point where the user has no effective choice but to continue use.
Threshold	In general, a threshold is a fixed location or value where an abrupt change is observed. In the sensory modalities, it is the minimum amount of stimulus energy necessary to elicit a sensory response.
Addiction	Addiction is an uncontrollable compulsion to repeat a behavior regardless of its consequences. Many drugs or behaviors can precipitate a pattern of conditions recognized as addiction, which include a craving for more of the drug or behavior, increased physiological tolerance to exposure, and withdrawal symptoms in the absence of the stimulus.
Chronic	Chronic refers to a relatively long duration, usually more than a few months.
Tremor	Tremor is the rhythmic, oscillating shaking movement of the whole body or just a certain part of it, caused by problems of the neurons responsible from muscle action.
Delirium tremens	Delirium tremens refers to a condition characterized by sweating, restlessness, disorientation, and hallucinations. It occurs in some chronic alcohol users when there is a

sudden decrease in usage.

Dementia	Dementia is progressive decline in cognitive function due to damage or disease in the brain beyond what might be expected from normal aging.
Habit	A habit is a response that has become completely separated from its eliciting stimulus. Early learning theorists used the term to describe S-R associations, however not all S-R associations become a habit, rather many are extinguished after reinforcement is withdrawn.
Personality trait	According to the Diagnostic and Statistical Manual of the American Psychiatric Association, a personality trait is a "prominent aspect of personality that is exhibited in a wide range of important social and personal contexts. ...".
Population	Population refers to all members of a well-defined group of organisms, events, or things.
Confabulation	Confabulation is the confusion of imagination with memory, or the confusion of true memories with false memories.
Senile dementia	Senile dementia is a state of mental deterioration caused by physical deterioration of the brain and characterized by impaired memory and intellect and by altered personality and behavior.
Visual acuity	Visual acuity is the eye's ability to detect fine details and is the quantitative measure of the eye's ability to see an in-focus image at a certain distance.
Executive function	The processes involved in regulating attention and in determining what to do with information just gathered or retrieved from long-term memory, is referred to as the executive function.
Survey	A method of scientific investigation in which a large sample of people answer questions about their attitudes or behavior is referred to as a survey.
Depression	In everyday language depression refers to any downturn in mood, which may be relatively transitory and perhaps due to something trivial. This is differentiated from Clinical depression which is marked by symptoms that last two weeks or more and are so severe that they interfere with daily living.
Short-term memory	Short-term memory is that part of memory which stores a limited amount of information for a limited amount of time (roughly 30-45 seconds). The second key concept associated with a short-term memory is that it has a finite capacity.
Long-term memory	Long-term memory is memory that lasts from over 30 seconds to years.
Presenile dementia	Dementia that appears before old age, between ages 40 and 60 is referred to as presenile dementia.
Seizure	A seizure is a temporary alteration in brain function expressed as a changed mental state, tonic or clonic movements and various other symptoms. They are due to temporary abnormal electrical activity of a group of brain cells.
Plaques	Plaques refer to small, round areas composed of remnants of lost neurons and beta-amyloid, a waxy protein deposit; present in the brains of patients with Alzheimer's disease.
Nerve	A nerve is an enclosed, cable-like bundle of nerve fibers or axons, which includes the glia that ensheath the axons in myelin. Neurons are sometimes called nerve cells, though this term is technically imprecise since many neurons do not form nerves.
Learning	Learning is a relatively permanent change in behavior that results from experience. Thus, to attribute a behavioral change to learning, the change must be relatively permanent and must result from experience.
Acetylcholine	The chemical compound acetylcholine was the first neurotransmitter to be identified. It plays a role in learning, memory, and rapid eye movement sleep and causes the skeletal muscle

fibers to contract.

Correlation	A statistical technique for determining the degree of association between two or more variables is referred to as correlation.
Receptor	A sensory receptor is a structure that recognizes a stimulus in the internal or external environment of an organism. In response to stimuli the sensory receptor initiates sensory transduction by creating graded potentials or action potentials in the same cell or in an adjacent one.
Hippocampus	The hippocampus is a part of the brain located inside the temporal lobe. It forms a part of the limbic system and plays a part in memory and navigation.
Gene	A gene is an ultramicroscopic area of the chromosome. It is the smallest physical unit of the DNA molecule that carries a piece of hereditary information.
Chromosome	The DNA which carries genetic information in biological cells is normally packaged in the form of one or more large macromolecules called a chromosome. Humans normally have 46.
Protein	A protein is a complex, high-molecular-weight organic compound that consists of amino acids joined by peptide bonds. It is essential to the structure and function of all living cells and viruses. Many are enzymes or subunits of enzymes.
Cholesterol	Cholesterol is a steroid, a lipid, and an alcohol, found in the cell membranes of all body tissues, and transported in the blood plasma of all animals. Cholesterol is an important component of the membranes of cells, providing stability; it makes the membrane's fluidity stable over a bigger temperature interval.
Genetic marker	A genetic marker is an inherited characteristic for which the chromosomal location of the responsible gene is known.
Stages	Stages represent relatively discrete periods of time in which functioning is qualitatively different from functioning at other periods.
Ion	An ion is an atom or group of atoms with a net electric charge. The energy required to detach an electron in its lowest energy state from an atom or molecule of a gas with less net electric charge is called the ionization potential, or ionization energy.
Role-playing	Role-playing refers to a technique that teaches people to behave in a certain way by encouraging them to pretend that they are in a particular situation; it helps people acquire complex behaviors in an efficient way.
Feedback	Feedback refers to information returned to a person about the effects a response has had.
Bipolar disorder	Bipolar Disorder is a mood disorder typically characterized by fluctuations between manic and depressive states; and, more generally, atypical mood regulation and mood instability.
Lithium	Lithium salts are used as mood stabilizing drugs primarily in the treatment of bipolar disorder, depression, and mania; but also in treating schizophrenia. Lithium is widely distributed in the central nervous system and interacts with a number of neurotransmitters and receptors, decreasing noradrenaline release and increasing serotonin synthesis.
Progestin	A hormone used to maintain pregnancy that can cause masculinization of the fetus is progestin.
Estrogen	Estrogen is a group of steroid compounds that function as the primary female sex hormone. They are produced primarily by developing follicles in the ovaries, the corpus luteum and the placenta.
Hormone	A hormone is a chemical messenger from one cell (or group of cells) to another. The best known are those produced by endocrine glands, but they are produced by nearly every organ

247

system. The function of hormones is to serve as a signal to the target cells; the action of the hormone is determined by the pattern of secretion and the signal transduction of the receiving tissue.

Sedative	A sedative is a drug that depresses the central nervous system (CNS), which causes calmness, relaxation, reduction of anxiety, sleepiness, slowed breathing, slurred speech, staggering gait, poor judgment, and slow, uncertain reflexes.
Dominant gene	In genetics, the term dominant gene refers to the allele that causes a phenotype that is seen in a heterozygous genotype.
Chorea	Chorea is the occurrence of continuous rapid, jerky, involuntary movements that may involve the face and limb and result in an inability to maintain a posture. It is also known as St. Vitus Dance disease and is seen mostly in children.
Delusion	A false belief, not generally shared by others, and that cannot be changed despite strong evidence to the contrary is a delusion.
Retrieval	Retrieval is the location of stored information and its subsequent return to consciousness. It is the third stage of information processing.
Intelligence test	An intelligence test is a standardized means of assessing a person's current mental ability, for example, the Stanford-Binet test and the Wechsler Adult Intelligence Scale.
Alcoholic	An alcoholic is dependent on alcohol as characterized by craving, loss of control, physical dependence and withdrawal symptoms, and tolerance.
Iris	The iris is the most visible part of the eye. The iris is an annulus (or flattened ring) consisting of pigmented fibrovascular tissue known as a stroma. The stroma connects a sphincter muscle, which contracts the pupil, and a set of dialator muscles which open it.
Clinical psychologist	A psychologist, usually with a Ph.D, whose training is in the diagnosis, treatment, or research of psychological and behavioral disorders is a clinical psychologist.
Genetic testing	Genetic testing allows the genetic diagnosis of vulnerabilities to inherited diseases, and can also be used to determine a person's ancestry. Every person carries two copies of every gene, one inherited from their mother, one inherited from their father.
Dopamine	Dopamine is critical to the way the brain controls our movements and is a crucial part of the basal ganglia motor loop. It is commonly associated with the 'pleasure system' of the brain, providing feelings of enjoyment and reinforcement to motivate us to do, or continue doing, certain activities.
Human genome	The complete sequence or mapping of genes in the human body and their locations is the human genome. It is made up of 23 chromosome pairs with a total of about 3 billion DNA base pairs.
Mutation	Mutation is a permanent, sometimes transmissible (if the change is to a germ cell) change to the genetic material (usually DNA or RNA) of a cell. They can be caused by copying errors in the genetic material during cell division and by exposure to radiation, chemicals, or viruses, or can occur deliberately under cellular control during the processes such as meiosis or hypermutation.
Glial	Glial cells are non-neuronal cells that provide support and nutrition, maintain homeostasis, form myelin, and participate in signal transmission in the nervous system.
Brain trauma	Brain Trauma, also called acquired brain injury, intracranial injury, or simply head injury, occurs when a sudden trauma causes damage to the brain.
Acute	Acute means sudden, sharp, and abrupt. Usually short in duration.
Chronic	Chronic disorders are characterized by slow onset and long duration. They are rare in early

Go to **Cram101.com** for the Practice Tests for this Chapter.

disorders	adulthood, they increase during middle adulthood, and they become common in late adulthood.
Concussion	Concussion, or mild traumatic brain injury (MTBI), is the most common and least serious type of brain injury. A milder type of diffuse axonal injury, concussion involves a transient loss of mental function. It can be caused by acceleration or deceleration forces, by a direct blow, or by penetrating injuries.
Contusion	Brain contusion, a form of traumatic brain injury, is a bruise of the brain tissue. Like bruises in other tissues, cerebral contusion can be caused by multiple microhemorrhages, small blood vessel leaks into brain tissue.
Psychological disorder	Mental processes and/or behavior patterns that cause emotional distress and/or substantial impairment in functioning is a psychological disorder.
Panic disorder	A panic attack is a period of intense fear or discomfort, typically with an abrupt onset and usually lasting no more than thirty minutes. The disorder is strikingly different from other types of anxiety, in that panic attacks are very sudden, appear to be unprovoked, and are often disabling. People who have repeated attacks, or feel severe anxiety about having another attack are said to have panic disorder.
Prognosis	A forecast about the probable course of an illess is referred to as prognosis.
Cognitive skills	Cognitive skills such as reasoning, attention, and memory can be advanced and sustained through practice and training.
Neurologist	A physician who studies the nervous system, especially its structure, functions, and abnormalities is referred to as neurologist.
Predisposition	Predisposition refers to an inclination or diathesis to respond in a certain way, either inborn or acquired. In abnormal psychology, it is a factor that lowers the ability to withstand stress and inclines the individual toward pathology.
Hypothesis	A specific statement about behavior or mental processes that is testable through research is a hypothesis.
Psychomotor retardation	Psychomotor retardation comprises a slowing down of thought and a reduction of physical movements in a person. This is most commonly seen in people with clinical depression where it indicates a degree of severity.
Mutism	Mutism refers to refusal or inability to talk.
Acute onset	Acute onset refers to the sudden beginning of a disease or disorder.
Central nervous system	The vertebrate central nervous system consists of the brain and spinal cord.
Syphilis	Syphilis is a sexually transmitted disease that is caused by a spirochaete bacterium, Treponema pallidum. If not treated, syphilis can cause serious effects such as damage to the nervous system, heart, or brain. Untreated syphilis can be ultimately fatal.
Cerebrospinal fluid	A solution that fills the hollow cavities of the brain and circulates around the brain and spinal cord is called cerebrospinal fluid.
Psychosis	Psychosis is a generic term for mental states in which the components of rational thought and perception are severely impaired. Persons experiencing a psychosis may experience hallucinations, hold paranoid or delusional beliefs, demonstrate personality changes and exhibit disorganized thinking. This is usually accompanied by features such as a lack of insight into the unusual or bizarre nature of their behavior, difficulties with social interaction and impairments in carrying out the activities of daily living.
Negative	An inverse relationship, often called a negative relationship, occurs when increases in one

relationship	variable are matched by decreases in another variable.
Amnestic disorder	Deterioration in the ability to transfer information from short- to long-term memory, in the absence of other dementia symptoms is called an amnestic disorder.
Cerebrovascular accident	Cerebrovascular accident refers to a sudden stoppage of blood flow to a portion of the brain, leading to a loss of brain function.
Epilepsy	Epilepsy is a chronic neurological condition characterized by recurrent unprovoked neural discharges. It is commonly controlled with medication, although surgical methods are used as well.
Cerebrum	The cerebrum (the portion of the brain that performs motor and sensory functions and a variety of mental activities) is divided into four lobes - the frontal, temporal, parietal and occipital lobes.
Antidepressant	An antidepressant is a medication used primarily in the treatment of clinical depression. They are not thought to produce tolerance, although sudden withdrawal may produce adverse effects. They create little if any immediate change in mood and require between several days and several weeks to take effect.
Multi-infarct dementia	Multi-infarct dementia can result from brain damage caused by stroke or transient ischemic attacks (also known as mini-strokes). It is characterized by sporadic and progressive loss of intellectual functioning caused by repeated temporary obstruction of blood flow in cerebral arteries.
Vascular dementia	Vascular dementia is a form of dementia resulting from brain damage caused by stroke or transient ischemic attacks (also known as mini-strokes). The specific symptoms will depend on the part of the brain damaged by the stroke or mini-stroke.
Impulse control	Deferred gratification is the ability of a person to wait for things they want. This trait is critical for life success. Those who lack this trait are said to suffer from poor impulse control, and often become criminals, as they are unwilling to work and wait for their paycheck.
Hypertension	Hypertension is a medical condition where the blood pressure in the arteries is chronically elevated. Persistent hypertension is one of the risk factors for strokes, heart attacks, heart failure and arterial aneurysm, and is a leading cause of chronic renal failure.
Syndrome	The term syndrome is the association of several clinically recognizable features, signs, symptoms, phenomena or characteristics which often occur together, so that the presence of one feature indicates the presence of the others.
Alcoholism	A disorder that involves long-term, repeated, uncontrolled, compulsive, and excessive use of alcoholic beverages and that impairs the drinker's health and work and social relationships is called alcoholism.
Thiamine	Thiamine, also known as vitamin B1, is a colorless compound with chemical formula $C_{12}H_{17}CIN_4OS$. Systemic thiamine deficiency can lead to myriad problems including neurodegeneration, wasting, and death. Well-known syndromes caused by lack of thiamine due to malnutrition or a diet high in thiaminase-rich foods include Wernicke-Korsakoff syndrome and beriberi, diseases also common in chronic abusers of alcohol.
Altered state of consciousness	Altered state of consciousness refers to a mental state other than ordinary waking consciousness, such as sleep, meditation, hypnosis, or a drug-induced state.
Hippocrates	Hippocrates was an ancient Greek physician, commonly regarded as one of the most outstanding figures in medicine of all time; he has been called "the father of medicine."

Go to **Cram101.com** for the Practice Tests for this Chapter.

Pathology	Pathology is the study of the processes underlying disease and other forms of illness, harmful abnormality, or dysfunction.
Guilt	Guilt describes many concepts related to a negative emotion or condition caused by actions which are believed to be, morally wrong. According to Freud, the avoidance of guilt is the basis for moral behavior.
Psychotherapy	Psychotherapy is a set of techniques based on psychological principles intended to improve mental health, emotional or behavioral issues.
Psychodynamic	Most psychodynamic approaches are centered around the idea of a maladapted function developed early in life (usually childhood) which are at least in part unconscious. This maladapted function (a.k.a. defense mechanism) does not do well in place of a normal/healthy one.
Socioeconomic Status	A family's socioeconomic status is based on family income, parental education level, parental occupation, and social status in the community. Those with high status often have more success in preparing their children for school because they have access to a wide range of resources.
Congenital	A condition existing at birth is referred to as congenital.
Prenatal	Prenatal period refers to the time from conception to birth.
Attitude	An enduring mental representation of a person, place, or thing that evokes an emotional response and related behavior is called attitude.
Amnesia	Amnesia is a condition in which memory is disturbed. The causes of amnesia are organic or functional. Organic causes include damage to the brain, through trauma or disease, or use of certain (generally sedative) drugs.
Schizophrenia	Schizophrenia is characterized by persistent defects in the perception or expression of reality. A person suffering from untreated schizophrenia typically demonstrates grossly disorganized thinking, and may also experience delusions or auditory hallucinations
Neurosis	Neurosis, any mental disorder that, although may cause distress, does not interfere with rational thought or the persons' ability to function.

Delusion	A false belief, not generally shared by others, and that cannot be changed despite strong evidence to the contrary is a delusion.
Perception	Perception is the process of acquiring, interpreting, selecting, and organizing sensory information.
Alcoholic	An alcoholic is dependent on alcohol as characterized by craving, loss of control, physical dependence and withdrawal symptoms, and tolerance.
Free will	The idea that human beings are capable of freely making choices or decisions is free will.
Consciousness	The awareness of the sensations, thoughts, and feelings being experienced at a given moment is called consciousness.
Emotion	An emotion is a mental states that arise spontaneously, rather than through conscious effort. They are often accompanied by physiological changes.
Affect	A subjective feeling or emotional tone often accompanied by bodily expressions noticeable to others is called affect.
Psychoactive substance	A psychoactive substance is a chemical that alters brain function, resulting in temporary changes in perception, mood, consciousness, or behavior. Such drugs are often used for recreational and spiritual purposes, as well as in medicine, especially for treating neurological and psychological illnesses.
Goal-directed behavior	Goal-directed behavior is means-end problem solving behavior. In the infant, such behavior is first observed in the latter part of the first year.
Substance abuse	Substance abuse refers to the overindulgence in and dependence on a stimulant, depressant, or other chemical substance, leading to effects that are detrimental to the individual's physical or mental health, or the welfare of others.
Addiction	Addiction is an uncontrollable compulsion to repeat a behavior regardless of its consequences. Many drugs or behaviors can precipitate a pattern of conditions recognized as addiction, which include a craving for more of the drug or behavior, increased physiological tolerance to exposure, and withdrawal symptoms in the absence of the stimulus.
Cocaine	Cocaine is a crystalline tropane alkaloid that is obtained from the leaves of the coca plant. It is a stimulant of the central nervous system and an appetite suppressant, creating what has been described as a euphoric sense of happiness and increased energy.
Heroin	Heroin is widely and illegally used as a powerful and addictive drug producing intense euphoria, which often disappears with increasing tolerance. Heroin is a semi-synthetic opioid. It is the 3,6-diacetyl derivative of morphine and is synthesised from it by acetylation.
Substance dependence	Drug addiction, or substance dependence is the compulsive use of drugs, to the point where the user has no effective choice but to continue use.
Maladaptive	In psychology, a behavior or trait is adaptive when it helps an individual adjust and function well within their social environment. A maladaptive behavior or trait is counterproductive to the individual.
Nervous system	The body's electrochemical communication circuitry, made up of billions of neurons is a nervous system.
Withdrawal symptoms	Withdrawal symptoms are physiological changes that occur when the use of a drug is stopped or dosage decreased.
Morphine	Morphine, the principal active agent in opium, is a powerful opioid analgesic drug. According to recent research, it may also be produced naturally by the human brain. Morphine is usually

Go to **Cram101.com** for the Practice Tests for this Chapter.

highly addictive, and tolerance and physical and psychological dependence develop quickly.

Syndrome	The term syndrome is the association of several clinically recognizable features, signs, symptoms, phenomena or characteristics which often occur together, so that the presence of one feature indicates the presence of the others.
Cell membrane	A component of every biological cell, the selectively permeable cell membrane is a thin and structured bilayer of phospholipid and protein molecules that envelopes the cell. It separates a cell's interior from its surroundings and controls what moves in and out.
Brain	The brain controls and coordinates most movement, behavior and homeostatic body functions such as heartbeat, blood pressure, fluid balance and body temperature. Functions of the brain are responsible for cognition, emotion, memory, motor learning and other sorts of learning. The brain is primarily made up of two types of cells: glia and neurons.
Amphetamine	Amphetamine is a synthetic stimulant used to suppress the appetite, control weight, and treat disorders including narcolepsy and ADHD. It is also used recreationally and for performance enhancement.
Anxiety	Anxiety is a complex combination of the feeling of fear, apprehension and worry often accompanied by physical sensations such as palpitations, chest pain and/or shortness of breath.
Tremor	Tremor is the rhythmic, oscillating shaking movement of the whole body or just a certain part of it, caused by problems of the neurons responsible from muscle action.
Central nervous system	The vertebrate central nervous system consists of the brain and spinal cord.
Mental disorder	Mental disorder refers to a disturbance in a person's emotions, drives, thought processes, or behavior that involves serious and relatively prolonged distress and/or impairment in ability to function, is not simply a normal response to some event or set of events in the person's environment.
Personality	Personality refers to the pattern of enduring characteristics that differentiates a person, the patterns of behaviors that make each individual unique.
Substance-related disorders	Substance-related disorders involve drugs such as alcohol and cocaine that are abused to such an extent that behavior becomes maladaptive. Social and occupational functioning are impaired, and control or abstinence becomes impossible.
Depressant	A depressant is a chemical agent that diminishes a body function or activity. The term is used in particular with regard to the central nervous system where these chemicals are known as neurotransmitters. They tend to act on the CNS by increasing the activity of a particular neurotransmitter known as gamma-aminobutyric acid (GABA).
Nerve	A nerve is an enclosed, cable-like bundle of nerve fibers or axons, which includes the glia that ensheath the axons in myelin. Neurons are sometimes called nerve cells, though this term is technically imprecise since many neurons do not form nerves.
Frontal lobe	The frontal lobe comprises four major folds of cortical tissue: the precentral gyrus, superior gyrus and the middle gyrus of the frontal gyri, the inferior frontal gyrus. It has been found to play a part in impulse control, judgement, language, memory, motor function, problem solving, sexual behavior, socialization and spontaneity.
Reasoning	Reasoning is the act of using reason to derive a conclusion from certain premises. There are two main methods to reach a conclusion, deductive reasoning and inductive reasoning.
Cerebellum	The cerebellum is located in the inferior posterior portion of the head (the hindbrain), directly dorsal to the brainstem and pons, inferior to the occipital lobe. The cerebellum is

Go to **Cram101.com** for the Practice Tests for this Chapter.

259

	a region of the brain that plays an important role in the integration of sensory perception and fine motor output.
Senses	The senses are systems that consist of a sensory cell type that respond to a specific kind of physical energy, and that correspond to a defined region within the brain where the signals are received and interpreted.
Acute	Acute means sudden, sharp, and abrupt. Usually short in duration.
Pupil	In the eye, the pupil is the opening in the middle of the iris. It appears black because most of the light entering it is absorbed by the tissues inside the eye. The size of the pupil is controlled by involuntary contraction and dilation of the iris, in order to regulate the intensity of light entering the eye. This is known as the pupillary reflex.
Hallucination	A hallucination is a sensory perception experienced in the absence of an external stimulus, as distinct from an illusion, which is a misperception of an external stimulus. They may occur in any sensory modality - visual, auditory, olfactory, gustatory, tactile, or mixed.
Paranoid	The term paranoid is typically used in a general sense to signify any self-referential delusion, or more specifically, to signify a delusion involving the fear of persecution.
Psychosis	Psychosis is a generic term for mental states in which the components of rational thought and perception are severely impaired. Persons experiencing a psychosis may experience hallucinations, hold paranoid or delusional beliefs, demonstrate personality changes and exhibit disorganized thinking. This is usually accompanied by features such as a lack of insight into the unusual or bizarre nature of their behavior, difficulties with social interaction and impairments in carrying out the activities of daily living.
Jung	Jung was in some aspects a response to Sigmund Freud's psychoanalysis. He proposed and developed the concepts of the extroverted and introverted personality, archetypes, and the collective unconscious. His work has been influential in psychiatry and in the study of religion, literature, and related fields.
Ethnic group	An ethnic group is a culture or subculture whose members are readily distinguishable by outsiders based on traits originating from a common racial, national, linguistic, or religious source. Members of an ethnic group are often presumed to be culturally or biologically similar, although this is not in fact necessarily the case.
Acculturation	Acculturation is the obtainment of culture by an individual or a group of people.
Population	Population refers to all members of a well-defined group of organisms, events, or things.
Alcoholism	A disorder that involves long-term, repeated, uncontrolled, compulsive, and excessive use of alcoholic beverages and that impairs the drinker's health and work and social relationships is called alcoholism.
Statistics	Statistics is a type of data analysis which practice includes the planning, summarizing, and interpreting of observations of a system possibly followed by predicting or forecasting of future events based on a mathematical model of the system being observed.
Statistic	A statistic is an observable random variable of a sample.
Metabolic rate	Metabolic rate refers to the rate at which the body burns calories to produce energy.
Chronic	Chronic refers to a relatively long duration, usually more than a few months.
Placenta	A membrane that permits the exchange of nutrients and waste products between the mother and her developing child but does not allow the maternal and fetal bloodstreams to mix is the placenta.
Fetus	A fetus develops from the end of the 8th week of pregnancy (when the major structures have

formed), until birth.

Fetal alcohol syndrome	A cluster of abnormalities that appears in the offspring of mothers who drink alcohol heavily during pregnancy is called fetal alcohol syndrome.
Binge drinking	Binge drinking refers to consuming 5 or more drinks in a short time or drinking alchohol for the sole purpose of intoxication.
Comorbidity	Comorbidity refers to the presence of more than one mental disorder occurring in an individual at the same time.
Hormone	A hormone is a chemical messenger from one cell (or group of cells) to another. The best known are those produced by endocrine glands, but they are produced by nearly every organ system. The function of hormones is to serve as a signal to the target cells; the action of the hormone is determined by the pattern of secretion and the signal transduction of the receiving tissue.
Theories	Theories are logically self-consistent models or frameworks describing the behavior of a certain natural or social phenomenon. They are broad explanations and predictions concerning phenomena of interest.
Detoxification	Detoxification in general is the removal of toxic substances from the body. It is one of the functions of the liver and kidneys, but can also be achieved artificially by techniques such as dialysis and (in a very limited number of cases) chelation therapy.
Delirium	Delirium is a medical term used to describe an acute decline in attention and cognition. Delirium is probably the single most common acute disorder affecting adults in general hospitals. It affects 10-20% of all adults in hospital, and 30-40% of older patients.
Society	The social sciences use the term society to mean a group of people that form a semi-closed (or semi-open) social system, in which most interactions are with other individuals belonging to the group.
Physical dependence	Physical dependence describes increased tolerance of a drug combined with a physical need of the drug to function. Abrupt cessation of the drug is typically associated with negative physical withdrawal symptoms. Physical dependence is distinguished from addiction. While addiction tends to describe psychological and behavioral attributes, physical dependence is defined primarily using physical and biological concepts.
Attention	Attention is the cognitive process of selectively concentrating on one thing while ignoring other things. Psychologists have labeled three types of attention: sustained attention, selective attention, and divided attention.
Metabolism	Metabolism is the biochemical modification of chemical compounds in living organisms and cells.
Enzyme	An enzyme is a protein that catalyzes, or speeds up, a chemical reaction. Enzymes are essential to sustain life because most chemical reactions in biological cells would occur too slowly, or would lead to different products, without enzymes.
Denial	Denial is a psychological defense mechanism in which a person faced with a fact that is uncomfortable or painful to accept rejects it instead, insisting that it is not true despite what may be overwhelming evidence.
Liver	The liver plays a major role in metabolism and has a number of functions in the body including detoxification, glycogen storage and plasma protein synthesis. It also produces bile, which is important for digestion. The liver converts most carbohydrates, proteing, and fats into glucose.
Gender	A gender difference is a disparity between genders involving quality or quantity. Though some

Go to **Cram101.com** for the Practice Tests for this Chapter.

difference	gender differences are controversial, they are not to be confused with sexist stereotypes.
Heredity	Heredity is the transfer of characteristics from parent to offspring through their genes.
Predisposition	Predisposition refers to an inclination or diathesis to respond in a certain way, either inborn or acquired. In abnormal psychology, it is a factor that lowers the ability to withstand stress and inclines the individual toward pathology.
Gene	A gene is an ultramicroscopic area of the chromosome. It is the smallest physical unit of the DNA molecule that carries a piece of hereditary information.
Neurotransmitter	A neurotransmitter is a chemical that is used to relay, amplify and modulate electrical signals between a neurons and another cell.
Neuron	The neuron is the primary cell of the nervous system. They are found in the brain, the spinal cord, in the nerves and ganglia of the peripheral nervous system. It is a specialized cell that conducts impulses through the nervous system and contains three major parts: cell body, dendrites, and an axon. It can have many dendrites but only one axon.
Receptor	A sensory receptor is a structure that recognizes a stimulus in the internal or external environment of an organism. In response to stimuli the sensory receptor initiates sensory transduction by creating graded potentials or action potentials in the same cell or in an adjacent one.
Synapse	A synapse is specialized junction through which cells of the nervous system signal to one another and to non-neuronal cells such as muscles or glands.
Protein	A protein is a complex, high-molecular-weight organic compound that consists of amino acids joined by peptide bonds. It is essential to the structure and function of all living cells and viruses. Many are enzymes or subunits of enzymes.
Nerve impulse	A nerve impulse is a change in the electric potential of a neuron; a wave of depolarization spreads along the neuron and causes the release of a neurotransmitter.
Ion	An ion is an atom or group of atoms with a net electric charge. The energy required to detach an electron in its lowest energy state from an atom or molecule of a gas with less net electric charge is called the ionization potential, or ionization energy.
Reinforcement	In operant conditioning, reinforcement is any change in an environment that (a) occurs after the behavior, (b) seems to make that behavior re-occur more often in the future and (c) that reoccurence of behavior must be the result of the change.
Brain imaging	Brain imaging is a fairly recent discipline within medicine and neuroscience. Brain imaging falls into two broad categories -- structural imaging and functional imaging.
Naltrexone	Naltrexone is an opioid receptor antagonist used primarily in the management of alcohol dependence and opioid dependence. It is marketed as its hydrochloride salt, naltrexone hydrochloride, under the trade name Revia.
Motivation	In psychology, motivation is the driving force (desire) behind all actions of an organism.
Disulfiram	Disulfiram is a drug used to support the treatment of chronic alcoholism by producing an acute sensitivity to alcohol.
Psychodynamic	Most psychodynamic approaches are centered around the idea of a maladapted function developed early in life (usually childhood) which are at least in part unconscious. This maladapted function (a.k.a. defense mechanism) does not do well in place of a normal/healthy one.
Longitudinal research	Research that studies the same subjects over an extended period of time, usually several years or more, is called longitudinal research.
Adolescence	The period of life bounded by puberty and the assumption of adult responsibilities is

Go to **Cram101.com** for the Practice Tests for this Chapter.

adolescence.

Friendship	The essentials of friendship are reciprocity and commitment between individuals who see themselves more or less as equals. Interaction between friends rests on a more equal power base than the interaction between children and adults.
Psychoanalyst	A psychoanalyst is a specially trained therapist who attempts to treat the individual by uncovering and revealing to the individual otherwise subconscious factors that are contributing to some undesirable behavor.
Self-concept	Self-concept refers to domain-specific evaluations of the self where a domain may be academics, athletics, etc.
Self-worth	In psychology, self-esteem or self-worth refers to a person's subjective appraisal of himself or herself as intrinsically positive or negative to some degree.
Variable	A variable refers to a measurable factor, characteristic, or attribute of an individual or a system.
Psychotherapy	Psychotherapy is a set of techniques based on psychological principles intended to improve mental health, emotional or behavioral issues.
Clinician	A health professional authorized to provide services to people suffering from one or more pathologies is a clinician.
Cognition	The intellectual processes through which information is obtained, transformed, stored, retrieved, and otherwise used is cognition.
Learning	Learning is a relatively permanent change in behavior that results from experience. Thus, to attribute a behavioral change to learning, the change must be relatively permanent and must result from experience.
Negative reinforcer	Negative reinforcer is a reinforcer that when removed increases the frequency of an response.
Positive reinforcer	In operant conditioning, a stimulus that is presented after a response that increases the likelihood that the response will be repeated is a positive reinforcer.
Sensation	Sensation is the first stage in the chain of biochemical and neurologic events that begins with the impinging of a stimulus upon the receptor cells of a sensory organ, which then leads to perception, the mental state that is reflected in statements like "I see a uniformly blue wall."
Norepinephrine	Norepinephrine is released from the adrenal glands as a hormone into the blood, but it is also a neurotransmitter in the nervous system. As a stress hormone, it affects parts of the human brain where attention and impulsivity are controlled. Along with epinephrine, this compound effects the fight-or-flight response, activating the sympathetic nervous system to directly increase heart rate, release energy from fat, and increase muscle readiness.
Peptides	Peptides are the family of molecules formed from the linking, in a defined order, of various amino acids.
Dopamine	Dopamine is critical to the way the brain controls our movements and is a crucial part of the basal ganglia motor loop. It is commonly associated with the 'pleasure system' of the brain, providing feelings of enjoyment and reinforcement to motivate us to do, or continue doing, certain activities.
Opioid	An opioid is any agent that binds to opioid receptors, found principally in the central nervous system and gastrointestinal tract.
Social anxiety	A feeling of apprehension in the presence of others is social anxiety.

Go to **Cram101.com** for the Practice Tests for this Chapter.

Depression	In everyday language depression refers to any downturn in mood, which may be relatively transitory and perhaps due to something trivial. This is differentiated from Clinical depression which is marked by symptoms that last two weeks or more and are so severe that they interfere with daily living.
Cognitive approach	A cognitive approach focuses on the mental processes involved in knowing: how we direct our attention, perceive, remember, think, and solve problems.
Cognitive-behavioral therapy	Cognitive-behavioral therapy refers to group of treatment procedures aimed at identifying and modifying faulty thought processes, attitudes and attributions, and problem behaviors.
Aversive conditioning	A behavior therapy technique in which undesired responses are inhibited by pairing offensive stimuli with them is aversive conditioning.
Classical conditioning	Classical conditioning is a simple form of learning in which an organism comes to associate or anticipate events. A neutral stimulus comes to evoke the response usually evoked by a natural or unconditioned stimulus by being paired repeatedly with the unconditioned stimulus.
Unconditioned response	An Unconditioned Response is the response elicited to an unconditioned stimulus. It is a natural, automatic response.
Unconditioned stimulus	In classical conditioning, an unconditioned stimulus elicits a response from an organism prior to conditioning. It is a naturally occurring stimulus and a naturally occurring response..
Conditioned stimulus	A previously neutral stimulus that elicits the conditioned response because of being repeatedly paired with a stimulus that naturally elicited that response, is called a conditioned stimulus.
Aversive stimulus	A stimulus that elicits pain, fear, or avoidance is an aversive stimulus.
Operant Conditioning	A simple form of learning in which an organism learns to engage in behavior because it is reinforced is referred to as operant conditioning. The consequences of a behavior produce changes in the probability of the behavior's occurence.
Habit	A habit is a response that has become completely separated from its eliciting stimulus. Early learning theorists used the term to describe S-R associations, however not all S-R associations become a habit, rather many are extinguished after reinforcement is withdrawn.
Conditioning	Conditioning describes the process by which behaviors can be learned or modified through interaction with the environment.
Covert sensitization	A form of aversion therapy in which the person is told to imagine undesirably attractive situations and activities while unpleasant feelings are being induced by imagery is covert sensitization.
Conditioned aversion	A learned dislike or conditioned negative emotional response to a particular stimulus is a conditioned aversion.
Controlled drinking	A behavioral approach to the treatment of alcoholism, designed to teach the skills necessary so that alcoholics can drink socially without losing control is referred to as controlled drinking.
Stages	Stages represent relatively discrete periods of time in which functioning is qualitatively different from functioning at other periods.
Relapse prevention	Extending therapeutic progress by teaching the client how to cope with future troubling situations is a relapse prevention technique.

Self-efficacy	Self-efficacy is the belief that one has the capabilities to execute the courses of actions required to manage prospective situations.
Guilt	Guilt describes many concepts related to a negative emotion or condition caused by actions which are believed to be, morally wrong. According to Freud, the avoidance of guilt is the basis for moral behavior.
Control group	A group that does not receive the treatment effect in an experiment is referred to as the control group or sometimes as the comparison group.
Social support	Social Support is the physical and emotional comfort given by family, friends, co-workers and others. Research has identified three main types of social support: emotional, practical, sharing points of view.
Psychopathology	Psychopathology refers to the field concerned with the nature and development of mental disorders.
Feedback	Feedback refers to information returned to a person about the effects a response has had.
Empathy	Empathy is the recognition and understanding of the states of mind, including beliefs, desires and particularly emotions of others without injecting your own.
Attitude	An enduring mental representation of a person, place, or thing that evokes an emotional response and related behavior is called attitude.
Early adulthood	The developmental period beginning in the late teens or early twenties and lasting into the thirties is called early adulthood; characterized by an increasing self-awareness.
Mood disorder	A mood disorder is a condition where the prevailing emotional mood is distorted or inappropriate to the circumstances.
Psychoactive drug	A psychoactive drug or psychotropic substance is a chemical that alters brain function, resulting in temporary changes in perception, mood, consciousness, or behavior. Such drugs are often used for recreational and spiritual purposes, as well as in medicine, especially for treating neurological and psychological illnesses.
Phencyclidine	Phencyclidine is a dissociative psychedelic drug formerly used as an anaesthetic agent. Although the primary psychoactive effects of the drug only last hours, total elimination from the body is prolonged, typically extending over weeks.
Hallucinogen	Certain drugs can affect the subjective qualities of perception, thought or emotion, resulting in altered interpretations of sensory input, alternate states of consciousness, or hallucinations. The term hallucinogen is often broadly applied, especially in current scientific literature, to some or all of these substances.
Tranquilizer	A sedative, or tranquilizer, is a drug that depresses the central nervous system (CNS), which causes calmness, relaxation, reduction of anxiety, sleepiness, slowed breathing, slurred speech, staggering gait, poor judgment, and slow, uncertain reflexes.
Barbiturate	A barbiturate is a drug that acts as a central nervous system (CNS) depressant, and by virtue of this produces a wide spectrum of effects, from mild sedation to anesthesia.
Marijuana	Marijuana is the dried vegetable matter of the Cannabis sativa plant. It contains large concentrations of compounds that have medicinal and psychoactive effects when consumed, usually by smoking or eating.
Nicotine	Nicotine is an organic compound, an alkaloid found naturally throughout the tobacco plant, with a high concentration in the leaves. It is a potent nerve poison and is included in many insecticides. In lower concentrations, the substance is a stimulant and is one of the main factors leading to the pleasure and habit-forming qualities of tobacco smoking.

Go to **Cram101.com** for the Practice Tests for this Chapter.

Insomnia	Insomnia is a sleep disorder characterized by an inability to sleep and/or to remain asleep for a reasonable period during the night.
Insight	Insight refers to a sudden awareness of the relationships among various elements that had previously appeared to be independent of one another.
Psychological dependence	Psychological dependence may lead to psychological withdrawal symptoms. Addictions can theoretically form for any rewarding behavior, or as a habitual means to avoid undesired activity, but typically they only do so to a clinical level in individuals who have emotional, social, or psychological dysfunctions, taking the place of normal positive stimuli not otherwise attained
Opium	Opium is a narcotic analgesic drug which is obtained from the unripe seed pods of the opium poppy. Regular use, even for a few days, invariably leads to physical tolerance and dependence. Various degrees of psychological addiction can occur, though this is relatively rare when opioids are properly used..
Narcotic	The term narcotic originally referred to a variety of substances that induced sleep (such state is narcosis). In legal context, narcotic refers to opium, opium derivatives, and their semisynthetic or totally synthetic substitutes.
Pituitary gland	The pituitary gland is an endocrine gland about the size of a pea that sits in the small, bony cavity at the base of the brain. The pituitary gland secretes hormones regulating a wide variety of bodily activities, including trophic hormones that stimulate other endocrine glands.
Enkephalins	Opiate-like brain chemicals that regulate reactions to pain and stress are enkephalins.
Endorphin	An endorphin is an endogenous opioid biochemical compound. They are peptides produced by the pituitary gland and the hypothalamus, and they resemble the opiates in their abilities to produce analgesia and a sense of well-being. In other words, they work as "natural pain killers."
Receptor site	A location on the dendrite of a receiving neuron that is tailored to receive a specific neurotransmitter is a receptor site.
Spinal cord	The spinal cord is a part of the vertebrate nervous system that is enclosed in and protected by the vertebral column (it passes through the spinal canal). It consists of nerve cells. The spinal cord carries sensory signals and motor innervation to most of the skeletal muscles in the body.
Analgesia	Analgesia refers to insensitivity to pain without loss of consciousness.
Opiates	A group of narcotics derived from the opium poppy that provide a euphoric rush and depress the nervous system are referred to as opiates.
Reliability	Reliability means the extent to which a test produces a consistent , reproducible score .
Epilepsy	Epilepsy is a chronic neurological condition characterized by recurrent unprovoked neural discharges. It is commonly controlled with medication, although surgical methods are used as well.
Diabetes	Diabetes is a medical disorder characterized by varying or persistent elevated blood sugar levels, especially after eating. All types of diabetes share similar symptoms and complications at advanced stages: dehydration and ketoacidosis, cardiovascular disease, chronic renal failure, retinal damage which can lead to blindness, nerve damage which can lead to erectile dysfunction, gangrene with risk of amputation of toes, feet, and even legs.
Sedative	A sedative is a drug that depresses the central nervous system (CNS), which causes calmness, relaxation, reduction of anxiety, sleepiness, slowed breathing, slurred speech, staggering

gait, poor judgment, and slow, uncertain reflexes.

Psychiatrist	A psychiatrist is a physician who specializes in the diagnosis and treatment of psychological disorders.
Stress-induced analgesia	Stress-induced analgesia refers to the reduced sensitivity to pain that occurs when one is subjected to highly arousing conditions.
Suicide	Suicide behavior is rare in childhood but escalates in adolescence. The suicide rate increases in a linear fashion from adolescence through late adulthood.
Anxiety disorder	Anxiety disorder is a blanket term covering several different forms of abnormal anxiety, fear, phobia and nervous condition, that come on suddenly and prevent pursuing normal daily routines.
Methadone	Methadone is a synthetic heroin substitute used for treating heroin addicts that acts as a substitute for heroin by eliminating its effects and the craving for it. Just like heroin, tolerance and dependence frequently develop.
Withdrawal effects	Withdrawal effects refer to the physiological, mental, and behavioral disturbances that can occur when a long-term user of a drug stops taking the drug.
Placebo	Placebo refers to a bogus treatment that has the appearance of being genuine.
Family therapy	Family therapy is a branch of psychotherapy that treats family problems. Family therapists consider the family as a system of interacting members; as such, the problems in the family are seen to arise as an emergent property of the interactions in the system, rather than ascribed exclusively to the "faults" or psychological problems of individual members.
Sigmund Freud	Sigmund Freud was the founder of the psychoanalytic school, based on his theory that unconscious motives control much behavior, that particular kinds of unconscious thoughts and memories are the source of neurosis, and that neurosis could be treated through bringing these unconscious thoughts and memories to consciousness in psychoanalytic treatment.
Local anesthetic	Local anesthetic drugs act mainly by inhibiting sodium influx through sodium-specific ion channels in the neuronal cell membrane, in particular the so-called voltage-gated sodium channels. When the influx of sodium is interrupted, an action potential cannot arise and signal conduction is thus inhibited.
Stimulant	A stimulant is a drug which increases the activity of the sympathetic nervous system and produces a sense of euphoria or awakeness.
Adrenaline	Adrenaline refers to a hormone produced by the adrenal medulla that stimulates sympathetic ANS activity and generally arouses people and heightens their emotional responsiveness.
Cerebral cortex	The cerebral cortex is the outermost layer of the cerebrum and has a grey color. It is made up of four lobes and it is involved in many complex brain functions including memory, perceptual awareness, "thinking", language and consciousness. The cerebral cortex receives sensory information from many different sensory organs eg: eyes, ears, etc. and processes the information.
Hypothalamus	The hypothalamus is a region of the brain located below the thalamus, forming the major portion of the ventral region of the diencephalon and functioning to regulate certain metabolic processes and other autonomic activities.
Paranoid schizophrenia	Paranoid schizophrenia is a type of schizophrenia characterized primarily by delusions-commonly of persecution-and by vivid hallucinations .
Hyperactivity	Hyperactivity can be described as a state in which a individual is abnormally easily excitable and exuberant. Strong emotional reactions and a very short span of attention is also typical for the individual.

Go to **Cram101.com** for the Practice Tests for this Chapter.

Paranoia	In popular culture, the term paranoia is usually used to describe excessive concern about one's own well-being, sometimes suggesting a person holds persecutory beliefs concerning a threat to themselves or their property and is often linked to a belief in conspiracy theories.
Mania	Mania is a medical condition characterized by severely elevated mood. Mania is most usually associated with bipolar disorder, where episodes of mania may cyclically alternate with episodes of depression.
Stroke	A stroke occurs when the blood supply to a part of the brain is suddenly interrupted by occlusion, by hemorrhage, or other causes
Domestic violence	Domestic violence is any violence between current or former partners in an intimate relationship, wherever and whenever the violence occurs. The violence may include physical, sexual, emotional or financial abuse.
Emotional abuse	There is no single accepted definition of emotional abuse which, like other forms of violence in a relationship, is based on power and domination.
Sympathetic	The sympathetic nervous system activates what is often termed the "fight or flight response". It is an automatic regulation system, that is, one that operates without the intervention of conscious thought.
Desensitization	Desensitization refers to the type of sensory or behavioral adaptation in which we become less sensitive to constant stimuli.
Incentive	An incentive is what is expected once a behavior is performed. An incentive acts as a reinforcer.
Antipsychotic	The term antipsychotic is applied to a group of drugs used to treat psychosis.
Critical thinking	Critical thinking is a mental process of analyzing or evaluating information, particularly statements or propositions that are offered as true.
Cardiovascular system	The human cardiovascular system comprises the blood, the heart, and a dual-circuit system of blood vessels that serve as conduits between the heart, the lungs, and the peripheral tissues of the body.
Psychedelic	A psychedelic experience is characterized by the perception of aspects of one's mind previously unknown, or by the creative exuberance of the mind.
Displacement	An unconscious defense mechanism in which the individual directs aggressive or sexual feelings away from the primary object to someone or something safe is referred to as displacement. Displacement in linguistics is simply the ability to talk about things not present.
Tactile	Pertaining to the sense of touch is referred to as tactile.
Hallucinogenic	Certain drugs can affect the subjective qualities of perception, thought or emotion, resulting in altered interpretations of sensory input, alternate states of consciousness, or hallucinations. The term hallucinogenic is often broadly applied, especially in current scientific literature, to some or all of these substances.
Psilocybin	A psychedelic drug extracted from the mushroom Psilocybe mexicana is called psilocybin. At low doses, hallucinatory effects occur, including walls that seem to breathe, a vivid enhancement of colors and the animation of organic shapes. At higher doses, experiences tend to be less social and more entheogenic, often catalyzing intense spiritual experiences.
Mescaline	Mescaline refers to a hallucinogenic drug derived from the mescal cactus. Users typically experience visual hallucinations and radically altered states of consciousness, often experienced as pleasurable and illuminating but occasionally as accompanied by feelings of

anxiety or revulsion.

Peyote	Peyote is a hallucinogen obtained from the root of the peyote cactus. The active ingredient is mescaline, an alkaloid.
Physiological changes	Alterations in heart rate, blood pressure, perspiration, and other involuntary responses are physiological changes.
Schizophrenia	Schizophrenia is characterized by persistent defects in the perception or expression of reality. A person suffering from untreated schizophrenia typically demonstrates grossly disorganized thinking, and may also experience delusions or auditory hallucinations
Psychotic behavior	A psychotic behavior is a severe psychological disorder characterized by hallucinations and loss of contact with reality.
Capillary	The capillary is the smallest of a body's blood vessels, measuring 5-10 im. They connect arteries and veins, and most closely interact with tissues.
Lungs	The lungs are the essential organs of respiration. Its principal function is to transport oxygen from the atmosphere into the bloodstream, and excrete carbon dioxide from the bloodstream into the atmosphere.
Hydrocarbon	A hydrocarbon is any chemical compound that consists only of the elements carbon (C) and hydrogen (H).
Cannabis	The hemp plant from which marijuana, hashish, and THC are derived is the cannabis.
Hashish	Hashish is a psychoactive drug derived from the Cannabis plant. It is used for its relaxing and mind-altering effects.
Tetrahydroca-nabinol	The major active chemical in marijuana and hashish is a tetrahydrocannabinol. A number of studies indicate that it may provide medical benefits for cancer and AIDS patients by increasing appetite and decreasing nausea, and by blocking the spread of some cancer-causing Herpes simplex viruses.
Carcinogen	A carcinogen is any substance or agent that promotes cancer. A carcinogen is often, but not necessarily, a mutagen or teratogen.
Prostate	The prostate is a gland that supplies most of the fluid that makes up semen, it is located at the base of the urinary bladder.
Testes	Testes are the male reproductive glands or gonads; this is where sperm develop and are stored.
Gland	A gland is an organ in an animal's body that synthesizes a substance for release such as hormones, often into the bloodstream or into cavities inside the body or its outer surface.
Ovulation	Ovulation is the process in the menstrual cycle by which a mature ovarian follicle ruptures and discharges an ovum (also known as an oocyte, female gamete, or casually, an egg) that participates in reproduction.
Placental barrier	The placental barrier between the fetus and the wall of the mother's uterus allows for the transfer of materials from mother, and eliminates waste products of fetus.
Chromosome	The DNA which carries genetic information in biological cells is normally packaged in the form of one or more large macromolecules called a chromosome. Humans normally have 46.
Multiple sclerosis	Multiple sclerosis affects neurons, the cells of the brain and spinal cord that carry information, create thought and perception, and allow the brain to control the body. Surrounding and protecting these neurons is a layer of fat, called myelin, which helps neurons carry electrical signals. MS causes gradual destruction of myelin (demyelination) in patches throughout the brain and/or spinal cord, causing various symptoms depending upon

	which signals are interrupted.
Chemotherapy	Chemotherapy is the use of chemical substances to treat disease. In its modern-day use, it refers almost exclusively to cytostatic drugs used to treat cancer.In its non-oncological use, the term may also refer to antibiotics.
Peripheral nervous system	The peripheral nervous system consists of the nerves and neurons that serve the limbs and organs. It is not protected by bone or the blood-brain barrier, leaving it exposed to toxins and mechanical injuries. The peripheral nervous system is divided into the somatic nervous system and the autonomic nervous system.
Acetylcholine	The chemical compound acetylcholine was the first neurotransmitter to be identified. It plays a role in learning, memory, and rapid eye movement sleep and causes the skeletal muscle fibers to contract.
Brain stem	The brain stem is the stalk of the brain below the cerebral hemispheres. It is the major route for communication between the forebrain and the spinal cord and peripheral nerves. It also controls various functions including respiration, regulation of heart rhythms, and primary aspects of sound localization.
Atherosclerosis	Process by which a fatty substance or plaque builds up inside arteries to form obstructions is called atherosclerosis.
Negative Reinforcement	During negative reinforcement, a stimulus is removed and the frequency of the behavior or response increases.
Neural network	A clusters of neurons that is interconnected to process information is referred to as a neural network.
Pathological gambling	Pathological gambling, as defined by American Psychiatric Association is an impulse control disorder associated with gambling. It is a chronic and progresive mental illness. It is estimated that 4-6% of gamblers are subject to the disease and that adolescents are three times more susceptible than adults.
Compulsion	An apparently irresistible urge to repeat an act or engage in ritualistic behavior such as hand washing is referred to as a compulsion.
Impulse control	Deferred gratification is the ability of a person to wait for things they want. This trait is critical for life success. Those who lack this trait are said to suffer from poor impulse control, and often become criminals, as they are unwilling to work and wait for their paycheck.
Psychodynamic therapy	Psychodynamic therapy uses a range of different techniques, applied to the client considering his or her needs. Most approaches are centered around the idea of a maladapted function developed early in life which are at least in part unconscious.
Behavioral therapy	The treatment of a mental disorder through the application of basic principles of conditioning and learning is called behavioral therapy.
Cognitive therapy	Cognitive therapy is a kind of psychotherapy used to treat depression, anxiety disorders, phobias, and other forms of mental disorder. It involves recognizing distorted thinking and learning how to replace it with more realistic thoughts and actions.
Abnormal behavior	An action, thought, or feeling that is harmful to the person or to others is called abnormal behavior.
Social skills	Social skills are skills used to interact and communicate with others to assist status in the social structure and other motivations.
Short-term memory	Short-term memory is that part of memory which stores a limited amount of information for a limited amount of time (roughly 30-45 seconds). The second key concept associated with a

Go to **Cram101.com** for the Practice Tests for this Chapter.

short-term memory is that it has a finite capacity.

Shaping

The concept of reinforcing successive, increasingly accurate approximations to a target behavior is called shaping. The target behavior is broken down into a hierarchy of elemental steps, each step more sophisticated then the last. By successively reinforcing each of the the elemental steps, a form of differential reinforcement, until that step is learned while extinguishing the step below, the target behavior is gradually achieved.

Go to **Cram101.com** for the Practice Tests for this Chapter.

Learning	Learning is a relatively permanent change in behavior that results from experience. Thus, to attribute a behavioral change to learning, the change must be relatively permanent and must result from experience.
Adolescence	The period of life bounded by puberty and the assumption of adult responsibilities is adolescence.
Maladaptive	In psychology, a behavior or trait is adaptive when it helps an individual adjust and function well within their social environment. A maladaptive behavior or trait is counterproductive to the individual.
Socialization	Social rules and social relations are created, communicated, and changed in verbal and nonverbal ways creating social complexity useful in identifying outsiders and intelligent breeding partners. The process of learning these skills is called socialization.
Personality	Personality refers to the pattern of enduring characteristics that differentiates a person, the patterns of behaviors that make each individual unique.
Society	The social sciences use the term society to mean a group of people that form a semi-closed (or semi-open) social system, in which most interactions are with other individuals belonging to the group.
Child abuse	Child abuse is the physical or psychological maltreatment of a child.
Clinician	A health professional authorized to provide services to people suffering from one or more pathologies is a clinician.
Attention-deficit/hype-activity disorder	Attention-deficit/hyperactivity disorder refers to a disorder that begins in childhood and is characterized by a persistent pattern of lack of attention, with or without hyperactivity and impulsive behavior.
Hyperactivity	Hyperactivity can be described as a state in which a individual is abnormally easily excitable and exuberant. Strong emotional reactions and a very short span of attention is also typical for the individual.
Self-esteem	Self-esteem refers to a person's subjective appraisal of himself or herself as intrinsically positive or negative to some degree.
Oppositional defiant disorder	Oppositional Defiant Disorder is an ongoing pattern pattern of disobedient, hostile, and defiant behavior toward authority figures that goes beyond the bounds of normal childhood behavior.
Conduct disorder	Conduct disorder is the psychiatric diagnostic category for the occurrence of multiple delinquent activities over a 6-month period. These behaviors include truancy, running away, fire setting, cruelty to animals, breaking and entering, and excessive fighting.
Depression	In everyday language depression refers to any downturn in mood, which may be relatively transitory and perhaps due to something trivial. This is differentiated from Clinical depression which is marked by symptoms that last two weeks or more and are so severe that they interfere with daily living.
Anxiety	Anxiety is a complex combination of the feeling of fear, apprehension and worry often accompanied by physical sensations such as palpitations, chest pain and/or shortness of breath.
Attention	Attention is the cognitive process of selectively concentrating on one thing while ignoring other things. Psychologists have labeled three types of attention: sustained attention, selective attention, and divided attention.
Clinical	The degree to which research findings have useful and meaningful applications to real

Go to **Cram101.com** for the Practice Tests for this Chapter.

significance	problems is called their clinical significance.
Personality disorder	A mental disorder characterized by a set of inflexible, maladaptive personality traits that keep a person from functioning properly in society is referred to as a personality disorder.
Mental retardation	Mental retardation refers to having significantly below-average intellectual functioning and limitations in at least two areas of adaptive functioning. Many categorize retardation as mild, moderate, severe, or profound.
Mood disorder	A mood disorder is a condition where the prevailing emotional mood is distorted or inappropriate to the circumstances.
Autism	Autism is a neurodevelopmental disorder that manifests itself in markedly abnormal social interaction, communication ability, patterns of interests, and patterns of behavior.
Population	Population refers to all members of a well-defined group of organisms, events, or things.
Social skills	Social skills are skills used to interact and communicate with others to assist status in the social structure and other motivations.
Punishment	Punishment is the addtion of a stimulus that reduces the frequency of a response, or the removal of a stimulus that results in a reduction of the response.
Antecedents	In behavior modification, events that typically precede the target response are called antecedents.
Feedback	Feedback refers to information returned to a person about the effects a response has had.
Neurotransmitter	A neurotransmitter is a chemical that is used to relay, amplify and modulate electrical signals between a neurons and another cell.
Brain	The brain controls and coordinates most movement, behavior and homeostatic body functions such as heartbeat, blood pressure, fluid balance and body temperature. Functions of the brain are responsible for cognition, emotion, memory, motor learning and other sorts of learning. The brain is primarily made up of two types of cells: glia and neurons.
Control group	A group that does not receive the treatment effect in an experiment is referred to as the control group or sometimes as the comparison group.
Adoption studies	Research studies that assess hereditary influence by examining the resemblance between adopted children and both their biological and their adoptive parents are referred to as adoption studies. The studies have been inconclusive about the relative importance of heredity in intelligence.
Anxiety disorder	Anxiety disorder is a blanket term covering several different forms of abnormal anxiety, fear, phobia and nervous condition, that come on suddenly and prevent pursuing normal daily routines.
Neuroimaging	Neuroimaging comprises all invasive, minimally invasive, and non-invasive methods for obtaining structural and functional images of the nervous system's major subsystems: the brain, the peripheral nervous system, and the spinal cord.
Frontal lobe	The frontal lobe comprises four major folds of cortical tissue: the precentral gyrus, superior gyrus and the middle gyrus of the frontal gyri, the inferior frontal gyrus. It has been found to play a part in impulse control, judgement, language, memory, motor function, problem solving, sexual behavior, socialization and spontaneity.
Cerebellum	The cerebellum is located in the inferior posterior portion of the head (the hindbrain), directly dorsal to the brainstem and pons, inferior to the occipital lobe. The cerebellum is a region of the brain that plays an important role in the integration of sensory perception and fine motor output.

Go to **Cram101.com** for the Practice Tests for this Chapter.

Norepinephrine	Norepinephrine is released from the adrenal glands as a hormone into the blood, but it is also a neurotransmitter in the nervous system. As a stress hormone, it affects parts of the human brain where attention and impulsivity are controlled. Along with epinephrine, this compound effects the fight-or-flight response, activating the sympathetic nervous system to directly increase heart rate, release energy from fat, and increase muscle readiness.
Dopamine	Dopamine is critical to the way the brain controls our movements and is a crucial part of the basal ganglia motor loop. It is commonly associated with the 'pleasure system' of the brain, providing feelings of enjoyment and reinforcement to motivate us to do, or continue doing, certain activities.
Stimulant	A stimulant is a drug which increases the activity of the sympathetic nervous system and produces a sense of euphoria or awakeness.
Central nervous system	The vertebrate central nervous system consists of the brain and spinal cord.
Methylphenidate	Methylphenidate is a central nervous system (CNS) stimulant. It has a "calming" effect on many children who have ADHD, reducing impulsive behavior and the tendency to "act out", and helps them concentrate on schoolwork and other tasks. Adults who have ADHD often find that it increases their ability to focus on tasks and organize their lives. Brand names include Ritalin, and Concerta.
Nervous system	The body's electrochemical communication circuitry, made up of billions of neurons is a nervous system.
Ritalin	Ritalin, a methylphenidate, is a central nervous system stimulant. It has a "calming" effect on many children who have ADHD, reducing impulsive behavior and the tendency to "act out", and helps them concentrate on schoolwork and other tasks.
Affect	A subjective feeling or emotional tone often accompanied by bodily expressions noticeable to others is called affect.
Suicide	Suicide behavior is rare in childhood but escalates in adolescence. The suicide rate increases in a linear fashion from adolescence through late adulthood.
Bipolar disorder	Bipolar Disorder is a mood disorder typically characterized by fluctuations between manic and depressive states; and, more generally, atypical mood regulation and mood instability.
Acute	Acute means sudden, sharp, and abrupt. Usually short in duration.
Reinforcement	In operant conditioning, reinforcement is any change in an environment that (a) occurs after the behavior, (b) seems to make that behavior re-occur more often in the future and (c) that reoccurence of behavior must be the result of the change.
Reinforcer	In operant conditioning, a reinforcer is any stimulus that increases the probability that a preceding behavior will occur again. In Classical Conditioning, the unconditioned stimulus (US) is the reinforcer.
Prognosis	A forecast about the probable course of an illess is referred to as prognosis.
Early adulthood	The developmental period beginning in the late teens or early twenties and lasting into the thirties is called early adulthood; characterized by an increasing self-awareness.
Psychopathology	Psychopathology refers to the field concerned with the nature and development of mental disorders.
Comorbidity	Comorbidity refers to the presence of more than one mental disorder occurring in an individual at the same time.
Placebo	Placebo refers to a bogus treatment that has the appearance of being genuine.

Go to **Cram101.com** for the Practice Tests for this Chapter.

Behavioral observation	A form of behavioral assessment that entails careful observation of a person's overt behavior in a particular situation is behavioral observation.
Stages	Stages represent relatively discrete periods of time in which functioning is qualitatively different from functioning at other periods.
Norms	In testing, standards of test performance that permit the comparison of one person's score on the test to the scores of others who have taken the same test are referred to as norms.
Graham	Graham has conducted a number of studies that reveal stronger socioeconomic-status influences rather than ethnic influences in achievement.
Substance abuse	Substance abuse refers to the overindulgence in and dependence on a stimulant, depressant, or other chemical substance, leading to effects that are detrimental to the individual's physical or mental health, or the welfare of others.
Mental disorder	Mental disorder refers to a disturbance in a person's emotions, drives, thought processes, or behavior that involves serious and relatively prolonged distress and/or impairment in ability to function, is not simply a normal response to some event or set of events in the person's environment.
Psychotherapy	Psychotherapy is a set of techniques based on psychological principles intended to improve mental health, emotional or behavioral issues.
Cognitive-behavior therapy	Cognitive-behavior therapy is a kind of psychotherapy used to treat depression, anxiety disorders, phobias, and other forms of mental disorder. It involves recognizing distorted thinking and learning to replace it with more realistic substitute ideas.
Behavior therapy	Behavior therapy refers to the systematic application of the principles of learning to direct modification of a client's problem behaviors.
Emotion	An emotion is a mental states that arise spontaneously, rather than through conscious effort. They are often accompanied by physiological changes.
Longitudinal study	Longitudinal study is a type of developmental study in which the same group of participants is followed and measured for an extended period of time, often years.
Epidemiology	Epidemiology is the study of the distribution and determinants of disease and disorders in human populations, and the use of its knowledge to control health problems.Epidemiology is considered the cornerstone methodology in all of public health research, and is highly regarded in evidence-based clinical medicine for identifying risk factors for disease and determining optimal treatment approaches to clinical practice.
Alcoholism	A disorder that involves long-term, repeated, uncontrolled, compulsive, and excessive use of alcoholic beverages and that impairs the drinker's health and work and social relationships is called alcoholism.
Substance dependence	Drug addiction, or substance dependence is the compulsive use of drugs, to the point where the user has no effective choice but to continue use.
Positive reinforcement	In positive reinforcement, a stimulus is added and the rate of responding increases.
Behavioral assessment	Direct measures of an individual's behavior used to describe characteristics indicative of personality are called behavioral assessment.
Social support	Social Support is the physical and emotional comfort given by family, friends, co-workers and others. Research has identified three main types of social support: emotional, practical, sharing points of view.
Late adolescence	Late adolescence refers to approximately the latter half of the second decade of life. Career

Go to **Cram101.com** for the Practice Tests for this Chapter.

	interests, dating, and identity exploration are often more pronounced in late adolescence than in early adolescence.
Schema	Schema refers to a way of mentally representing the world, such as a belief or an expectation, that can influence perception of persons, objects, and situations.
Affective	Affective is the way people react emotionally, their ability to feel another living thing's pain or joy.
Attachment	Attachment is the tendency to seek closeness to another person and feel secure when that person is present.
Separation anxiety	Separation anxiety is a psychological condition in which an individual has excessive anxiety regarding separation from home, or from those with whom the individual has a strong attachment.
Early childhood	Early childhood refers to the developmental period extending from the end of infancy to about 5 or 6 years of age; sometimes called the preschool years.
Pervasive developmental disorder	The diagnostic category pervasive developmental disorder refers to a group of disorders characterized by delays in the development of multiple basic functions including socialization and communication.
Panic disorder with agoraphobia	In panic disorder with agoraphobia the person may experience severe panic attacks during situations where they feel trapped, insecure, out of control, or too far from their personal comfort zone. During severe bouts of anxiety, the person is confined not only to their home, but to one or two rooms and they may even become bedbound until their over-stimulated nervous system can quiet down, and their adrenaline levels return to a more normal level.
Schizophrenia	Schizophrenia is characterized by persistent defects in the perception or expression of reality. A person suffering from untreated schizophrenia typically demonstrates grossly disorganized thinking, and may also experience delusions or auditory hallucinations
Neglected children	Neglected children are infrequently nominated as a best friend but are not disliked by their peers.
Bowlby	Bowlby, a developmental psychologist of the psychoanalytic tradition, was responsible for much of the early research conducted on attachment in humans. He identified three stages of separation: protest, despair, and detachment.
Psychological disorder	Mental processes and/or behavior patterns that cause emotional distress and/or substantial impairment in functioning is a psychological disorder.
Secure attachment	With secure attachment, the infant uses a caregiver as a secure base from which to explore the environment. Ainsworth believes that secure attachment in the first year of life provides an important foundation for psychological development later in life.
Infancy	The developmental period that extends from birth to 18 or 24 months is called infancy.
Social phobia	An irrational, excessive fear of public scrutiny is referred to as social phobia.
In vivo	In vivo is used to indicate the presence of a whole/living organism, in distinction to a partial or dead organism, or a computer model. In vivo research is more suited to observe an overall effect than in vitro research, which is better suited to deduce mechanisms of action.
Biological predisposition	The genetic readiness of animals and humans to perform certain behaviors is a biological predisposition.
Developmental level	An individual's current state of physical, emotional, and intellectual development is called the developmental level.
Stress disorder	A significant emotional disturbance caused by stresses outside the range of normal human

	experience is referred to as stress disorder.
Reexperiencing	Careful and systematic visualizing and reliving of traumatic life events in order to diminish their power and emotional effects as a means of treating dissociative identity disorder or posttraumatic stress disorder is called reexperiencing.
Obsessive-compulsive disorder	Obsessive-compulsive disorder is an anxiety disorder manifested in a variety of forms, but is most commonly characterized by a subject's obsessive drive to perform a particular task or set of tasks, compulsions commonly termed rituals.
Compulsion	An apparently irresistible urge to repeat an act or engage in ritualistic behavior such as hand washing is referred to as a compulsion.
Obsession	An obsession is a thought or idea that the sufferer cannot stop thinking about. Common examples include fears of acquiring disease, getting hurt, or causing harm to someone. They are typically automatic, frequent, distressing, and difficult to control or put an end to by themselves.
Date rape	Date rape refers to non-consensual sexual activity between people who are already acquainted, or who know each other socially where it is alleged that consent for sexual activity was not given, or was given under duress.
Tics	Tics are a repeated, impulsive action, almost reflexive in nature, which the person feels powerless to control or avoid.
Antidepressant	An antidepressant is a medication used primarily in the treatment of clinical depression. They are not thought to produce tolerance, although sudden withdrawal may produce adverse effects. They create little if any immediate change in mood and require between several days and several weeks to take effect.
Toddler	A toddler is a child between the ages of one and three years old. During this period, the child learns a great deal about social roles and develops motor skills; to toddle is to walk unsteadily.
Stroke	A stroke occurs when the blood supply to a part of the brain is suddenly interrupted by occlusion, by hemorrhage, or other causes
Socioeconomic Status	A family's socioeconomic status is based on family income, parental education level, parental occupation, and social status in the community. Those with high status often have more success in preparing their children for school because they have access to a wide range of resources.
Alcoholic	An alcoholic is dependent on alcohol as characterized by craving, loss of control, physical dependence and withdrawal symptoms, and tolerance.
Major mood disorder	A major mood disorder is characterized by a severely depressed mood that persists for at least two weeks. Episodes may start suddenly or slowly and can occur several times through a person's life. The disorder may be categorized as "single episode" or "recurrent" depending on whether previous episodes have been experienced before.
Eating disorders	Psychological disorders characterized by distortion of the body image and gross disturbances in eating patterns are called eating disorders.
Logical thought	Drawing conclusions on the basis of formal principles of reasoning is referred to as logical thought.
Serotonin	Serotonin, a neurotransmitter, is believed to play an important part of the biochemistry of depression, bipolar disorder and anxiety. It is also believed to be influential on sexuality and appetite.
Cognitive-	Cognitive-behavioral therapy refers to group of treatment procedures aimed at identifying and

Go to **Cram101.com** for the Practice Tests for this Chapter.

behavioral therapy	modifying faulty thought processes, attitudes and attributions, and problem behaviors.
Rape	Rape is a crime where the victim is forced into sexual activity, in particular sexual penetration, against his or her will.
Phobia	A persistent, irrational fear of an object, situation, or activity that the person feels compelled to avoid is referred to as a phobia.
Self-instructional training	A cognitive-behavioral approach that tries to help people improve their overt behavior by changing how they silently talk to themselves is called self-instructional training.
Relaxation training	Relaxation training is an intervention technique used for tics. The person is taught to relax the muscles involved in the tics.
Stimulus	A change in an environmental condition that elicits a response is a stimulus.
Dysthymic disorder	A dysthymic disorder is a form of the mood disorder of depression characterized by a lack of enjoyment/pleasure in life that continues for at least two years. It differs from clinical depression in the severity of the symptoms.
Major depression	Major depression is characterized by a severely depressed mood that persists for at least two weeks. Episodes of depression may start suddenly or slowly and can occur several times through a person's life. The disorder may be categorized as "single episode" or "recurrent" depending on whether previous episodes have been experienced before.
Psychiatrist	A psychiatrist is a physician who specializes in the diagnosis and treatment of psychological disorders.
Night terror	A night terror is a parasomnia sleep disorder characterized by extreme terror and a temporary inability to regain full consciousness. The subject wakes abruptly from the fourth stage of sleep, with waking usually accompanied by gasping, moaning, or screaming. It is often impossible to fully awaken the person, and after the episode the subject normally settles back to sleep without waking.
Nightmare	Nightmare was the original term for the state later known as waking dream, and more currently as sleep paralysis, associated with rapid eye movement (REM) periods of sleep.
Motivation	In psychology, motivation is the driving force (desire) behind all actions of an organism.
Major depressive disorder	The diagnosis of a major depressive disorder occurs when an individual experiences a major depressive episode and depressed characteristics, such as lethargy and depression, last for 2 weeks or longer and daily functioning becomes impaired.
Hypomanic episode	A hypomanic episode is a less severe and less disruptive version of a manic episode that is one of the criteria for several mood disorders.
Chronic	Chronic refers to a relatively long duration, usually more than a few months.
Social development	The person's developing capacity for social relationships and the effects of those relationships on further development is referred to as social development.
Correlation	A statistical technique for determining the degree of association between two or more variables is referred to as correlation.
Attributional style	One's tendency to attribute one's behavior to internal or external factors, stable or unstable factors, and so on is their attributional style.
Interpersonal therapy	A brief psychotherapy designed to help depressed people better understand and cope with problems relating to their interpersonal relationships is referred to as interpersonal therapy.

Cognitive therapy	Cognitive therapy is a kind of psychotherapy used to treat depression, anxiety disorders, phobias, and other forms of mental disorder. It involves recognizing distorted thinking and learning how to replace it with more realistic thoughts and actions.
Tic disorder	A tic disorder is a repeated, impulsive action, almost reflexive in nature, which the actor feels powerless to control or avoid. They can be triggered by an emotional state (stress is a common trigger) or sensation, or can happen for no obvious reason.
Transient tic disorder	A transient tic disorder is a childhood disorder that lasts longer than four weeks but less than one year and is characterized by involuntary, repetitive, and nonrhythmic movements or vocalizations.
Coprolalia	Coprolalia is involuntary swearing that is an occasional but rare characteristic of Tourette syndrome patients.
Receptor	A sensory receptor is a structure that recognizes a stimulus in the internal or external environment of an organism. In response to stimuli the sensory receptor initiates sensory transduction by creating graded potentials or action potentials in the same cell or in an adjacent one.
Gene	A gene is an ultramicroscopic area of the chromosome. It is the smallest physical unit of the DNA molecule that carries a piece of hereditary information.
Child development	Scientific study of the processes of change from conception through adolescence is called child development.
Attitude	An enduring mental representation of a person, place, or thing that evokes an emotional response and related behavior is called attitude.
Generalization	In conditioning, the tendency for a conditioned response to be evoked by stimuli that are similar to the stimulus to which the response was conditioned is a generalization. The greater the similarity among the stimuli, the greater the probability of generalization.
Cultural values	The importance and desirability of various objects and activities as defined by people in a given culture are referred to as cultural values.
Behavior modification	Behavior Modification is a technique of altering an individual's reactions to stimuli through positive reinforcement and the extinction of maladaptive behavior.
Play therapy	Play therapy is often used to help the diagnostician to try to determine the cause of disturbed behavior in a child. Treatment therapists then used a type of systematic desensitization or relearning therapy to change the disturbing behavior, either systematically or in less formal social settings.
Trauma	Trauma refers to a severe physical injury or wound to the body caused by an external force, or a psychological shock having a lasting effect on mental life.
Family therapy	Family therapy is a branch of psychotherapy that treats family problems. Family therapists consider the family as a system of interacting members; as such, the problems in the family are seen to arise as an emergent property of the interactions in the system, rather than ascribed exclusively to the "faults" or psychological problems of individual members.
Acquisition	Acquisition is the process of adapting to the environment, learning or becoming conditioned. In classical conditoning terms, it is the initial learning of the stimulus response link, which involves a neutral stimulus being associated with a unconditioned stimulus and becoming a conditioned stimulus.
Behavioral therapy	The treatment of a mental disorder through the application of basic principles of conditioning and learning is called behavioral therapy.
Stereotype	A stereotype is considered to be a group concept, held by one social group about another.They

Go to **Cram101.com** for the Practice Tests for this Chapter.

are often used in a negative or prejudicial sense and are frequently used to justify certain discriminatory behaviors. This allows powerful social groups to legitimize and protect their dominant position

Post-traumatic stress disorder

Post-traumatic stress disorder is a term for the psychological consequences of exposure to or confrontation with stressful experiences, which involve actual or threatened death, serious physical injury or a threat to physical integrity and which the person found highly traumatic.

Go to **Cram101.com** for the Practice Tests for this Chapter.

Autistic disorder	An autistic disorder is a neurodevelopmental disorder that manifests itself in markedly abnormal social interaction, communication ability, patterns of interests, and patterns of behavior.
Mental retardation	Mental retardation refers to having significantly below-average intellectual functioning and limitations in at least two areas of adaptive functioning. Many categorize retardation as mild, moderate, severe, or profound.
Autism	Autism is a neurodevelopmental disorder that manifests itself in markedly abnormal social interaction, communication ability, patterns of interests, and patterns of behavior.
Pervasive developmental disorder	The diagnostic category pervasive developmental disorder refers to a group of disorders characterized by delays in the development of multiple basic functions including socialization and communication.
Affect	A subjective feeling or emotional tone often accompanied by bodily expressions noticeable to others is called affect.
Childhood disintegrative disorder	Childhood disintegrative disorder is a rare condition characterized by late onset (>3 years of age) of developmental delays in language, social function, and motor skills. It has some similarity to autism, but an apparent period of fairly normal development is often noted before a regression in skills or a series of regressions in skills.
Cognitive development	The process by which a child's understanding of the world changes as a function of age and experience is called cognitive development.
Severe mental retardation	A limitation in mental development as measured on the Wechsler Adult Intelligence Scale with scores between 20 -34 is called severe mental retardation.
Kanner	Kanner was known for his work related to autism. He was the first physician in the United States to be identified as a child psychiatrist and his first textbook, Child Psychiatry in 1935, was the first English language textbook to focus on the psychiatric problems of children.
Maintenance of sameness	Maintenance of sameness is a necessity among people with autism that their familiar environments remain unchanged. They become upset when changes are introduced.
Psychosis	Psychosis is a generic term for mental states in which the components of rational thought and perception are severely impaired. Persons experiencing a psychosis may experience hallucinations, hold paranoid or delusional beliefs, demonstrate personality changes and exhibit disorganized thinking. This is usually accompanied by features such as a lack of insight into the unusual or bizarre nature of their behavior, difficulties with social interaction and impairments in carrying out the activities of daily living.
Laboratory setting	Research setting in which the behavior of interest does not naturally occur is called a laboratory setting.
Down syndrome	Down syndrome encompasses a number of genetic disorders, of which trisomy 21 (a nondisjunction, the so-called extrachromosone) is the most representative, causing highly variable degrees of learning difficulties as well as physical disabilities. Incidence of Down syndrome is estimated at 1 per 660 births, making it the most common chromosomal abnormality.
Syndrome	The term syndrome is the association of several clinically recognizable features, signs, symptoms, phenomena or characteristics which often occur together, so that the presence of one feature indicates the presence of the others.
Fixation	Fixation in abnormal psychology is the state where an individual becomes obsessed with an attachment to another human, animal or inanimate object. Fixation in vision refers to maintaining the gaze in a constant direction. .

Learning	Learning is a relatively permanent change in behavior that results from experience. Thus, to attribute a behavioral change to learning, the change must be relatively permanent and must result from experience.
Simile	A simile is a figure of speech in which the subject is compared to another subject.
Insight	Insight refers to a sudden awareness of the relationships among various elements that had previously appeared to be independent of one another.
Trial and error	Trial and error is an approach to problem solving in which one solution after another is tried in no particular order until an answer is found.
Instinct	Instinct is the word used to describe inherent dispositions towards particular actions. They are generally an inherited pattern of responses or reactions to certain kinds of situations.
Autistic savant	An autistic savant is a person who expresses extraordinary mental abilities, often in the fields of numerical calculation (not to be confused with mathematics), but also sometimes in art or music.
Cognitive skills	Cognitive skills such as reasoning, attention, and memory can be advanced and sustained through practice and training.
Task analysis	The procedure of identifying the component elements of a behavior chain is called task analysis.
Trait	An enduring personality characteristic that tends to lead to certain behaviors is called a trait. The term trait also means a genetically inherited feature of an organism.
Cognition	The intellectual processes through which information is obtained, transformed, stored, retrieved, and otherwise used is cognition.
Executive function	The processes involved in regulating attention and in determining what to do with information just gathered or retrieved from long-term memory, is referred to as the executive function.
Theory of mind	A theory of mind considers the nature of mind, and its structure and processes
Attention	Attention is the cognitive process of selectively concentrating on one thing while ignoring other things. Psychologists have labeled three types of attention: sustained attention, selective attention, and divided attention.
Feedback	Feedback refers to information returned to a person about the effects a response has had.
Brain	The brain controls and coordinates most movement, behavior and homeostatic body functions such as heartbeat, blood pressure, fluid balance and body temperature. Functions of the brain are responsible for cognition, emotion, memory, motor learning and other sorts of learning. The brain is primarily made up of two types of cells: glia and neurons.
Working Memory	Working memory is the collection of structures and processes in the brain used for temporarily storing and manipulating information. Working memory consists of both memory for items that are currently being processed, and components governing attention and directing the processing itself.
Functional play	Piaget's and Smilansky's concept of functional play is the lowest cognitive level of play, involving repetitive muscular movements.
Hypothesis	A specific statement about behavior or mental processes that is testable through research is a hypothesis.
Affective	Affective is the way people react emotionally, their ability to feel another living thing's pain or joy.
Abnormal	An action, thought, or feeling that is harmful to the person or to others is called abnormal

Go to **Cram101.com** for the Practice Tests for this Chapter.

305

behavior	behavior.
Variability	Statistically, variability refers to how much the scores in a distribution spread out, away from the mean.
Coding	In senation, coding is the process by which information about the quality and quantity of a stimulus is preserved in the pattern of action potentials sent through sensory neurons to the central nervous system.
Social play	Play that involves social interactions with peers is called social play. It increases affiliation with peers, releases tension, advances cognitive development, and increases exploration.
Central nervous system	The vertebrate central nervous system consists of the brain and spinal cord.
Clinician	A health professional authorized to provide services to people suffering from one or more pathologies is a clinician.
Occipital lobe	The occipital lobe is the smallest of four true lobes in the human brain. Located in the rearmost portion of the skull, the occipital lobe is part of the forebrain structure. It is the visual processing center.
Monozygotic	Identical twins occur when a single egg is fertilized to form one zygote, calld monozygotic, but the zygote then divides into two separate embryos. The two embryos develop into foetuses sharing the same womb. Monozygotic twins are genetically identical unless there has been a mutation in development, and they are almost always the same gender.
Dizygotic	Fraternal twins (commonly known as "non-identical twins") usually occur when two fertilized eggs are implanted in the uterine wall at the same time. The two eggs form two zygotes, and these twins are therefore also known as dizygotic.
Gene	A gene is an ultramicroscopic area of the chromosome. It is the smallest physical unit of the DNA molecule that carries a piece of hereditary information.
Correlation	A statistical technique for determining the degree of association between two or more variables is referred to as correlation.
Personality trait	According to the Diagnostic and Statistical Manual of the American Psychiatric Association, a personality trait is a "prominent aspect of personality that is exhibited in a wide range of important social and personal contexts. ...".
Shyness	A tendency to avoid others plus uneasiness and strain when socializing is called shyness.
Population	Population refers to all members of a well-defined group of organisms, events, or things.
Personality	Personality refers to the pattern of enduring characteristics that differentiates a person, the patterns of behaviors that make each individual unique.
Anxiety	Anxiety is a complex combination of the feeling of fear, apprehension and worry often accompanied by physical sensations such as palpitations, chest pain and/or shortness of breath.
Schizophrenia	Schizophrenia is characterized by persistent defects in the perception or expression of reality. A person suffering from untreated schizophrenia typically demonstrates grossly disorganized thinking, and may also experience delusions or auditory hallucinations
Hallucination	A hallucination is a sensory perception experienced in the absence of an external stimulus, as distinct from an illusion, which is a misperception of an external stimulus. They may occur in any sensory modality - visual, auditory, olfactory, gustatory, tactile, or mixed.
Delusion	A false belief, not generally shared by others, and that cannot be changed despite strong

307

evidence to the contrary is a delusion.

Anatomy	Anatomy is the branch of biology that deals with the structure and organization of living things. It can be divided into animal anatomy (zootomy) and plant anatomy (phytonomy). Major branches of anatomy include comparative anatomy, histology, and human anatomy.
Deinstitutio-alization	The transfer of former mental patients from institutions into the community is referred to as deinstitutionalization.
Observational learning	The acquisition of knowledge and skills through the observation of others rather than by means of direct experience is observational learning. Four major processes are thought to influence the observational learning: attentional, retentional, behavioral production, and motivational.
Experimental group	Experimental group refers to any group receiving a treatment effect in an experiment.
Control group	A group that does not receive the treatment effect in an experiment is referred to as the control group or sometimes as the comparison group.
Reinforcer	In operant conditioning, a reinforcer is any stimulus that increases the probability that a preceding behavior will occur again. In Classical Conditioning, the unconditioned stimulus (US) is the reinforcer.
Obsession	An obsession is a thought or idea that the sufferer cannot stop thinking about. Common examples include fears of acquiring disease, getting hurt, or causing harm to someone. They are typically automatic, frequent, distressing, and difficult to control or put an end to by themselves.
Adaptive behavior	An adaptive behavior increases the probability of the individual or organism to survive or exist within its environment.
Antidepressant	An antidepressant is a medication used primarily in the treatment of clinical depression. They are not thought to produce tolerance, although sudden withdrawal may produce adverse effects. They create little if any immediate change in mood and require between several days and several weeks to take effect.
Antipsychotic	The term antipsychotic is applied to a group of drugs used to treat psychosis.
Stimulant	A stimulant is a drug which increases the activity of the sympathetic nervous system and produces a sense of euphoria or awakeness.
Seizure	A seizure is a temporary alteration in brain function expressed as a changed mental state, tonic or clonic movements and various other symptoms. They are due to temporary abnormal electrical activity of a group of brain cells.
Recessive gene	Recessive gene refers to an allele that causes a phenotype (visible or detectable characteristic) that is only seen in a homozygous genotype (an organism that has two copies of the same allele). Thus, both parents have to be carriers of a recessive trait in order for a child to express that trait.
Metabolism	Metabolism is the biochemical modification of chemical compounds in living organisms and cells.
Chromosome	The DNA which carries genetic information in biological cells is normally packaged in the form of one or more large macromolecules called a chromosome. Humans normally have 46.
Nervous system	The body's electrochemical communication circuitry, made up of billions of neurons is a nervous system.
Dendrite	A dendrite is a slender, typically branched projection of a nerve cell, or "neuron," which

Go to **Cram101.com** for the Practice Tests for this Chapter.

conducts the electrical stimulation received from other cells to the body or soma of the cell from which it projects. This stimulation arrives through synapses, which typically are located near the tips of the dendrites and away from the soma.

Learning disability	A learning disability exists when there is a significant discrepancy between one's ability and achievement.
Autistic spectrum	The autistic spectrum is the idea that autism is a developmental and behavioral syndrome that results from certain combinations of traits. At the severe end of the spectrum is low-functioning autism, which can cause severe-profound impairments in many areas, to a milder form of autism known as Asperger's syndrome and finally a shading into typicality and perhaps then hypersocialization.
Intelligence test	An intelligence test is a standardized means of assessing a person's current mental ability, for example, the Stanford-Binet test and the Wechsler Adult Intelligence Scale.
Bipolar disorder	Bipolar Disorder is a mood disorder typically characterized by fluctuations between manic and depressive states; and, more generally, atypical mood regulation and mood instability.
Psychopathology	Psychopathology refers to the field concerned with the nature and development of mental disorders.
Heterogeneous	A heterogeneous compound, mixture, or other such object is one that consists of many different items, which are often not easily sorted or separated, though they are clearly distinct.
Variable	A variable refers to a measurable factor, characteristic, or attribute of an individual or a system.
Homogeneous	In biology homogeneous has a meaning similar to its meaning in mathematics. Generally it means "the same" or "of the same quality or general property".
Regression	Return to a form of behavior characteristic of an earlier stage of development is called regression.
Alfred Binet	Alfred Binet published the first modern intelligence test, the Binet-Simon intelligence scale, in 1905. Binet stressed that the core of intelligence consists of complex cognitive processes, such as memory, imagery, comprehension, and judgment; and, that these developed over time in the individual.
Mendel	Mendel is often called the "father of genetics" for his study of the inheritance of traits in pea plants. Mendel showed that there was particulate inheritance of traits according to his laws of inheritance.
Genetics	Genetics is the science of genes, heredity, and the variation of organisms.
Eugenics	The field concerned with improving the hereditary qualities of the human race through social control of mating and reproduction is called eugenics.
Psychometric	Psychometric study is concerned with the theory and technique of psychological measurement, which includes the measurement of knowledge, abilities, attitudes, and personality traits. The field is primarily concerned with the study of differences between individuals
Mental illness	Mental illness is the term formerly used to mean psychological disorder but less preferred because it implies that the causes of the disorder can be found in a medical disease process.
Attitude	An enduring mental representation of a person, place, or thing that evokes an emotional response and related behavior is called attitude.
Genetic disorder	A genetic disorder is a disease caused by abnormal expression of one or more genes in a person causing a clinical phenotype.

Dominant gene	In genetics, the term dominant gene refers to the allele that causes a phenotype that is seen in a heterozygous genotype.
Mutation	Mutation is a permanent, sometimes transmissible (if the change is to a germ cell) change to the genetic material (usually DNA or RNA) of a cell. They can be caused by copying errors in the genetic material during cell division and by exposure to radiation, chemicals, or viruses, or can occur deliberately under cellular control during the processes such as meiosis or hypermutation.
Lobotomy	A lobotomy is the intentional severing of the prefrontal cortex from the thalamic region of the brain. The frontal lobe of the brain controls a number of advanced cognitive functions, as well as motor control. Today, lobotomy is very infrequently practised. It may be a treatment of last resort for obsessive-compulsive sufferers, and may also be used for people suffering chronic pain.
Lobes	The four major sections of the cerebral cortex: frontal, parietal, temporal, and occipital are called lobes.
Threshold	In general, a threshold is a fixed location or value where an abrupt change is observed. In the sensory modalities, it is the minimum amount of stimulus energy necessary to elicit a sensory response.
Pathology	Pathology is the study of the processes underlying disease and other forms of illness, harmful abnormality, or dysfunction.
Phenylalanine	Phenylalanine is an essential amino acid. The genetic disorder phenylketonuria is an inability to metabolize phenylalanine.
Congenital	A condition existing at birth is referred to as congenital.
Uterus	The uterus or womb is the major female reproductive organ. The main function of the uterus is to accept a fertilized ovum which becomes implanted into the endometrium, and derives nourishment from blood vessels which develop exclusively for this purpose.
Fragile X syndrome	Fragile X Syndrome is the most common inherited cause of mental retardation, and the most common known cause of autism. Fragile X syndrome is a genetic disorder caused by mutation of the FMR1 gene on the X chromosome, a mutation found in 1 out of every 2000 males and 1 out of every 4000 females.
X chromosome	The sex chromosomes are one of the 23 pairs of human chromosomes. Each person normally has one pair of sex chromosomes in each cell. Females have two X chromosomes, while males have one X and one Y chromosome. The X chromosome carries hundreds of genes but few, if any, of these have anything to do directly with sex determination.
Y chromosome	The Y chromosome is one of the two sex chromosomes in humans and most other mammals. The sex chromosomes are one of the 23 pairs of human chromosomes. The Y chromosome contains the fewest genes of any of the chromosomes. It contains the genes that cause testis development, thus determining maleness. It is usually contributed by the father.
Moderate mental retardation	Moderate mental retardation is a limitation in mental development. Scores on IQ tests range between 35-50. People with this degree of retardation are often institutionalized, and their training is focused on self-care rather than on development of intellectual skills.
Nondisjunction	Nondisjunction is the failure of a chromosome to split correctly during meiosis. This results in the production of gametes which have either more or less of the usual amount of genetic material, and is a common mechanism for trisomy or monosomy. Nondisjunction can occur in the meiosis I or meiosis II phases of cellular reproduction.
Trisomy	A condition wherein there are three rather than the usual pair of homologous chromosomes within the cell nucleus is referred to as trisomy.

Embryo	A developed zygote that has a rudimentary heart, brain, and other organs is referred to as an embryo.
Adolescence	The period of life bounded by puberty and the assumption of adult responsibilities is adolescence.
Short-term memory	Short-term memory is that part of memory which stores a limited amount of information for a limited amount of time (roughly 30-45 seconds). The second key concept associated with a short-term memory is that it has a finite capacity.
Telegraphic speech	Telegraphic speech refers to the use of short and precise words to communicate. Young children's two- and three-word utterances characteristically are telegraphic.
Perception	Perception is the process of acquiring, interpreting, selecting, and organizing sensory information.
Reasoning	Reasoning is the act of using reason to derive a conclusion from certain premises. There are two main methods to reach a conclusion, deductive reasoning and inductive reasoning.
Physical therapy	Physical therapy is a health profession concerned with the assessment, diagnosis, and treatment of disease and disability through physical means. It is based upon principles of medical science, and is generally held to be within the sphere of conventional medicine.
Dementia	Dementia is progressive decline in cognitive function due to damage or disease in the brain beyond what might be expected from normal aging.
Neurofibrillary tangles	Neurofibrillary tangles are pathological protein aggregates found within neurons in cases of Alzheimer's disease.
Senile plaques	Senile plaques are clumps of A-beta peptides commonly found in Alzheimer's disease on microscopic examination of brain tissue.
Amniocentesis	Amniocentesis is a medical procedure used for prenatal diagnosis, in which from the amnion around a developing fetus a small amount of amniotic fluid is extracted. It is usually offered when there may be an increased risk for genetic conditions in the pregnancy.
Prenatal	Prenatal period refers to the time from conception to birth.
Tangles	Tangles are twisted fibers that build up inside nerve cells.
Fetus	A fetus develops from the end of the 8th week of pregnancy (when the major structures have formed), until birth.
Ultrasound	Ultrasound is sound with a frequency greater than the upper limit of human hearing, approximately 20 kilohertz. Medical use can visualise muscle and soft tissue, making them useful for scanning the organs, and obstetric ultrasonography is commonly used during pregnancy.
False positive	A false positive, also called a Type I error, exists when a test incorrectly reports that it has found a result where none really exists.
Heredity	Heredity is the transfer of characteristics from parent to offspring through their genes.
Malnutrition	Malnutrition is a general term for the medical condition in a person or animal caused by an unbalanced diet—either too little or too much food, or a diet missing one or more important nutrients.
Chronic	Chronic refers to a relatively long duration, usually more than a few months.
Measles	Measles, also known as rubeola, is a common disease caused by a virus of the genus Morbillivirus. Complications with measles are relatively common, ranging from relatively common and less serious diarrhea, to pneumonia and encephalitis. Complications are usually

Go to **Cram101.com** for the Practice Tests for this Chapter.
And, **NEVER** highlight a book again!

	more severe amongst infants and adults who catch the virus.
Rubella	An infectious disease that, if contracted by the mother during the first three months of pregnancy, has a high risk of causing mental retardation and physical deformity in the child is called rubella.
Human immunodeficiency virus	The human immunodeficiency virus is a retrovirus that primarily infects vital components of the human immune system. It is transmitted through penetrative and oral sex; blood transfusion; the sharing of contaminated needles in health care settings and through drug injection; and, between mother and infant, during pregnancy, childbirth and breastfeeding.
Syphilis	Syphilis is a sexually transmitted disease that is caused by a spirochaete bacterium, Treponema pallidum. If not treated, syphilis can cause serious effects such as damage to the nervous system, heart, or brain. Untreated syphilis can be ultimately fatal.
Placenta	A membrane that permits the exchange of nutrients and waste products between the mother and her developing child but does not allow the maternal and fetal bloodstreams to mix is the placenta.
Tranquilizer	A sedative, or tranquilizer, is a drug that depresses the central nervous system (CNS), which causes calmness, relaxation, reduction of anxiety, sleepiness, slowed breathing, slurred speech, staggering gait, poor judgment, and slow, uncertain reflexes.
Fetal alcohol syndrome	A cluster of abnormalities that appears in the offspring of mothers who drink alcohol heavily during pregnancy is called fetal alcohol syndrome.
Trauma	Trauma refers to a severe physical injury or wound to the body caused by an external force, or a psychological shock having a lasting effect on mental life.
Low birth weight	Low birth weight is a fetus that weighs less than 2500 g (5 lb 8 oz) regardless of gestational age.
Encephalitis	Encephalitis is an acute inflammation of the brain, commonly caused by a viral infection.
Deprivation	Deprivation, is the loss or withholding of normal stimulation, nutrition, comfort, love, and so forth; a condition of lacking. The level of stimulation is less than what is required.
Tumor	A tumor is an abnormal growth that when located in the brain can either be malignant and directly destroy brain tissue, or be benign and disrupt functioning by increasing intracranial pressure.
Normal distribution	A normal distribution is a symmetrical distribution of scores that is assumed to reflect chance fluctuations; approximately 68% of cases lie within a single standard deviation of the mean.
Alcoholic	An alcoholic is dependent on alcohol as characterized by craving, loss of control, physical dependence and withdrawal symptoms, and tolerance.
Diabetes	Diabetes is a medical disorder characterized by varying or persistent elevated blood sugar levels, especially after eating. All types of diabetes share similar symptoms and complications at advanced stages: dehydration and ketoacidosis, cardiovascular disease, chronic renal failure, retinal damage which can lead to blindness, nerve damage which can lead to erectile dysfunction, gangrene with risk of amputation of toes, feet, and even legs.
Early Intervention	Early intervention is a process used to recognize warning signs for mental health problems and to take early action against factors that put individuals at risk.
Motor skills disorder	Motor skills disorder is characterized by marked impairment in the development of motor coordination that is not accounted for by a physical disorder.
Learning	A disorder characterized by a discrepancy between one's academic achievement and one's

disorder	intellectual ability is referred to as a learning disorder.
Child development	Scientific study of the processes of change from conception through adolescence is called child development.
Mental disorder	Mental disorder refers to a disturbance in a person's emotions, drives, thought processes, or behavior that involves serious and relatively prolonged distress and/or impairment in ability to function, is not simply a normal response to some event or set of events in the person's environment.
Motivation	In psychology, motivation is the driving force (desire) behind all actions of an organism.
Achievement test	A test designed to determine a person's level of knowledge in a given subject area is referred to as an achievement test.
IQ test	An IQ test is a standardized test developed to measure a person's cognitive abilities ("intelligence") in relation to their age group.
Society	The social sciences use the term society to mean a group of people that form a semi-closed (or semi-open) social system, in which most interactions are with other individuals belonging to the group.
Dyslexia	Dyslexia is a neurological disorder with biochemical and genetic markers. In its most common and apparent form, it is a disability in which a person's reading and/or writing ability is significantly lower than that which would be predicted by his or her general level of intelligence.
Acquisition	Acquisition is the process of adapting to the environment, learning or becoming conditioned. In classical conditoning terms, it is the initial learning of the stimulus response link, which involves a neutral stimulus being associated with a unconditioned stimulus and becoming a conditioned stimulus.
Mild mental retardation	Mild mental retardation refers to a limitation in mental development measured on IQ tests with scores between 55 and 70. Children with such a limitation are considered the educable mentally retarded and are usually placed in special classes.
Early childhood	Early childhood refers to the developmental period extending from the end of infancy to about 5 or 6 years of age; sometimes called the preschool years.
Infancy	The developmental period that extends from birth to 18 or 24 months is called infancy.
Social skills training	Social skills training refers to a behavior therapy designed to improve interpersonal skills that emphasizes shaping, modeling, and behavioral rehearsal.
Social skills	Social skills are skills used to interact and communicate with others to assist status in the social structure and other motivations.
Friendship	The essentials of friendship are reciprocity and commitment between individuals who see themselves more or less as equals. Interaction between friends rests on a more equal power base than the interaction between children and adults.
Social support	Social Support is the physical and emotional comfort given by family, friends, co-workers and others. Research has identified three main types of social support: emotional, practical, sharing points of view.
Masturbation	Masturbation is the manual excitation of the sexual organs, most often to the point of orgasm. It can refer to excitation either by oneself or by another, but commonly refers to such activities performed alone.
Psychological disorder	Mental processes and/or behavior patterns that cause emotional distress and/or substantial impairment in functioning is a psychological disorder.

Go to **Cram101.com** for the Practice Tests for this Chapter.

Conduct disorder	Conduct disorder is the psychiatric diagnostic category for the occurrence of multiple delinquent activities over a 6-month period. These behaviors include truancy, running away, fire setting, cruelty to animals, breaking and entering, and excessive fighting.
Hyperactivity	Hyperactivity can be described as a state in which a individual is abnormally easily excitable and exuberant. Strong emotional reactions and a very short span of attention is also typical for the individual.
Depression	In everyday language depression refers to any downturn in mood, which may be relatively transitory and perhaps due to something trivial. This is differentiated from Clinical depression which is marked by symptoms that last two weeks or more and are so severe that they interfere with daily living.
Dysthymic disorder	A dysthymic disorder is a form of the mood disorder of depression characterized by a lack of enjoyment/pleasure in life that continues for at least two years. It differs from clinical depression in the severity of the symptoms.
Mood disorder	A mood disorder is a condition where the prevailing emotional mood is distorted or inappropriate to the circumstances.
Personality disorder	A mental disorder characterized by a set of inflexible, maladaptive personality traits that keep a person from functioning properly in society is referred to as a personality disorder.
Problem solving	An attempt to find an appropriate way of attaining a goal when the goal is not readily available is called problem solving.
Self-image	A person's self-image is the mental picture, generally of a kind that is quite resistant to change, that depicts not only details that are potentially available to objective investigation by others, but also items that have been learned by that person about himself or herself.
Social development	The person's developing capacity for social relationships and the effects of those relationships on further development is referred to as social development.
Stages	Stages represent relatively discrete periods of time in which functioning is qualitatively different from functioning at other periods.
Mainstreaming	Mainstreaming refers to educating mentally retarded students in regular rather than special schools by placing them in regular classes for part of the day or having special classrooms in regular schools.
Phenylketonuria	Phenylketonuria is a genetic disorder in which an individual cannot properly metabolize amino acids. The disorder is now easily detected but, if left untreated, results in mental retardation and hyperactivity.

Mental disorder	Mental disorder refers to a disturbance in a person's emotions, drives, thought processes, or behavior that involves serious and relatively prolonged distress and/or impairment in ability to function, is not simply a normal response to some event or set of events in the person's environment.
Insanity	A legal status indicating that a person cannot be held responsible for his or her actions because of mental illness is called insanity.
Maladaptive	In psychology, a behavior or trait is adaptive when it helps an individual adjust and function well within their social environment. A maladaptive behavior or trait is counterproductive to the individual.
Reflection	Reflection is the process of rephrasing or repeating thoughts and feelings expressed, making the person more aware of what they are saying or thinking.
Society	The social sciences use the term society to mean a group of people that form a semi-closed (or semi-open) social system, in which most interactions are with other individuals belonging to the group.
Heredity	Heredity is the transfer of characteristics from parent to offspring through their genes.
Brain	The brain controls and coordinates most movement, behavior and homeostatic body functions such as heartbeat, blood pressure, fluid balance and body temperature. Functions of the brain are responsible for cognition, emotion, memory, motor learning and other sorts of learning. The brain is primarily made up of two types of cells: glia and neurons.
Trait	An enduring personality characteristic that tends to lead to certain behaviors is called a trait. The term trait also means a genetically inherited feature of an organism.
Population	Population refers to all members of a well-defined group of organisms, events, or things.
Social support	Social Support is the physical and emotional comfort given by family, friends, co-workers and others. Research has identified three main types of social support: emotional, practical, sharing points of view.
Group therapy	Group therapy is a form of psychotherapy during which one or several therapists treat a small group of clients together as a group. This may be more cost effective than individual therapy, and possibly even more effective.
Impulse control	Deferred gratification is the ability of a person to wait for things they want. This trait is critical for life success. Those who lack this trait are said to suffer from poor impulse control, and often become criminals, as they are unwilling to work and wait for their paycheck.
Schizophrenia	Schizophrenia is characterized by persistent defects in the perception or expression of reality. A person suffering from untreated schizophrenia typically demonstrates grossly disorganized thinking, and may also experience delusions or auditory hallucinations
Attention	Attention is the cognitive process of selectively concentrating on one thing while ignoring other things. Psychologists have labeled three types of attention: sustained attention, selective attention, and divided attention.
Enzyme	An enzyme is a protein that catalyzes, or speeds up, a chemical reaction. Enzymes are essential to sustain life because most chemical reactions in biological cells would occur too slowly, or would lead to different products, without enzymes.
Abnormal behavior	An action, thought, or feeling that is harmful to the person or to others is called abnormal behavior.
Juvenile delinquency	Juvenile delinquency refers to a broad range of child and adolescent behaviors, including socially unacceptable behavior, status offenses, and criminal acts.

323

Attitude	An enduring mental representation of a person, place, or thing that evokes an emotional response and related behavior is called attitude.
Personality	Personality refers to the pattern of enduring characteristics that differentiates a person, the patterns of behaviors that make each individual unique.
Psychosis	Psychosis is a generic term for mental states in which the components of rational thought and perception are severely impaired. Persons experiencing a psychosis may experience hallucinations, hold paranoid or delusional beliefs, demonstrate personality changes and exhibit disorganized thinking. This is usually accompanied by features such as a lack of insight into the unusual or bizarre nature of their behavior, difficulties with social interaction and impairments in carrying out the activities of daily living.
Role model	A person who serves as a positive example of desirable behavior is referred to as a role model.
Family therapy	Family therapy is a branch of psychotherapy that treats family problems. Family therapists consider the family as a system of interacting members; as such, the problems in the family are seen to arise as an emergent property of the interactions in the system, rather than ascribed exclusively to the "faults" or psychological problems of individual members.
Variable	A variable refers to a measurable factor, characteristic, or attribute of an individual or a system.
Maladjustment	Maladjustment is the condition of being unable to adapt properly to your environment with resulting emotional instability.
Control group	A group that does not receive the treatment effect in an experiment is referred to as the control group or sometimes as the comparison group.
Depression	In everyday language depression refers to any downturn in mood, which may be relatively transitory and perhaps due to something trivial. This is differentiated from Clinical depression which is marked by symptoms that last two weeks or more and are so severe that they interfere with daily living.
Anxiety	Anxiety is a complex combination of the feeling of fear, apprehension and worry often accompanied by physical sensations such as palpitations, chest pain and/or shortness of breath.
Mental retardation	Mental retardation refers to having significantly below-average intellectual functioning and limitations in at least two areas of adaptive functioning. Many categorize retardation as mild, moderate, severe, or profound.
Prenatal	Prenatal period refers to the time from conception to birth.
Epilepsy	Epilepsy is a chronic neurological condition characterized by recurrent unprovoked neural discharges. It is commonly controlled with medication, although surgical methods are used as well.
Learning	Learning is a relatively permanent change in behavior that results from experience. Thus, to attribute a behavioral change to learning, the change must be relatively permanent and must result from experience.
Affect	A subjective feeling or emotional tone often accompanied by bodily expressions noticeable to others is called affect.
Low birth weight	Low birth weight is a fetus that weighs less than 2500 g (5 lb 8 oz) regardless of gestational age.
Alcoholic	An alcoholic is dependent on alcohol as characterized by craving, loss of control, physical dependence and withdrawal symptoms, and tolerance.

Go to **Cram101.com** for the Practice Tests for this Chapter.

Clinician	A health professional authorized to provide services to people suffering from one or more pathologies is a clinician.
Child abuse	Child abuse is the physical or psychological maltreatment of a child.
Emotional abuse	There is no single accepted definition of emotional abuse which, like other forms of violence in a relationship, is based on power and domination.
Self-image	A person's self-image is the mental picture, generally of a kind that is quite resistant to change, that depicts not only details that are potentially available to objective investigation by others, but also items that have been learned by that person about himself or herself.
Cognition	The intellectual processes through which information is obtained, transformed, stored, retrieved, and otherwise used is cognition.
Punishment	Punishment is the addtion of a stimulus that reduces the frequency of a response, or the removal of a stimulus that results in a reduction of the response.
Statistic	A statistic is an observable random variable of a sample.
Counselor	A counselor is a mental health professional who specializes in helping people with problems not involving serious mental disorders.
Mental illness	Mental illness is the term formerly used to mean psychological disorder but less preferred because it implies that the causes of the disorder can be found in a medical disease process.
Emotion	An emotion is a mental states that arise spontaneously, rather than through conscious effort. They are often accompanied by physiological changes.
Survey	A method of scientific investigation in which a large sample of people answer questions about their attitudes or behavior is referred to as a survey.
Statistics	Statistics is a type of data analysis which practice includes the planning, summarizing, and interpreting of observations of a system possibly followed by predicting or forecasting of future events based on a mathematical model of the system being observed.
Early Intervention	Early intervention is a process used to recognize warning signs for mental health problems and to take early action against factors that put individuals at risk.
Community intervention	An approach to treating and preventing disorders by directing action at the organizational, agency, and community levels rather than at individuals is called a community intervention.
Tact	The word tact, another of Skinner's intentionally "nonsense" words, comes from the notion of the child's making "conTACT" with the nonverbal environment. The tact is verbal behavior that is under the control of the nonverbal environment and includes nouns, actions, adjectives, pronouns, relations, and others.
Behavioral therapy	The treatment of a mental disorder through the application of basic principles of conditioning and learning is called behavioral therapy.
Clinical method	Studying psychological problems and therapies in clinical settings is referred to as the clinical method. It usually involves case histories, pathology, or non-experimentally controlled environments.
Psychotherapy	Psychotherapy is a set of techniques based on psychological principles intended to improve mental health, emotional or behavioral issues.
Delusion	A false belief, not generally shared by others, and that cannot be changed despite strong evidence to the contrary is a delusion.
Phobia	A persistent, irrational fear of an object, situation, or activity that the person feels

Go to **Cram101.com** for the Practice Tests for this Chapter.

327

compelled to avoid is referred to as a phobia.

Community psychology	Community psychology is the study of how to use the principles of psychology to create communities of all sizes that promote mental health of their members.
Adaptation	Adaptation is a lowering of sensitivity to a stimulus following prolonged exposure to that stimulus. Behavioral adaptations are special ways a particular organism behaves to survive in its natural habitat.
Clinical psychologist	A psychologist, usually with a Ph.D, whose training is in the diagnosis, treatment, or research of psychological and behavioral disorders is a clinical psychologist.
Paraprofessional	A paraprofessional is an individual lacking a doctoral degree but trained to perform certain functions usually reserved for clinicians.
Socioeconomic	Socioeconomic pertains to the study of the social and economic impacts of any product or service offering, market intervention or other activity on an economy as a whole and on the companies, organization and individuals who are its main economic actors.
Psychiatrist	A psychiatrist is a physician who specializes in the diagnosis and treatment of psychological disorders.
Bipolar disorder	Bipolar Disorder is a mood disorder typically characterized by fluctuations between manic and depressive states; and, more generally, atypical mood regulation and mood instability.
Halfway house	A halfway house is a term for a drug rehabilitation or sex offender center, where drug users or sex offenders respectively are allowed to move more freely than in a prison but are still monitored by staff and/or law enforcement. There is often opposition from neighborhoods where halfway houses attempt to locate.
Paranoid	The term paranoid is typically used in a general sense to signify any self-referential delusion, or more specifically, to signify a delusion involving the fear of persecution.
Antipsychotic	The term antipsychotic is applied to a group of drugs used to treat psychosis.
Lithium	Lithium salts are used as mood stabilizing drugs primarily in the treatment of bipolar disorder, depression, and mania; but also in treating schizophrenia. Lithium is widely distributed in the central nervous system and interacts with a number of neurotransmitters and receptors, decreasing noradrenaline release and increasing serotonin synthesis.
Diabetes	Diabetes is a medical disorder characterized by varying or persistent elevated blood sugar levels, especially after eating. All types of diabetes share similar symptoms and complications at advanced stages: dehydration and ketoacidosis, cardiovascular disease, chronic renal failure, retinal damage which can lead to blindness, nerve damage which can lead to erectile dysfunction, gangrene with risk of amputation of toes, feet, and even legs.
Chronic	Chronic refers to a relatively long duration, usually more than a few months.
Partial hospitalization	Partial hospitalization is a type of program used to treat mental illness and substance abuse. In partial hospitalization, the patient continues to reside at home, but commutes to a treatment center up to seven days a week. Since partial hospitalization focuses on the overall treatment of the individual, rather than purely on his or her safety, the program is not used for people who are acutely suicidal.
Deinstitutio- alization	The transfer of former mental patients from institutions into the community is referred to as deinstitutionalization.
Acute	Acute means sudden, sharp, and abrupt. Usually short in duration.
Civil commitment	Civil commitment is the practice of using legal means or forms as part of a mental health law to commit a person to a mental hospital, insane asylum or psychiatric ward against their will

Go to **Cram101.com** for the Practice Tests for this Chapter.

	or over their protests. Many but not all countries have mental health laws governing involuntary commitment.
Paranoia	In popular culture, the term paranoia is usually used to describe excessive concern about one's own well-being, sometimes suggesting a person holds persecutory beliefs concerning a threat to themselves or their property and is often linked to a belief in conspiracy theories.
Insanity defense	In a criminal trial, the insanity defense is a possible defense by excuse, via which defendants may argue that they should not be held criminally liable for breaking the law, as they were mentally ill or mentally incompetent at the time of their allegedly "criminal" actions.
Irresistible impulse	In jurisprudence, irresistible impulse is a defense by excuse, in this case some sort of insanity, in which the defendant argues that they should not be held criminally liable for their actions that broke the law, because they could not control those actions.
Personality disorder	A mental disorder characterized by a set of inflexible, maladaptive personality traits that keep a person from functioning properly in society is referred to as a personality disorder.
Perception	Perception is the process of acquiring, interpreting, selecting, and organizing sensory information.
Suicide	Suicide behavior is rare in childhood but escalates in adolescence. The suicide rate increases in a linear fashion from adolescence through late adulthood.
Informed consent	The term used by psychologists to indicate that a person has agreed to participate in research after receiving information about the purposes of the study and the nature of the treatments is informed consent. Even with informed consent, subjects may withdraw from any experiment at any time.
Involuntary commitment	Involuntary commitment is the practice of using legal means or forms as part of a mental health law to commit a person to a mental hospital, insane asylum or psychiatric ward against their will or over their protests. Many but not all countries have mental health laws governing involuntary commitment.
Least restrictive alternative	The legal principle according to which a committed mental patient must be treated in a setting that imposes as few restrictions as possible on his or her freedom is the so-called least restrictive alternative.
Domestic violence	Domestic violence is any violence between current or former partners in an intimate relationship, wherever and whenever the violence occurs. The violence may include physical, sexual, emotional or financial abuse.
Right to treatment	A legal principle according to which a committed mental patient must be provided some minimal amount of professional intervention, enough to afford a realistic opportunity for meaningful improvement, is the right to treatment.
Free choice	Free choice refers to the ability to freely make choices that are not controlled by genetics, learning, or unconscious forces.
Psychoactive substance	A psychoactive substance is a chemical that alters brain function, resulting in temporary changes in perception, mood, consciousness, or behavior. Such drugs are often used for recreational and spiritual purposes, as well as in medicine, especially for treating neurological and psychological illnesses.
Abnormal psychology	The scientific study whose objectives are to describe, explain, predict, and control behaviors that are considered strange or unusual is referred to as abnormal psychology.
Social skills	Social skills are skills used to interact and communicate with others to assist status in the

Go to **Cram101.com** for the Practice Tests for this Chapter.

social structure and other motivations.

Social norm   A social norm, is a rule that is socially enforced. In social situations, such as meetings, they are unwritten and often unstated rules that govern individuals' behavior. A social norm is most evident when not followed or broken.

Go to **Cram101.com** for the Practice Tests for this Chapter.